JESUS & THE TWISTED GENERATION

JESUS & THE TWISTED GENERATION

A Killer Stripper, A Cult Comedian & Rock'n'Roll

IDA SPUTUM

Library of Congress Control Number:		2022922594
ISBN:	Hardcover	978-1-6698-3350-5
	Softcover	978-1-6698-3349-9
	eBook	978-1-6698-3348-2

This book is a work of non-fiction. Unless otherwise noted, the author and the publisher make no explicit guarantees as to the accuracy of the information contained in this book and in some cases, names of people and places have been altered to protect their privacy.

Any people depicted in stock imagery provided by Getty Images are models, and such images are being used for illustrative purposes only.
Certain stock imagery © Getty Images.

Print information available on the last page.

Rev. date: 12/17/2022

To order additional copies of this book, contact:
Xlibris
AU TFN: 1 800 844 927 (Toll Free inside Australia)
AU Local: (02) 8310 8187 (+61 2 8310 8187 from outside Australia)
www.Xlibris.com.au
Orders@Xlibris.com.au
848800

JESUS & THE TWISTED GENERATION: A KILLER STRIPPER, A CULT COMEDIAN & ROCK N ROLL.

From a childhood of drug smuggling, porn, violence and rock'n'roll, to an adulthood of more violence, GBH, stripping, punk, drugs, DRAMA CLUB, rock'n'roll, rape, alienation, mental institutions, invention, abortions, kidnap by press, infamy, plus heinously unfunny comedians, (names of some places and people are changed to protect the publisher from lawsuits brought by the guilty), Bob Crumpton, Franklyn Chancer. Funny ones too; John Cooper-Clarke, Ian Cognito, Barbara Nice, Andy Robinson and Milo McCabe get a mention. Olympic skier Alan Schoenberger and wild Aaron Barschak. Leading to repentance, redemption and salvation in Jesus Christ.

Ida Sputum takes you to the dark heart of comedy, out of its anus and into fertiliser, leaving you refreshed and hopeful for the human spirit. Finishing with a story of my great friend, the late and lovely rocker, Dave Kusworth and more to be continued.

This book is dedicated to Billy Button 1961-2021.

The only man that ever told a rapist to leave me alone. Billy was a musician and always wore a cape he'd had specially designed. With his cape flying he kicked off the rapist's front door and marched up to his flat where the rapist cowered behind his door chain. "LEAVE IDA ALONE! There's loads more of us". (There was only ever Billy, no other man would help). All I'd asked of the rapist was to be left alone, but the rapist had seen me in town and spat red drink all over me. The rapist called the cops and the cops let us go free. The rapist never dared to even look at me again.

Billy Button I love you forever.

To Adele Cooper, you made my father's final years wonderful in his super shed in your garden with your fantastic meals and great friendship. Thank you.

To Judy Davis, thank you for respecting me.

To Jodie Mercer, Nicole Ford & Jade Douglas thank you for your computer skills in making this book.

BIRTH;

Medical professionals were amazed when, unaided, I climbed out of mother with a merry cry of, "Make way boys!!! I'm coming through!", seized a medical instrument, severed my own umbilical cord, tottered out of Derby City Hospital, ran to the Social Services and put myself up for adoption pronto.

Aah... would that it were, would that it were.

Oh who am I trying to kid? Sat here like I'm some middle-class writer, all poised as if pensively staring out of a picture window at my wildly bucolic garden, as befitting a woman of my years and inclinations. HA! Really, the other night, naked due to the Australian heat, and the heat from a naked Australian who remains platonic, I confronted three hooded men in my backyard. One had a dagger in his hand.

"WHADDYA DOING!??", I roared. Breaking my frangipani, they scarpered over the 6ft fence that hems my home. (I don't like being hemmed).

They ran down the back lane screaming about the scary nude Teletubby, yelling, "My eyes!! Take my eyes! Therapy!" Unlike my striptease dancing days, medication has given me a belly and I don't care. All they got was a tobacco pouch off the outside table.

I've been in fight or flight mode for 53 years damn it. 50 years staunchly UNMEDICATED I'll have you know! Those punks haven't a clue of the monsters I've fought, I thought. (I generally lost against the monsters, but mentally I just about survived!). Then yesterday and this morning I found piss all over my front door, festooning the flywire, a urine waterfall flowing down the path. Big bladder! LOADS of piss. Or maybe they all pissed in unison? Just to let me know they're kings of this manor. Anyway, the police on the phone added it to my incident number. A month I've been here. Somehow I'll get this book written.

Tony Martin, jailed for defending his English farm from robbers, 'I feel you' man.

(I'd like to report that the piss transpired to be from the reticulated garden sprinkler and all's well, but I can't. The sprinkler doesn't hit the door. It was yellow piss from miscreants.

UK CLASS SYSTEM;.

Aged about seven, on seeing a famous comedy sketch with John Cleese, and the Two Ronnies, Barker and Corbet, acting as men who were working class, middle class and upper class, I asked my dad which class are we? His answer was clever. He thought for a moment and replied with a smile, "Lucky. We're just lucky". That was enough for me. No socioeconomic bracket for me thank you very much. I was lucky. Magic! Hurrah! Happily deluded and would continue to disregard the class system forever. Or try to.

BIRTH; Take 2. Reality.

In fact birth was ooooh! Difficult.

1964 September, Sunday 6.00am. Derby City Hospital. Evicted by forceps from my happy place inside mother. A sense of foreboding must have informed me as my cranium was gripped by cold steel prongs, leaving bruises and crossed eyes for days. Weighing eight pounds, three ounces, the eldest child of five, I popped out to the cacophony of hospital implements on metal dishes and echoing voices, a surge of sounds, like water leaving your eardrums at the swimming pool. Our twenty year old mother needed eight stitches which I was regularly reminded of throughout my contact with her. Eight eight eight!

It was better inside than out.

Inside, the rosy glow of the English Midlands summer could be seen through the membranes of mothers tummy. Outside I was called, 'a mistake', and given a plastic bottle of formula. (Lucky to get anything these days!)

Perfectly healthy, I was placed in an incubator, a perspex cloche over me like a display in a museum. There weren't any cots left at the maternity hospital. So unlike the other incubating babies, my eyes were wide open and I could see a man in a white coat with a clipboard. As it goes.

If he'd interviewed me I'd have said, "Aren't I supposed to be breastfed roundabout now?" (At the Pompidou Centre in Paris as a child, I saw the painting by Jackson Pollock entitled 'Birth'. Perfectly capturing my experience of being born).

By the age of seven, sporadic physical attacks from mother left me with the countenance of one who lived with gun-less guerilla warfare. Standard fare. Never knew when or why. Cold. Like the Pink Panther and Kato his sparring partner, except not evenly matched in size or height and I wasn't paying mother to train me in Martial Arts.

Her favourite trick was to grab my head and smash it against the porcelain bathroom sink of whichever house we lived in.

I'd try to fight and pull my head away but she was much bigger with a strong hold on my head. Confusion, head-ringing pain, then back outside to play with our street gang(s) again. Didn't occur to me to discuss it with anyone, being a child I just absorbed it as what mums did. Child-line didn't exist and Mum always told me not to tell tales. Her stock response to most things I said was "Don't tell tales!" But like all psychos, mother had her neutral days towards me. (I fondly liked to believe). Dad hit me too but rarely and never full force.

DEAR READER, you may say, "WHO CARES about your childhood, your young friends, your God-given talents, the porn and strange people in your childhood home? We want famous people and the salacious details of your adult life!"

My reply is that you may skip ahead and also have a hard look at yourselves. But you'd be missing the point that without my autonomous discipline to train myself in gymnastics and art, I would not have had the God-given strength of character and humour to survive the violent cracks to my cranium from my mother and ensuing onslaught of further cranial and bodily abuse until I was rendered to the state of just a maggot in the dirt. The cultures I saw as a child gave me a sense of perspective. It's the foundation of my life so please bear with me.

I didn't look at the little girl at school behind the bike sheds, showing her bottom to boys for a packet of crisps and think to myself, "That looks like a healthy career!" It just ended up that way.

Thank you.

It's easy to see in retrospect why stripping seemed such a breeze for me. At first when I saw naked hippies in the Welsh countryside commune aged 7, I felt a frisson of naughtiness. Then it became natural. The porn and the naked nubile life models in my father's office, used as a studio by artist Donald Newton, added to the normalisation of nudity and when aged 17 I found a job as a stripper in Soho, it seemed strange that other people were dressed and paid me to be as God intended the first people to be in the Garden of Eden. How bizarre! The seediness and danger of the stripping world only dawned on me much later, the hard way.

DADDY; Warm.

A friendly personality. His parents sent him to a Jesuit school as a day boy. Generally placid but once seen to hit my violent mother with a broom handle when I was 12. A one off occurrence. A man called Sid was present and he did nothing. When asked why, Sid replied to mother that he thought she might like it. She didn't. What a plonker Sid was. (Mum didn't mind hitting me though). Eight years with the Merchant Navy, then dad ran his own business and was absent frequently with long-distance lorry driving. I'd go with him occasionally, around Ireland

and South Wales, hiding in the cab under a blanket at the factory gate-house because children weren't allowed in. Then up I'd pop once inside the factory and watch the forklift unload the grinding wheels off the lorry. Dad always returned with a load too. (Never run an empty lorry).

Once he took 3 daughters in the cab around Ireland and had us sleeping on the flatbed under tarpaulin tented over crates. We also stayed in The Falls Hotel in the luscious southern countryside, as he liked to show us the high life too. "My girls will be able to sleep in ditches and the finest hotels!" he cried.

On the way back he left us three in the dark cab on the docks while he went to the pub. My little sisters wet themselves and were fractious at the length of time Dad was gone. Aged 8, I was the oldest and suddenly began singing loosely to the tune of Rolf Harris's 'Two Little Boys';

"Did you think I would leave you siiiiitting in this 'orriiibull lorreeeey? I've got Esme on my right, wetting with all her might and Rachel on my left, wetting her bloomin' vest. And I'm in the middle, drowning in the piddle, so can I have a rubber ring! Soon we will be saaillling back to Holyhead and then we will drive on slowly and bump into our beds!" Daddy finally returned and we giggled all the way home.

HASHISH

Dad developed a side-line in hashish smuggling from Morocco and used his family as a cover. At that time he had three young daughters and a wife, all of whom he would take on exciting family holidays to North Africa in a ricketty transit van, later a comfy caravanette.

Driving for days through France and Spain, (where gun-toting police ripped the cladding off the inside of the van doors and found nothing because Daddy had a special way with roof-racks), to the big boat, which floated past the monkeys on the Rock of Gibraltar, as it made its balmy evening journey to Tangiers.

The boat was full of soldiers, I don't know why. It was 1971 or '72, I was seven.

Dad had spent ages building a roof-rack on the van in our back garden. None of us, including mother, knew why. Only on our arrival back in UK did Dad announce that he'd smuggled tens of thousands of pounds worth of dope in the rack. Mother went into spasm, "Oh Geoffrey, how could you do this! We could've been imprisoned!"

Dad replied that what she didn't know didn't hurt her and our 'happy family' holiday vibe was a better cover.

MOROCCO; Life-changing.

Seeing the children my age deftly weaving intricate carpets in dimly lit cellar rooms in Fez medina, and the shanty towns of North Africa; people living in cobbled together plastic sheeting, corrugated iron, cardboard and bits of wood, smoke rising from endless hovels for ages as we drove through with local children hanging on the outside of the van until Dad accelerated and they'd jump off, lucky Westerners in a white van; it suddenly dawned on me that (A) there was sod all I could do about it, and (B) I was extremely lucky.

Running water, electricity and big buildings full of food called shops meant; that no matter how precariously and perilously my life unfolded in the West, I could always fall back on the perspective that at least I didn't live in a shanty town, or inside a boulder!

Yes inside a boulder.

Silent rocks on mountain sides in dust and scrub in the middle of the Atlas range, with nothing as far as the heat-hazy horizon but mountains like fish scales over-lapping each other with helter-skelter roads winding steeply around them, like a '70s Mordillo poster.

We drove through those mountains on bendy barrier-less roads for what seemed like ever. Stopping at night to sleep in the van in desolate places. Seeing no other vehicles, just car wrecks at the bottom of gorges.

Yet in that empty barren terrain I felt we were being watched. But we couldn't be, because nobody was there. Just boulders with random black holes in them, it was ludicrous to think anyone could actually live in them. Could they?

Then whilst driving we emptied my two year old sister's potty out of the back door and accidentally threw out the pot too. As we watched the plastic potty bounce down the road, suddenly human figures in black robes appeared in the road, grabbed the blue plastic potty and began a tug-o-war with it, trying to snatch it off each other.

It's carved into my brain that people somehow survived out there,... on what?! Spiders? Lizards? Where was their water? I still don't know. Waiting and watching inside boulders. Conserving their coolness.

That's when I knew how amazingly tough human beings could be.

One night, asleep on a mountain we were robbed, although the only opening to the van was a tiny slit of window wedged open by a knife for air. A huge staff and a metal hook were in the van the next day left by the robber. Four adults and three children covering every spare surface of the van didn't feel a thing throughout the robbery. How did they do it? Shadow people. Very strong, like the blind fisherman all wrapped up in black on the empty beach, who caught fish by tying a string to his toe and feeling the tug of the fish. We girls accidentally startled him by tripping over his long string so he thought he'd got a fish.

A sight that haunts me to this day is seeing a ring of Moroccan men and boys around a living octopus on the beach, its beak opening and closing to stay alive and its big intelligent eyes staring sadly. A youth threw sand in its eyes and to see it helplessly blinking the sand out of its eyes was the saddest thing. As a seven year old I didn't know what to do. I hope it was thrown in the sea.

Our 'bathing suits' in a Muslim country were blue school P.E. pants, nothing else. We got locked on the beach as the large metal gates of that campsite were shut to the beach at night. We knew nobody could hear our calls. So I led my little sister along the wall of the campsite and through the street in our P.E. pants being stared at in what looked to be disdain by the local men in their djellabas, until we found the front drive through gates of the camp. At night I stared at a lamp covered in praying mantis's then suddenly one flew down and boxed my chest with little machine gun punches.

We saw so many strong people, a man with no nose, just holes in his face. A woman walking in the mountains very far from any town without legs, just bits of car tyres strapped to her stumps and a huge bundle on her back and two big staffs in her hands to lean on. We pulled over to give her a lift but she scuttled away. Next day we saw her 50 miles away in Fez medina, begging. Miraculous.

A tall man in a djellaba had eyes like a chameleon. Every day he carried a tray of biscuits on his head, calling "ALLAH COOKIE! ALLAH COOKIE!". We'd buy from him and watch amazed as he crossed a road by looking in both directions at once, his head forward under his tray. Had he trained himself? Were his eyes always like that?

Me and the second eldest sister went walking on a bridge by ourselves. It overlooked a wide dried up riverbed full of thousands of boulders. Far in the distance I saw some maroon clothes sticking out from behind a boulder. I told my sister that it was a dead body. We told our parents who told the police, and it turned out I was right. It was a murdered man.

SCHOOL; Couldn't wait to go.

Had to kill time at home until I was just turned six. I used to stare at the new estate being built across the road on the other side of the sewer.

The roof tiles finally went on to the estate where Catholic schoolboy Bob Crumpton would grow up. There's only so much Jimmy Young on the radio a child can take and there were no tears from me on the first day of school, that's for sure.

Everybody usually has a school in their past. I mostly liked my infant and junior school years, so excuse me if I indulge in the very foundations of my life which kept me nearly sane in the tumultuous approaching years.

Apart from the badly cracked backroom ceiling falling on my head and into my breakfast, concussing me, and the vicious maternal violence; I spent some of my happiest years until I was twelve. Eight whole years of relative peace!

Our family was intact. School was enjoyable, I had good friends and neighbours, used my talents in dancing, gymnastics and art, met talented adults and people from all over the world as our house was a boarding house and full of friends. Blessed.

(I'd warned Dad repeatedly that the ceiling would fall, but Dad heard the Jehova's Witnesses say the end of the world was coming in '73 and he thought the ceiling didn't matter. After the ceiling hit me I walked through the room along the walls. Bit late for that!),

One night Dad put cigarettes in my 5 year old mouth and got me to light them, oh how Mum and Dad laughed.

Dad taped a map of the world on the wall and taught us all the countries before we could read, until he could point to anywhere and we'd know off by heart the shapes and names of the places. As we got older we'd read the map and get the answers. Ecuador on the equator, and he'd say, "Ahhh you're cheating now you can read!"

Dad said his favourite country that he visited in his Merchant Navy days was New Zealand. A lot of the place names have long since changed,

Ceylon is now Sri Lanka, Persia is Iran, Yugoslavia is now lots of countries. Plenty of other names have changed since then.

He was a busy man but I've always remembered Dad telling me about being in the tropics onboard a big ship with a dead shark hung between the railings on the deck. Its mouth was hanging open, its flesh was cut off, partly leaving the exposed skeleton bleaching all day in the blazing sun.

A sailor had a knife which he put inside the sharks mouth against its teeth and said he could make a necklace out of them when SLAM! The shark's jaws gnashed shut! The blade of the knife was broken on the deck.

Obviously I learned not to put my hand in a dead shark's jaws. Sharks have tiny brains and run almost entirely on killer reflexes that may remain even when brain dead.

(To extrapolate on Dad's shark tale, from experience I know that you should also never try to reason with psychopathic bullies or ever give them another chance like I did with 'comedian' Bob Crumptton. Only because of a comment from my mother when I left him at 18. She said "You're so hard!"

Her words echoed in my mind when he turned up again when I was 20. Sadly, I had STILL wanted to believe in her although she too was a bully. Trusting her came at a most horrendous far-reaching price as you will see if you read on).

Another time Dad took me aside in a rare moment and told me the story of his experience with jealousy. As a boy of seven in Norton-on-Hales village he had a little girlfriend and she was his world. One day she began playing with another boy and dad felt terrible. He forgot it and carried on life until he was in the Merchant Navy. His beautiful Chinese girlfriend started hanging out with the Purser instead of Dad. The horrible feeling that this gave him suddenly reminded him of all those years ago as a boy. He realised it was a mad feeling as he didn't own the Chinese girl. It was a free world. He vowed to never be jealous again.

THIS STORY GAVE ME NO CLUE as to HOW VIOLENTLY, NASTILY AND DEVIOUSLY jealousy could manifest in people. I was completely deluded for years that jealousy was just a mildly bad feeling that people could rationalise away.

I thought that Mum would think the same way as Dad as she was married to him, and that people generally would reason their way out of jealous feelings as rationally and logically as my Dad. SO sadly deluded.

After many travesties until I was far too old I'd logically reason like Dr Spock, "Why would anyone in my family be jealous of me? They know my life, they're not stupid and wouldn't want to be me for quids!"

IF ANY YOUNGSTERS EVER SEE THIS, LET ME TELL YOU; JEALOUSY IS EVIL AND ENTIRELY IRRATIONAL. GOD SAYS 'DO NOT COVET THY NEIGHBOURS ASS'.

(DONKEY!)

Everything at school was easy except maths. I peaked in exam placing at 28th out of 32. When Marie Haymer, my best school friend moved out of town, I found a new best friend in the infants playground, Diana Wilson. From six to twelve years old we were a strong team.

She was pretty and wearing a navy nurses cape made by her sewing genius mother. Diana was (is?) of Jamaican descent. She was a lovely colour, rosy golden, amber brown.

Colours and shapes were my speciality, along with gymnastics, dance and diving which I loved. As a kamikaze baby of 15 months, throwing myself off the adult diving board into the lovely bubbling deep water at Market Drayton Outdoor Pools, I remember the screams. Dad dived in and saved me. All I said for his efforts was, "Daddy's hair's fallen off". He never bothered with a comb-over again.

Dad showed me how to dive by making a tiny hole in the water which your whole body passes through with barely a ripple. I represented the school at diving with Michael 'Wardy' Ward representing the boys, and I fell like a stack of bricks in the pool.

Diana was the cleverest girl in the class and the best runner, violinist, ballet dancer and mathematician. She eventually became Head Girl of the entire Junior school. I was picked for the prophetic title of Vice Captain.

We remained best friends for years until I moved house at the end of Juniors to a tiny house, which was raided by police, who found nothing. Daddy had a way with burying Tupperware containers in the garden. Metal-detector proof.

ART?

In the infant school, I became aware that realism was the standard by which our art was judged. It wasn't deemed 'good art' unless it leaned towards realism. Ludicrous. But I capitalised on it.

Realising early that the sky went down to the horizon and wasn't just a blue line across the top of the paper, and because I put eyelashes on a picture of my best friend, the teachers showed my work to the Head Mistress.

From then on I was summoned out of normal classes to do colouring in with Jameel, who was also good at staying inside the black lines. That didn't last long, I wanted to do my own lines.

Dean Sutton asked me to draw a nude lady one day, so I did and gave it to him, I was six. He then snidely said, "Om! I'm telling Miss!".

Weirdo, I thought and forgot about it.

Then an almighty roar came from the teacher! "QUIET EVERYBODY! NOW!! IDA SPUTUM COME TO THE FRONT!" So I did and she hit me.

In her other shaking hand she held out my picture and said, "THIS FILTH BELONGS IN THE BIN!!" She ripped it up and put it in the bin.

Stunned I went and sat down, thinking the equivalent of, "WTF?!". (But I never swore). Mother kindly told the teacher that I was being brought up with a healthy, relaxed view of nudity thank you.

Junior school was the same. "Who's the class artist, there's always one?" the new teacher would ask at the start of the year. "IDA!" the class would chorus. It was nice to get some recognition even if it was just for being a human camera. We all had to draw ourselves in our projected future job. I drew a parachutist. Mr Flynn asked us all which picture was different to the rest? Silence. He said, "Ida's picture is the only one with the feet facing forward". Yes, all the other pictures had the feet sideways in ballet 1st or 2nd position.

Sat alone in the huge school assembly hall / gym at a lonely old fashioned single desk, charged to make art for the school, I was too overwhelmed by the emptiness and size of the place and the oddness of being singled out to make more than a few scratches on the paper, the leg of a sad clown. Miss Wardle wanted to keep my colourful Easter picture of a bird for the school but as usual I gave it to Mum instead.

Kiss chase in the playground with Andrew Cartwright, Simon Twistle, and Mark Taylor from the RAF Camp. Oh hilarity.

BIKE; Best present I've ever had.

LOVED adventuring on it. Advice; - don't put your tiddlers (little fish) in tap water. They look like they're racing about loving it, but they're actually in paroxysms of pain and go belly up, dead from the chemicals.

BIG SECONDARY SCHOOL; Bloody hell. 'Shit got real'.

THOUSANDS of kids in loads of classes. Stairs. Grownup looking students from the 5th and 6th years. I asked a couple of oldies sitting on the grass, "Why isn't anyone playing here?"

One replied disdainfully, "This is secondary school, we don't play". LOADS of books to carry in satchel style bags which almost gave you curvature of the spine as you lugged them home on Shanks pony. School rucksacks weren't around back then. Loads of tramping from class to class. Bells, always bells!

By this time my school report had gone from, MATHS; "Ida tries hard but achieves little", to "Ida doesn't try or appear to care anymore".

Graph-paper, grey squares, bars on a cage. No room for artistic interpretation in maths. No freedom of expression. There was only one answer and they already knew it. So why ask me?!

On the way home down the alleyway from secondary school, I found a little cream puppy dog amongst the ankle-socked legs, nobody seemed to notice him. So I put my books in my friends bag, (how kind), and tucked Charlie into mine.

WRONGNESS

I was allowed to keep Charlie, walked him, fed him and one day he had a bloody period and we knew he was Charlie girl. When I got home from school one Spring day Charlie was gone. Mum said Charlie must have run away. But I knew Charlie wouldn't do that. She must've been dognapped or run over. I grieved for Charlie.

A few years later, mother told me Dad was dead. I was 19 and believed her because he'd been hospitalised before. So I mourned Dad. well he had a good innings etc.

As I turned 25, my dead Dad rang my Birmingham bedsit payphone from the grave. I nearly had a cow. Mum had lied. I sped over to Arnhem, Holland where he'd been all along. He told me that Charlie girl, my dog, had NOT run away, mum had killed her out of spite.

By then I was finally allowing the penny to drop.... that just maybe,. mother hadn't got my best interests at heart.

I was a very slow learner when it came to facing facts about mother. The clues were all there. Hitting my head where the bruises were mostly hidden under my hair etc. Beating me with the buckle end of a leather belt. Confused, I wanted to believe the best of my own mother. As one does.

After all, I had big ideas, I was a big-eyed dear, big eyed deer, (Bambi in the jungle), and intended to keep mum in the style my father had accustomed her to. Style which drastically diminished when we were suddenly homeless at age 14 and given the key to a council house.

Greyness everywhere on the council estate. The buildings, even the gates were grey, like wire versions of math graph-paper. Oh God, it was an aesthetic pebble-dash nightmare. Day-dreams of painting the outside of our home in vivid hues or just white.

PREAMBLE; Where, when, what.

Directly after my birth in Derby, my parents lodged with a Yugoslavian family in Leicester, whose eldest daughter was named Ida, and so I was named. Also because dad had a girlfriend named Ida whilst travelling with the Navy. My middle name was Simone after Dad's Jewish friend, Simon Nadle who'd told Dad to marry Mum after getting her pregnant at a party. If I'd been a boy they'd have called me Simon.

Then for a few winter months we three lived in a caravan at Hopton Pools. I was making a lot of noise and my parents eventually realised that there wasn't a hole in the rubber teat for the milk to come out of my bottle. Dad cut a hole for me. Silence. Although a baby, I remember the steam of breath and a wall of snow when Dad opened the caravan door, and him digging a path through it in the dark early morning.

Soon we moved into another caravan in my father's parents' back garden until I was four. My first sister arrived when I was 15 months. She was put in my cot and I was put into a little bed to sleep. Of course being so young, I regularly fell off it in the night, trapped upside down, spreadeagled down the crack between the bed and wall in the dark, crying for help. The parents would laugh at me, "Like a little starfish wedged down the side".

To be fair they put cushions on the floor on the other side of the bed but I always fell down the gap by the wall. Putting the bed mattress itself on the floor evaded them. When I could toddle I'd climb up the drawer handles under my parents bed and try to get in, but there wasn't room. I'd listen to them breathe.

But they were mellow happy years, if you like staring at orange slugs and playing with Geoffrey Mellor, the boy next-door. Granny had 1950's petticoats to dress up in.

Mother kept her distance which I became used to. I felt the yearning for her attention be cauterised and die off inside. So it felt almost painful on the rare occasions she ever did actually touch me in a non-threatening way. And they wondered why I was "self contained"?! Bah!

Aged four we moved into a big Victorian pile, two storeys high. Corporation Street, Sandiford.

CORPORATION STREET; Multi-cultural.

Our house was between a Mental Hospital opposite us, and behind us was a sewerage plant across the back lane by the new allotments.

When it started to stink everybody in the street was badly affected except me. No olfactory sense at all. My sisters could announce the existence of food in their vicinity without seeing the food first. What magical ability was this? They had fully working noses.

The smell of mothballs that I played with as a baby in the caravan is the only smell I've ever known. Aged one, I was unattended on my Aunt's stairs and tumbled to the bottom onto my head and was hospitalised. Zero smellability ever since.

One night as my sister and I lay across a single bed, Mum gave us bottle's to feed ourselves and left to go out dancing at Stafford's nightclub, saying as she left "You look like a pair of little old men with your bottles".

The room was dark as we lay there.

In the flickering glow of the fire in the grate, I saw a very tall man standing against the wall by the door. He had curly blonde shortish hair and strong features. He was resting his hands on the hilt of a large sword in front of him, about waist height, balanced on its tip on the floor. He had bare muscular legs, leather sandals and a white tunic which was belted. He had huge feathery, still, white wings that could be seen framing him, folded behind. He stared straight ahead. I had no fear at all. I now realise that he was an angel.

As toddlers in the 60's we two children would scrawm around on the floor of the hairdresser's and play on the big empty vinyl seats, as Mum had her long bleached blonde hair piled up and arranged in an intricate basket work bun on top of her head. At home I'd watch her reflection in the mirror as she painted on her elaborate eye make-up before going out dancing with her friends.

Mum would always say how people had said to her as a child, "Look at your lovely almond shaped eyes!"

Wonderful and sometimes strange people abounded at Corporation Street.

It was run as a boarding house with lodgers in the two spare attic rooms. Also my mother ran a nursery at Corporation Street. So we had all kinds of little ones tottering around.

Dad was away on lorry runs two weeks a month or more. Mother cooked at night, which I was barred from learning about.

"Get out Ida! When I got married I couldn't boil an egg!" A cycle breaker mother wasn't.

We had Nigerian nurses stay, Bernice and Franca who cooked their fish with scales left on and eyeballs rolling on the plate. They were apoplectic to see their first ever snow; in their sing-song voices they said, "What about the birds??! How can they eat?"

They would let me in their room and sing old English songs to me like. 'Johnny's So Long at the Fayre', in lovely dulcet voices and brushed my long hair. They allowed me to play with their Afro wigs too.

We had young party girls and boys staying. Carlos was 18 and banned from his adoptive parents house.

For some prescient reason, I'd think, "There but for the grace of God go I", or similar. (God didn't exist in our Darwinian house).

Deep down I realised that all was not well with mother and I was lucky not to be an orphan like Carlos. Cold chills radiated from her but I didn't know what to do about it.

People mentioned my very long wavy chestnut hair in favourable ways. Mum took me to the hairdressers and ordered them to chop it off short like a boys with a side parting. I didn't mind. It grew back like a rampant plant.

But whilst it was short, I'd go off looking for adventure on my bike as usual in my navy tracksuit and holey canvas pumps that were held together by two plastic white stripes and laces and play with whoever was up the rec. "I like your socks Ida!" said Susan Dodd, as my shoes were actually just red socks with laces. Ha!

A lad said, "You always wear that tracksuit". I replied, "I wear dresses too". He spluttered, "Ugh! HE wears dresses!" I said, "I'M A GIRL! Look, I've got earrings!" "Boys can wear earrings". I rode off before they got my trousers off me for proof!

On the way home I pulled into the public ladies loo by the allotment. An old man said, "Boys aren't allowed in there sonny!"

Persian men stayed and would pinch our little faces as a greeting. "Hellooooo...Are you alriiiiiiight!?" They went back to Persia, (now Iran), with gold and diamond watches from the catalogue without paying. They couldn't believe credit existed for such luxuries and that nobody would cut off their hands, as was the penalty in Persia for theft.

Guitarists were often around making up songs about the family and playing acoustic guitar. Dave Mac (McIntyre) was a favourite. He taught me how to play the title song of the '70s children's TV show, 'Tales Of the Riverbank' on guitar. Dave was a good friend to me. He ended up lorry driving for Dad for years...until he was decapitated by a load coming through his cab's back window. Mum smiled as she told me.

People passed in and out, up and down stairs around the clock. A woman into transcendental meditation was found sitting with a sleeping bag over her head under my parents beautifully handmade platform bed. An eternal higher education student, Brian Leighfield constructed the bed with dad. It was sanded to mirror smooth with a curling wooden staircase.

Hari Krishna, Vishnu, Shiva, Chinese astrology, Buddha, Alan Watts, Zen Buddhism, Gore Vidal,

Beckett, Rosa Luxembourg, Eric Fromm, Hieronymous Bosch, 'The Ragged Trousered Philanthropists' keeping it surreal with Dali and Escher, Carlos Casteneda. Just a few of the authors, artists and fads wafting through the place with the cannabis fumes. God didn't get a look in. I was brainwashed by the New Age agenda that there were many paths to God but we were all allegedly ex-monkeys anyway.

I'd stare at the Hieronymous Bosch triptych on the wall. The first panel had the Garden of Eden, so serene. The middle and largest panel represented our fall from grace with all kinds of twisted images, and the final panel was horrific hell on earth. I wasn't told this, it was obvious. But I did not understand that I was living in the twisted central large panel.

The music was awesome, from Steve Gibbons who Dad loved, (whom I was acquainted with in my adult B'ham life and knew his songs from his album 'Any Road Up'), Bob Dylan, I loved his 'Desire' album and knew every word, especially Hurricane and Isis. Ian Dury, Frank Zappa, Pink Floyd, The Beatles and Stones, Tangerine Dream (? sounded like a toilet flushing backwards to me), Little Feat, Mozart, poets John Cooper-Clarke, (whom I'd meet as an adult), and Beckett,

Monty Python, Steely Dan, Bob Marley, Eagles, Kevin Ayers, Wings, Captain Beefheart,

Beethoven and Mozart, loads more, a cornucopia. (Steve Gibbons loved Bob Dylan too and created a show called 'The Dylan Project' when I was an adult).

If any adult knew they were part of the predictable results of a Tavistock Institute psyop, (psychological operation through culture/media), they never mentioned it around me. Tavistock Institute type places just love to think they're in control don't they?!

Dad enjoyed driving through town, the windows down in the Merc playing Ian Dury full blast singing, "Arseholes, baaastards, facking cants and pricks!", at the passers by.

For over a week a man sat on our sofa, amenable enough, as people came and went to work / school / the pub / ate etc. He smiled and didn't say much.

A bunch of people were in the kitchen talking to mother about him. "Isn't he with you?"...

"No I thought he was Woody's friend".....

"No he's not with me"...

"He's with Jan isn't he?"...

"I think he's Dave's mate?"...

"Does anybody know him?"

Then they approached the sofa guy...."Hi, ...err.. who ARE you?"

He replied, "Oh I just walked in off the street".

"Well can you go now please?" And he left no problem. Thank God he was harmless. Not a child sex-trafficker.

We had an artist stay with us named Donald Newton who would nude sketch the young women that came to the house. My dad's office was used as 'the studio'.

The office was on the first floor, part of an extension with a new bathroom and a bidet upstairs for washing your bum in. (Oh my friends and I had a riot with the bidet, squirting the ceiling with 'douche'). The bathroom and office were built on top of a new kitchen, shower and laundry downstairs. We even had a waste disposal unit which mangled cutlery, and a water softener. From a falling down tip, it became a 'des res', way ahead of its time for a town like Stafford in the early '70s.

Just saying. Materialism was rife. At a party there, a big Mama Cass type hippy lady called Sally Gardner sat on the floor, almost under our mahogany dining table, and told me we were very 'bourgois'.

Mum and Dad brought us up to sound like Midlands newsreaders. They were strict in not letting us sound like our friends. Style over substance some may say.

To try and be heard in such a busy place I talked very fast like a machine gun to get it all out before the adults' attention left me.

"SLOW down Ida!" Mum would say until I had cracked the art of m-ea-s-u-r-e-d..... e-n-u-n-c-i-a-t-i-o-n. Dad commented to mum, "You'll give her a stammer next".

When an attic room became empty I finally got my own room, replete with a heavy, rasping breather of a ghost that tried to tip me off my bed. The Nigerians heard my screams and rescued me by turning the light on. Our house was well known for ghosts amongst the inhabitants. (Ghosts followed me into my 40's until I learned why and how to get rid. More of that later).

It amused me tremendously to open the back attic window and slide down the roof tiles in my nightie until i was on the flat roof of the extension, then hang down off the edge of the gutter until I could reach mums first-floor bedroom window, at right-angle to the extension, then knock on the top corner of her window.

Her face looking up from her bedroom was a picture of mock shock. To list all my reckless escapades would look like I'm proudly showing off my stupidity. Just do not attempt to zip-line off the top of a towering pine-tree with a bandaged and stitched slashed artery in your hand from a skating accident with a glass door. It's a hell of a way to fall and it will bust your stitches. Then you'll get up as if you meant to fall on purpose.

Generally I entertained myself without recourse to adults. Art, dance and acrobatics, attaining the B.A.G.A (British Amateur Gymnastics Assoc.) badges.

Dad knocked through a dividing wall, (the first person in our street to do so). The new living room allowed me at least five consecutive cartwheels before hitting furniture. The staircase was where I learned the splits by taking five steps at a time. The wall is where I learned to walk my hands down backwards until I was in a crab. Until I did it without the wall. Then tied myself in a knot for something to do. Diana gave me all her 'Famous Five' books and I read a bit of Tolkien, 'Where The Wild Things Are', Dr Seuss, C.S.Lewis and dad's books like Alan Watt's book on Zen Buddhism.

Usually only a couple of pages. Never bothered with Noam Chomsky. I read a few pages of 'Emanuelle' or 'Apple-bottom book' as I called it due to the lady's bottom on the cover with an apple peel curling off it with a snake's head. Some bollocks about a woman who had sex everywhere, even on a plane.

Played outside a lot, often upside-down, and got Distinction in Ballet. Honours in tap. OH LA DI bloody DA! Hark at me!

Miss Porter the dance teacher at Sandiford School Of Dance told Dad that some children just learned deportment, but that some, including me, could be professional. All that came to an end when I was 11 or 12 as life at home was too chaotic for me to go.

For years if I saw ballet on TV I'd cry. But later, on hearing of the damage to ballerina's hips and feet I knew I'd had a lucky escape.

ACID

One sunny afternoon Mum was watching Persian rugs being made with a loom on TV. She seemed more enthusiastic than usual,

"Oh Geoffrey, aren't they clever how they get the colours to move?". Dad agreed with her that it was indeed amazing. I thought so too. Beautiful. Then mum was in the kitchen freaking out that her hands looked like a bunch of bananas. Dad was calming her down.

Turns out dad had put LSD, an acid trip, in mum's tea unbeknownst to her or anyone. Not a good idea, she nearly went mad. And was justifiably cross with dad. But she was more fun whilst tripping.

Both parents were on acid in London driving the Merc with me and all the children in the back, including a little girl called Maddy 'The Baddy' Coburn, (who still remembers being in her pyjamas the whole trip).

We'd been at the Divine Light festival at an indoor London stadium to see the guru Maharishi. We drove lost for hours around London until dad had the bright idea of paying a black cab to drive in front of him to our destination.

Dad asked the cabby to get out of his cab at every traffic light and come to dad's window to remind him that he was following the cab. Very cooperative cabby.

It was a relief to me as, up to then, I'd been expected to get directions and tell them to my parents who'd forget everything I said. I was nine. I recall mum freaking out at some automatically opening glass doors.

The Maharishi hadn't impressed me. He was very materialistic. going on about his diamond and gold cuff-links. "So what?" I thought, looking at all the hippies on their knees to him.

Dad was in the kitchen one day and announced to Mum that he wanted to be a guru and she should follow him. Mum replied "No, I'm doing the washing up, I don't want to follow you". Deflated Dad said, "If my own wife won't follow me, who will?"

My vivid nightmares involved me being at the wheel of a bus full of my siblings, not being able to drive and teetering out of control and just about keeping from crashing.

Everyday the milkman would deliver bottles of milk, and every morning the bottles were empty on the doorstep when we went to fetch them. Mother lay in wait to see why.

She spied a very tall mental patient in pyjamas from over the road, gulping each bottle down. She asked the milkman to knock and put the bottles in her hands.

We had coalmen bringing sacks of coal on a lorry for our fires. There was a rag-and-bone man on a horse-drawn wagon looking for old tat and selling it too. He was Mr Boswell. My dad taught him to drive when the horse became outmoded. Mr Boswell couldn't read so dad taught him every road symbol and he passed his test. Mr Massey next-door got tired of his bike so dad taught him to drive too.

We children were taught to speak up for ourselves. At Junior School the older children were tasked with serving the food out to their table of younger ones. My servers didn't ever give me enough so I told my Dad that I wanted more. He said, "Tell them not me!" So I did and was called an "outspoken child", by the servers. Like Oliver Twist.

One evening dad brought home a long-haired blonde young Welshman named Colin Brick whom he'd picked up hitchhiking. Colin was also taught to drive by dad.

Colin was an amazing drummer and guitarist, also a brilliant artist who made magical paintings of glowing people in sunsets. If the family ever saw a dramatic sunset we'd say "That's a Colin sky". His photography was off the scale brilliant too.

Dad and I would go down to Cardiff to Colin's flat which he shared with Clare, a curly, smiley, pretty nurse. Her nose ran clear liquid due to the medical cocaine that she got from her work. (We were in Colin's cushiony exotic flat when the news of Elvis's death broke). Brilliant music at Colin's, like Frank Zappa and The Doors. When police raided his flat they trashed it, even destroying sealed unopened film.

(Colin was eventually jailed but Dad always stayed free until his death. Like my father, I too have always avoided a criminal record in any country. Lucky as Australia isn't taking crims anymore).

Colin, Clare, Dad and our family went into smuggling together and the couple travelled with us to Morocco.

During the first trip to Morocco they shared our van. The second time they travelled separately in a red Audi because pretty Clare was crying and left our vehicle on the first trip because she "couldn't take anymore" sniping from mum. I do not blame Clare at all.

We were all sick of mum's moaning, e.g. "Why can't Clare change her knickers in the cafe toilet like I do?!" Only us girls could see Clare quickly change in the van anyway so what difference did it make? Nobody knows.

Another time Dad took the family and Dave Mole (a lovely man), all around Southern Ireland in a caravanette. BEAUTIFUL. LUSH. Tralee...what a melodious name for a town. The Listowel Folk Festival with youngsters playing snare drums and bodhrans in the streets and the pubs continually open except for an hour lock-in per day. Orange tiger lilies growing wild on the grass verges of the lanes. But Dad still couldn't stop Mum's endless moaning.

"The roads are too bumpy! Stop it Geoffrey! You're doing it on purpose!" We all loved the ricketty lanes.

BLAH BLAH BLAH she whined until it was just white noise nagging our brains. As we pulled over in paradise, still the complaints escalated and Dave was politely smiling as if it was all a silly joke that would end soon. Gradually his face became ashen.

I felt like saying, "Sorry Dave, it doesn't end. This is how she stays. ZERO sense of humour about herself or anything". ON she continued most depressingly, ruining life for all. Dave couldn't stand anymore and said, "I'm off for some air!" Lucky Dave, I mused. He was an adult and could go where he pleased. We were trapped children.

Dad kissed the famous Blarney Stone which is supposed to imbue the kisser with the gift of the gab. Talk about over-egging the pudding.

On another family trip to Ireland, our parents left us to sleep in the caravanette while they went to a country pub. Dad was saying, "No need to lock it, it's Ireland". Mum was saying, "Oh I think so".

After a while I could hear a creepy male voice talking to the second oldest sister who was in a bunk along the downstairs window. "Are you alone? Are you on holiday".

I was with the third child in the big bed over the cab, so I couldn't see him but the sound he made drove me to start shouting, "GO AWAY!" and all the children joined in.

The man came into view pulling on the back door handle, saying "Let me in!" His deep set eyes under frowning bushy white eyebrows made him look like an angry evil baboon. Then he went to try the front doors and I hoped dearly that Mum had locked the door. She had! He disappeared.

We were crying when our parents got back.

The pub landlord got a description of him, (bald with white hair and a big nose), and said, "That's Jeck, with the plumy nose, he was in the bar and overheard you saying your kids are in the car-park so he went out. I'll get the Garda". THANK GOD Mum locked us in. Dad had a really clueless side. We children always remembered Jeck and would scare each other, saying "Jeck is coming!".

NEIGHBOURING CHILDREN; Great!

I could rave on about all our neighbourhood gang. Smiling 'Cabbage' (David Rowley), Lucille, Robert and Christine Massey, handsome Alan Phillips, (ANOTHER older Headboy), and his two older beautiful sisters, Susan and Joanne who baby-sat us, Bindu the Hindu and baby Sonny. Lucien Zaraski the bi-lingual Polish boy next-door. The doctor's children who lived in the hospital grounds.

GREAT HAPPY LONG DAYS OF SUMMER HOLIDAYS. Rarely indoors.

Yes I could go on about our games, dens in the old allotment and seeing the ceremonial costumes the pretty Massey girls wore for Holy Communion because they were Catholics. We were sandwiched between two Catholic families whose children went to St Patrick's Catholic School.

We went to the comprehensive school across the road.

Oh it'd be endless if I mentioned all the children I liked. Sorry to miss you out, (if you'd even read this or want to be in a book like this). Suzanne Tyres and Claire Lancaster, two blonde cuties who played football with me on the Rec. Susan Dodd who was funny. Andrew Talbot who represented the school at football and became Head Boy alongside Head Girl Diana. My finest footballing moment was tackling the ball off Talbot up the Rec.

Banger-ball and two-bally on the wall, holding funerals for small dead animals we found, bikes and games straight after morning holiday TV, 'Champion The Wonder Horse', 'The Banana Splits' and 'The Double-Deckers'. The game '40-40 IN', or British Bulldog as some called it. We were hardly ever in our houses.

I remember feeling rock solid inside.

Lucien 'Lucheek' Zaraski's Dad would only let one child at a time in their huge garden. My boyfriend Alan Phillips, the older Head Boy at my school, told Lucheek to, "Just let Ida in but nobody else".

I replied "I don't want to come in if we all can't". We all turned our backs and walked away. Solidarity! In later years that memory buried in my battered brain reminded me that I was strong in the face of temptation.

Mrs Zaraski always took sweets off us and gave us peeled carrots to eat.

It was great spending time at Diana's house having sleepovers. But she was never invited by my mother to sleep at our house. Diana's mother, Hazel, was ten/fifteen years older than mine and she had a lot of time for us. She was so warm compared to the mum I had at home. Hazel would cook peas and rice for us and teach us songs. Diana loved The Jackson Five, so did I. It was easy to just BE around there. We were given loads of attention by Hazel Wilson.

We'd dance around a garden hole full of leaves, laughing our heads off singing, "Witches brew, witches brew, how about you for the witches brew?" We'd run races and I'd come soooo close to being level with her, but was ALWAYS pipped before the post!

One day I ran into Diana's bedroom and was confronted by a pale little girl in the dressing-table mirror. I was taken aback then realised it was me.

Living with Jamaicans and no mirrors, I'd felt warm, strong and colourful like them. The mirror told me that I wasn't Jamaican at all. Diana's mother Hazel Wilson never left me out of anything, even giving me a hair wrap at bedtime like Diana and her big sister, Princess Leonora.

In later years it struck me what Diana's Dad, Benny Wilson must have gone through at work in the factory. As a child, I saw another black man walking down the lane after work and some rude children giggling, shouting, "BIG NIG NOG!"

I'd never heard that expression before. The man didn't react and kept steadfastly walking. Very strong I thought, and very wrong of the children.

Later it hit me that Benny always sat quietly alone in the front room after work and was probably exhausted from jibes all day. He never let it show to his daughters. Great man.

Bob Crumpton; First meeting.

Gillian McAusland, a Scottish girl in my class lived down the road. Her mum was lovely too. One day on our bikes, she introduced me to an older boy, about 11, very shy, on his Chopper bike. He blushed bright red under his mop of dark brown curls, and lived over the allotments on the newly built council estate.

I'd no idea that our paths would cross again when I turned 17. He would become the first man I ever lived with and would later become a celebrated comedian in the UK, using the name Bob Crumpton.

The first local child to be run over by a car was 4 year old Jonathan who lived a couple of doors closer to Prospect Road. He lived but his leg was damaged. The next local child to be run over was a little boy from the new estate, across Prospect Road. We all heard that he was very badly hurt in hospital. Then the tragic news of his death. I had no idea that he was the little brother of Bob Crumpton until I was 17 and recognised his sweet smiling face in a school photo at Bob's parents house.

As an adult I appeared semi-naked on a TV show with the words 'CARS SUCK' emblazoned across my buttocks in honour of those injured and killed children.

HOME AGAIN; Danger!

All was not good inside the house. Blazing rows between the parents. One sunny day Icame in from a bike mission to find myself in the middle of a killer row. "GET OUT! IDA! GET OUT!" yelled mum.

"Why should she? This is her home", countered Dad. "Stay where you are Ida!"

"GET OUT!!!"

"Stay in".

I didn't know whether to come or go. Then mum got hold of me and flung me through the hall door, SLAMMING it to shake the house. My finger hurt, but I didn't look as my parents row was more upsetting. Then I looked at my hand and saw my right forefinger was hanging off, all flat. I opened the hall door to a barrage of, "GET OUT!!" from mother. Then I held up my hand and said, "...but my finger.."

Dad saw it and whisked me to hospital, tears in his eyes. (Sweet). He saw a wild eyed doctor, didn't like him and demanded the Consultant, who wouldn't be free for hours.

"My daughter's a pianist!" said Dad. "She must regain feeling!" (Lie). So I was quickly bandaged and went to the cafe over the road to wait hours for the Consultant.

FINALLY the finger was stitched and dealt with. At home, mother just rolled her eyes and never said a word to me about it, like it was all my fault. Oh dear.

Had to go back to hospital for checks, where I was asked how my piano playing was going.

Dumbfounded, I suddenly remembered the lie and quietly said, "Fine thank you".

The home rows were appalling. Dad would go out to get cigarettes and not come home for days. He looked exhausted and weary. Mother looked like a manic bird of prey. A pterodactyl with mad steely eyes. At the time her physical attacks seemed random, but in hindsight the lodgers were always out at work.

But there were fun times as the whole family would unite in raucous song on car drives singing “DERBYSHIRE BORN. DERBYSHIRE BRED! STRONG IN THE ARM, THICK IN THE HEAD”.

I was the only one born in Derby. They were happy and that’s the main thing.

PORN; A diet of soft porn.

Porn crackers, porn on the cob, porn on toast, porn.

When I was eight or younger, mother came into the bedroom I shared with two sisters and said, “Come and look at THIS Ida!”

She led me to her bedroom, and lifted the hinged lid of the bench seating under her platform bed. What could it be?

“PORN!” said my mother, pointing at stacks of magazines with titles like Penthouse, Men Only, Hustler etc. “There’s over four hundred pounds worth here that your Daddy has spent!”

Didn’t know how best to react, speechless. Didn’t understand the significance of porn. Mother opened the pages to show me wide open vaginas and all the women with their mouths half open.

Still didn’t understand.

Why show me?

I felt I was meant to look at these strange magazines of models with vacant looking stares and names ending in ‘i’. So I did. Daddy didn’t have anything to say about it either.

Regularly I sat under my parents bed engrossed in the photos and articles. One about fellatio which I pronounced in my head to rhyme with 'the patio'. I was only eight for goodness sake. Written by a man, this fictional girl decided she preferred fellatio to hot-dogs. Hard to get my head around. Sorry, not funny.

But they stayed in my head, the images. Lots and lots and lots of vaginas and mention of the word "clit" and "clitoris", but no directions as to where it was. Inside? I vaguely guessed.

It transpired that very few men knew where the clitoris was when I grew up. I blamed porn and its supercilious, sleazy, smug, empty articles. Also deficient sex education in schools. But I'm not bitter.

A boy showed me where my clitoris was when I was the ripe old age of 21! Up to then I'd been wriggling around all night whilst the males snored having ejaculated whilst I hadn't, but we didn't realise it.

The boys/men called me a "nymphomaniac", when all along, I just wasn't always satisfied with wham bam. Oh I liked it a lot but it's not the same as a serious orgasm. (Now I won't have sex outside marriage and have been a born again virgin for years).

Daddy said, "Ida, making love is the most natural thing in the world". This caused me to be a slag. Well it greatly contributed.

We had Desiderata on our wall everywhere we went for years, a tract on how to conduct life, allegedly found in a church. We knew it well as it ended up on the toilet wall, so we read it everyday. "Be on good terms with all people as far as possible without surrender. Even the dull and ignorant, they too have their story". (They sure do).

It's not bad but it's NEW AGE, and says to be at peace with your God whatever you conceive that to be. As I found out in person, there's only Jesus that actually shows up. As you'll see if you stick with this book.

I'd have been better served by Proverbs in the Bible. Not read the Bible fully yet but it contains really good advice. I had zero advice from my family. Except my Dad kindly told us, "You can do anything!" Oh and he told us to use the outside cutlery first and work our way inwards when dining in posh restaurants.

There were no penises in the porn mags and there was no moral code regarding sex in our house. Anything went. I entered Dave's attic room when he lived with us and him and Jan were having sex. Mum was doing it with a teacher's husband. She'd bend over to 'do something' in a mini dress in front of him flashing her knickers in the middle of the day when I was seven. (A move I incorporated into my stripping). Dad was doing it with an eighteen year old down South. On a family trip without mother, we three girls went in the ostentatious cream left-hand drive Mercedes (that made it look like a child was driving), to a Cornish hotel that dad wanted to do some kind of deal with. I walked into a hotel room in the middle of the day followed by a hotel owner's wife. Luckily she stopped at the doorway and couldn't see round the corner into the room. She left. When I got round the corner inside the room and saw the 'love making', I was shocked but stayed cool and told dad he better be more careful because an owner nearly caught him. Both the nubile and my dad interrogated me to find out how much the owner had seen. They were appeased that their cover wasn't blown.

That night I went to bed and cried with childish loyalty to my mother. A bunch of hippies crowded my bed, and told me it was ok, my mum did it as well. "No she doesn't", I cried. But I was wrong, she did. She just couldn't stand dad doing it as well. Double standards. (That last sentence was superfluous).

DEAR READER;

never tell your child crossly, "YOU'RE JUST LIKE YOUR DAD / MUM!!" It makes children feel worthless when their parent calls them fundamentally rubbish because of who they're 50% related to.

BTW. I can't afford Word with the spellchecker and am writing on Notebook, so all my good spelling so far is natural. But although I love spelling I'm not a grammar Nazi to others.

(Amendment: I've now got Libre Office & my only mistakes were triptych and pterodactyl).

ALLIANCE STREET. Why?

Who could understand why mum was set on leaving Corporation St. for a tiny box in Alliance St.? Twelve years old, different area so all new friends at school. Don't worry I won't list them.

The Diamondette cheerleader team practised at the local social club and I became the Diamondette that was held up on top of the pyramid of girls whilst in the splits. When I fell towards the parquet floor they held on to my legs so I was hanging upside down. We marched in the town pageant and danced in open air competitions on local common grounds. I cartwheeled while the girls danced in unison. Unthinkably I'd become one of those marching girls who smack their legs to the beat until their thighs are red, whom my sisters and I used to think were mad as they paraded through Stafford High Street, hitting their legs like that.

Mum had a new bathroom in Alliance Street in which to smash my skull on the sink, at the back of the house with frosted windows. Perfect for her. She'd drag me in there and smash every bit of me. On my bed in absolute agony afterwards, I'd be thinking "?" kiboshed. But of course I just absorbed it, got on with life and didn't tell tales. WELL I'M TELLING NOW woman.

I witnessed Dad take you (Mum) from a caravan to a massive house which he extended to make a downstairs shower, laundry and kitchen, an upstairs office where Dad's suited accountant Richard would go, and a new upstairs bathroom. I saw him pour the concrete on the new massive kitchen floor so we walked on planks. Far ahead of the times, it was open through a big entrance to the huge lounge. You had hundreds of pounds worth of mahogany dining table, a Chesterfield sofa, a leather wing-backed chair, a massive velvet sofa, Persian intricate rugs, a beautiful rug bought in Morocco on the wall, books galore, music, art, gold, silver, a bidet, an exquisitely made platform bed, the list of your riches goes on. AND an ancient pull out door bell attached to a wire with a real old bell on a coil of metal in a stunningly tiled Victorian hall. We were so lucky and we all appreciated what Dad had created. Yet you only wanted more, sulked and moaned and battered your child and set your mind on destroying me entirely by banning me from my own siblings that I loved as much as my own breath. Answer to God. (Reader you will see later how much worse she became and nothing I tried would stop her).

Dad had a diamond needle Pioneer sound system at the new box house, the bass from a speaker boomed right under my box bedroom and shook me in my bed 'til late each night, (as soon as I got into a rhythm to sleep, the rhythm would switch), but I still had to go to school.

We were raided by police. Barbara, the lady of the B'ham couple who were staying with us, went to prison. Not sure about her guitarist boyfriend Alan. David Bowie resonated out of the speakers thanks to them. We looked after their daughter Lisa. Dad stayed free. Sad for Barbara who was a LOVELY funny woman. I slept in the windowless roof space with chipboard across the beams to walk on.

A nosy teacher would come snooping when I was off school. I'd hide and peek at her staring at the house. At school she'd ask questions like, "How many live in your house? Eight? Isn't that a lot of people to be in such a tiny house?". As if it was her business, or I had any control. I'd shrug.

Dad took all of us to London while Mum was in a Harley Street Clinic having an abortion of her fourth child. We went to the Planetarium and fell asleep. It was a cold bleak feeling when we arrived at the clinic to see Mum in her private room. I felt even more lucky to be alive.

My new secondary school was very flash and a far walk. It was the school chosen for Prince Charles to visit. Broken tiles were fixed, tennis courts were resurfaced, paint applied. We were all sent home to keep the place looking tidy for his visit. I served out two years at that school. Ignored the bitchy lonely girl who didn't like me being 'good at art' and hissed nasty names at me when the teacher wasn't looking.

At this school I was in the Olympic Gymnastic class after school and was singled out of my day class to play an instrument after they tested us all wearing headphones to see if we could differentiate between very similar tones. 100% correct and I was sent with a boy named Vincent who'd been singled out of another class, to see a music teacher. We two could choose a French Horn or a violin. Violins at school sounded awful. Not realising that with practise a violin could sound amazing and are also lightweight and don't make your hand wet, we went for the very heavy horn, stupidly.

We would be summoned out of our classes to go to a sports changing room among the football boots to have French Horn lessons, just Vincent, me and the teacher.

The French Horn case was massive and looked like a toilet. 54 Alliance Street was too tiny to practise a horn. Nobody liked hearing it.

ROLLERSKATING was what I lived for. Saturday mornings at the rink with Julie Bates where we learned to spin around in style.

Had fun bringing choice pages of porn to school to show the two boys who sat behind me. One page was called 'GUMS' and had a Barbara Cartland look-a-like covered in powder and make-up with her flaccid boobs and legs wide open for the camera. Those boys called me Kate Bush due to my mass of long hair. It occurred to me that Kate Bush had a good idea of how to make a living. Records!

The school netball team I was in played an away game at a school called Rising Stream. Our team couldn't believe how shabby it was. Rubble and old wooden huts outside an ageing school building, litter and no fancy pants stuff like we had at Graham Balfour.

Three months later Rising Stream would suddenly be my new school. DA DA DAAAA!

AUSTRALIA. Now 2018;

Aah, excuse me, here comes my 'Street To Home' worker, Suzanne Lambert. Sue is a London girl who knows what must be done to keep me ticking over. Brilliant helper, straight talker, great person and a good laugh. Sue is organising for me to have a dog. It will be great to have a dog of my own after all these years since Charlie, also it will bark at burglars. Sue took me to Church to get a food parcel and the allowance of three free clothes.

"Now DON'T give these away Ida! These are for YOU! You'll have nothing left, giving all your stuff away!"

Sue gets very exasperated at my delusion that I'm Elvis, giving presents to everyone. (Janice Connolly aka Mrs Barbara Nice, the Birmingham comedian used to say, "Shes a giver! She gives too much!" of my enthusiasm for comedy shows:-).

My explanation for giving stuff, besides Jesus of course, is the picture by Salvadore Dali entitled, "The Weaning of The Furniture". The lady in the picture is sitting desolate on a beach with a hole in her body the shape of a chest of drawers, as if her furniture was her life and she's gutted about losing it.

So I choose to test myself by giving good stuff away, gold, silver, leather, ANYTHING, to prove the stuff doesn't own me. I was suffocated with stuff for years, especially in London. Retro this, handmade leather that.

A plethora of fine hats, boots, leopard skin coat and objet d'art from decades ago.

Then I read a passage in the Bible where Jesus says to 'get rid of all your stuff and follow me'. He also said it's easier for a camel to get through the eye of the needle than for a rich man to enter Heaven.

So I took all my stuff to Brick Lane London and gave it away for donations which I gave to the Iraq shop for the bombed babies. A friend said I was "mad" and "neither rich nor a man". I reasoned, "we in the West are ALL rich".

I was nicked for unlicensed trading and fined 100 pounds. I disputed the case using Common Law and Iraq shop receipts and won.

It was hard initially to part with things but became easier and easier to freely give special stuff that I loved. New stuff always appears to fill the vacuum. God is good.

AND you get to spoil people who don't get many nice presents. Never again will I be ruled by possessions. My ancient 2nd hand cowboy boots that I painted are in London awaiting my return! HA! But I'd give them away too. We come to Earth naked and leave with nothing.

(BUT I DO NOT WANT TO LIVE IN A WORLD WHERE WE ARE NOT FREE TO BUY AND TRADE WHAT WE WANT, I just don't set too much importance on stuff)

SO MUCH HELP IN AUSTRALIA!!! MORE THAN I'VE EVER HAD!!

Then Aidan, my 6ft four Australian born, half Irish, half Aussie ex-husband came around on Good Friday. I went to hug him hello and he typically responded with,

"GET AWAY FROM ME WOMAN WITH YOUR FLESH BANDITRY!!!"

He's given up booze, smokes and gambling. His discipline is incredible. He now drinks only purified water from the Reverse Osmosis filter he set up here. I'm trying to emulate him. Twice in my life I've stopped smoking for 4 months. Once when I was 33, then began again after being pressured into an abortion. Once in Australia on the organic farm whilst Aidan still smoked. But I started again in the city. Aidan's Irish accent comes out occasionally in very florid language and crazy made up words. He made me wee on my sofa, I was laughing so hard and I had to wash it. He sees straight through me in a laser beam hilariously funny way and is super masculine. On the organic farm in a couple of hours he single-handedly dug a 6 ft deep, 20+ ft long trench for pipes.

(As I'm editing this in Feb 2022, the powers that be want to make man into machine. HEY you power mad bastards! Aidan's already an organic machine better than any cyborg ingredients you can inject into people!)

We both worked from dawn to dusk picking all kinds of fruit. Excellent after being in London.

He drove me around today in his heart-stopping style and chose and bought me some delicious shopping; salmon, french bread, olives, blue cheese and lots of real coffee. He's a rustic chef and has pushed my culinary education further back. He always gives me the best of organic food and brings me books about The Bible too, plus he plays wild guitar.

He's vastly better than he was when I ran away from him a couple of years ago. He used to chuck the Bible against the wall when I met him. Back in those days he fought speeding cars in the dark in the middle of the road, as if bullfighting. Heart attack material. Now he loves Jesus and God. He was born in August 1978 a Leo and I'm from September 1964, Virgo. You do the maths.

When we first met in a Perth backpackers hostel he was about 32 and I was in my late 40's but we couldn't tell how old we were. As he began standing up, he kept getting higher and higher until he was the tallest most perfect man I'd ever seen. A living work of art.

He said, "How's this for a deal, I cook you a steak, you give me something to cook it in and wash up?"

GAME ON!

He's amassed so many tickets, (as the Aussies call certificates), since I met him that he's now in 'The Purple Circle' at work because he can drive ANY vehicle, any size. He'd walk 30km as the crow flies across fields and over fences to get to his tests on time when we had nothing. He ALWAYS walks as the crow flies and I'd be dragging my big case over walls and fences for miles. He'd help me chuck it over walls. Eventually our lifestyle led me to have just an onboard flight case with my papers inside. Oh we've had intense ups and downs in our cowboy bush-wacker hats but after everything I'll always have massive respect for that young man. He'd say, "Little lady, I'm going to put some roses in your cheeks". And he DID!

We saw loads of WA in the first few years of our marriage, working and travelling. We never saw TV, (I've not had a TV for 15 years), just lay on a mattress looking out the big open backdoor of our van at amazing sunsets over the sea, like staircases to the moon. The best time of my life. Sleeping on beaches, in villages, (waking up eyeball to eyeball with a deadly brown snake), in vans, hotels, back-packer hostels, farms, shared houses, flats, even a mansion. Whilst on the move I was also doing paperwork for immigration in libraries and cafes.

Aidan could never compromise with anyone and never backed down. Leading us to be sleeping on beaches and waking up with a deadly brown snake staring me in the face 6cms from my eyeballs. I wrote it again! As my eyes focused and I realised that what I'd thought was a stick was a snake, for a few moments I was mesmerised by the intricate beauty of the snake's tiny scales and brown eye staring at me. Then I jolted back to reality and the fact that it wasn't a DVD, press rewind, eject, this was a killer! Man did I jump up fast!

Aidan gambled and drank like nobody I'd ever met who was still alive. After a couple of years of me being gone, he reformed himself like night into day. Only pure water, no smoking and instead of throwing my Bible at the wall, he gave me Biblical literature and prayed. AMAZING. He is an amazing character. I will return to the Aborigines whom we lived with for a year.

Since I ran away from Aidan I've been in a Women's Refuge, a mental institution again after taking Champix, then stayed with a friend in Denmark WA until my place came up in a psychiatric hostel called 'Ngulla Mia', which means 'Our Place' in Aboriginal. (Hair-raising at times with a psycho hurling a cup at my head, but great and they even gave me driving lessons!).

Then I went to Sunflower Villas where the staff come to your own personal villa and remind you to take your medication.

Wow! Now I'm HERE! In my own groovy, cheap rent govt flat or 'unit' as the Aussies say, and I have outreach workers. WHAT AN AMAZING COUNTRY! But back to the story of UK,

(Australia and Aidan deserve their own book!)

RISING STREAM HIGHSCHOOL; insane.

Just turned fifteen I started at my new shabby school from my new home on Highfields estate, the dour council estate. We'd become homeless and the council handed my parents the keys to Attlee Crescent. It occurred to me that the architect of Highfields didn't like people. Mental cruelty is what it was design wise, (and believe me I tried to enhance it in my head).

My first week at Rising Stream High I was corralled into a fight over a boy behind the library after school. Loads of blood-thirsty strangers crowded round for the spectacle.

It transpired that 'Basher', the Bates brother I'd hung out with over summer on the estate, was already the boyfriend of Denise, a girl from a different area. Basher Bates friendship with me was just NOT ON!

The fact that only Basher had known of Denise's existence was out the window. Like a bizarre ritual the fight was on. Feeling like I was in 'Stupid Land', reluctantly I did my bit and it was over in a flash, with ringing ears on the way home. The disappointed crowd dissipated. I'm not sure who won.

MARIE-ANTOINETTE Ida

Denise became a good fun friend after that. We sat next to each other in Home Ec. Our Home Ec teacher didn't like working. Mrs Mopdale and her side-kick assistant Mrs Leakin would stalk other classrooms requesting, "Big strong boys needed to help in the Home Economics room please".

These boys would be excused from their respective classes and lured to sit in the Home Ec top kitchen around a table full of cake and tea with Mrs Mopdale and Mrs Leakin.

They'd all be talking and jolly, eating away without a care that all us Home Ec girls in our little kitchen areas were doing nothing! Just entertaining ourselves, yawning, drawing cartoon pictures of Mrs Mopdale without a bottom and boobs sagging to her stomach. It was a lesson-free zone.

One day I could take no more of this power abuse. I stood up. "Mrs Moppdale, I would like some cake and tea please". Appdale muttered darkly to Leakin. "Get Ida some tea and cake". "Mrs Moppdale" I continued, "Also my friend Denise would like tea and cake please, in fact the entire class wants tea and cake thank you".

Chastened, Mrs Mopdale made sure every girl was included. Ha!

There was a Mexican stand-off type situation between the posh girls and the girls from my estate. Suspicion of the unknown on both sides. The poshies were called "snobs", and the council girls were called "dangerous". I was the coloured intersection of the Venn Diagram because I knew both sides of life.

The posh girls only visited me a couple of times as their mums, "don't like the area". Well I lived in it, so tough shit all round. Then I remembered being 'posh' myself back at Corporation St., and our family had no problem at all with me playing on the council estate.

So after I'd decorated our mouldy Highfields bathroom, I vowed to refuse to be ashamed over my new environment anymore, or the fact that I had free school dinners and just couldn't afford the food the posh girls bought at lunchtime from the shops. I had my free dinner queue pals.

The posh girl's parents didn't mind me visiting them, just not the other way round. They had horses, detached houses and their dads owned car dealerships.

I loved going to see Linda Owen at her Renault Garage and listening to 'Young Americans' by David Bowie; and disco dancing with her on Tuesday nights at The Top Of The World, wearing outfits made for us by the great Alexandra Gribbin.

Dawn Gilbert's dad owned a book factory where we worked in summer assembling bargain bags of books and crayons. Factory life was repetitive and people laughed at me for wanting to finish up my bargain bag before leaving for tea break. I soon realised there was no point in taking pride in work in the factory.

Nicky Shaw was super posh, horses AND her dad ran Shaws Garage. Very beautiful and in my maths group and was also in the coloured intersection of the Venn diagram because her boyfriend lived on Highfields estate.

We sat by each other in maths and spent lessons being entertained by the boys who sat behind us.

Steve 'Dabz' Davis and Mark Forsythe who was Nicky's boyfriend from Highfields.

Mark and Dabz were the funniest pair I'd ever met and could keep such straight faces whilst being hilarious. Dabz looked like a man with his sideburns. He was Fonzy alright. A king, and Marilyn, an Italian girl, was his queen. Dabz 'n' Maz. Totally beyond all that school could throw at them.

There was a dimly lit turd coloured corridor at Rising Stream, with coats hanging in the alcoves blocking out light from the tiny high windows. How could they make a place of learning look as if we were all poos jostling down an anal passage to get out??

My coat was in the upper cloakroom where my posh classmates hung out and my body was in the lower cloakroom where the posh girls didn't go. When the Highfields estate girls got over my so called 'posh' voice, we skint people got on very well. We were good neighbours, and they were full of funny sayings to each other;

"Come over 'ere!" "No you come 'ere the busfare's cheaper!" "What d'you want, a medal or a chest to put it on?!" "What you lookin' at?" "Dunno the label's dropped off".

Special thanks for helping me stay alive to Sheila Dunn and family who trusted my hair-cutting skill. Sheila played eclectic punk records including The Slits and Janet Kay's 'Silly Games' in her busy bedroom and she stuck up for me against mum's boyfriend. Cheers to Heather Faulkener for being a laugh, Marie 'Muz' for being so cute, and Tania Warburton and family. Tania played 'Supremes' records which we'd sing loudly in the street on our way downtown. "Aint no mountain high enough!" Tania was Highfields answer to Marilyn Monroe. I'll never forget.

ATTLEE CRESCENT: Highfields estate.

Mum was pregnant again with a fourth little girl when we moved in. We'd lost our Alliance street owned home and were homeless until the council gave us the keys to Attlee Crescent. The floors were exposed concrete with broken tiles. Fake brick wallpaper was on the downstairs wall. Our visitors were encouraged to paint graffiti on it. Mark Styles, a college lecturer wrote, 'DON'T DILLY DALI ON THE WAY' and 'CANUTE IS ALL WET'.

A Scottish hippy postman, O'Leery, visited us, surveyed the family and said to dad in a wheedling accent,...

"Nice set-up you've got here Geoff...".

Dad and I didn't realise how ominous that was. (It was not a 'nice set-up'. It was a family that Dad had poured his heart, soul and hard work into. O'Leery had no effing clue).

My dad was around for my first month at Rising Stream secondary school. Mum said they'd never been so happy. Less was more. Police arrived one morning and only dad and I were in.

The Police had a series of cleverly stacked photos to catch dad out with. Eg. "Who is this man?" The photo depicted a South American named Flaco in front of the Mannequin De Piss in Brussels.

Flaco was connected to my father through cocaine smuggling. (We all drove to Belgium and Flaco asked us all to wear gold watches for him as we went through customs then we gave them back on the other side).

Dad made a big show of not having his glasses, trying to focus on the photo, he said he really couldn't see. The police then showed another pic with us kids in the frame with Flaco in Brussels.

"Well he seems to be very friendly with your children Mr Sputum".

Then dad showed me the photo and said, "Oh yes Ida! Isn't that Ima the Irish fiddle player?' Frozen feeling I took the hint, "Sandra's boyfriend", I replied. LIE. We knew Ima and Sandra but they were Irish looking from Dublin.

Then the police showed a picture of the Mercedes. Dad claimed no knowledge. Then they showed another pic of it and asked if Dad knew why it was outside our old small house crushing next-door's greenhouse? (Mum had reversed it and smashed the fence down and crushed the neighbours greenhouse). Dad wriggled his way out of it again with claims of not having his glasses. Stress.

It was magic mushroom season, so dad sent us children out to the fields beyond the council estate. We'd been trained on what kind of shroom to pick. As dusk came it got easier and easier to find them as we were near the electricity pylon and it made the phosphorus in the mushrooms glow. There were mushrooms drying out on mesh trays on every lampshade in the house. Dad ate nothing but.

At school I was hanging out with an Afghan coated hippy girl named Brandy Butter. At first I thought she didn't belong in our classroom as she looked like a sixth former and was wearing the brown sixth former's uniform. She was extremely well-developed, and looked like an hour-glass with long thick chestnut hair and a face like actress Judy Geeson.

The posh girls who'd first adopted me as their friend, pointed at Brandy and told me, "We don't associate with her!" When I asked why not, they just said, "because we don't".

An unsatisfactory reason, so I became friends with Brandy. She walked home from school my way until just before the council estate. But she was fully allowed to visit my home and we'd go out at night to visit older boys that she knew, 16, 17 year old prog rock heads, whom she slept with. Randy Brandy. We heard the bands Gong, Hawkwind and Led Zepplin's Stairway To Heaven.

I was happy that she liked my dad and liked visiting us in her tight pink corduroy jeans. It was a cold, rainy Autumn and dad would give her a lift home most nights.

For some reason the TV was in mum and dad's room and we'd all sit on the big cushion covered mattress. Sat on the edge, I looked around and Brandy and dad's hands were on each others thighs.

They smiled.

"Weirdness afoot", I thought. I shrugged it off kind of.

One day I went downstairs to find Dad and Brandy locked in an embrace, kissing. I was thunderstruck. Refused to speak to Brandy for ages.

Although dad could have stopped her, him being the adult. But he probably encouraged her. I had encouraged her myself with my enthusiastic tales of Daddy's exploits and his ability to pick up heavy things. He had fine, chiselled looking muscles. But they did what they did....whatever it was? She was 14, I'd just turned 15.

ALONE WITH MOTHER & O'LEERY; Grim

Dad went to Holland to regain our fortune and I was alone at home with mother and sisters. Every week school mates would ask,

"Is your dad back yet?" "No but he will be soon", I'd answer brightly.

Dad wrote to us, sent some money and I sent him a funny reply about fat Mr Weeble across the road baring his body again, making me wish for snow and a photo-booth pic of me. Dad wrote back that I already had boyfriends in Holland. Then I heard nothing for months.

The classmates continued asking if I'd heard from my dad, by then I'd sadly reply, "No". Wistfully dreaming of going down town and bumping into him.

Little did I realise that Dad's presence at home and the frequent presence of the lodgers who lived with us and friends had stemmed the tide of abuse from my mother. Dad and his associates had held back my mother's hell so it had only appeared in flashes when there were no viewers around, as the lodgers all worked in the day. Left alone with her, I had no preparation for the following.

O'Leery moved into the house, bringing copious amounts of booze with him. We children didn't really have an issue either way. We were used to not being consulted by then and we were too busy with our own lives and new school, also we were used to lots of people around. But O'Leery wanted to be noticed. Particularly by me.

O'Leery liked hitting me and screaming at me "MORON!" repeatedly at the top of his lungs in his laborious Scottish accent, like a full force deafening wind tunnel in my face. I knew it was wrong. That was Mum's job. He wasn't even related!

Mum never intervened. I used to think very confusedly, "Mum is my mum, so she's allowed to smash me. Mum must love me really, she's just not able to deal with horrible men".

My estate friends met my mum and told me straight out, "Your mums a bitch!" I wish it was so clear-cut from my side, but she was the only mum I'd ever had and I was used to surviving on abuse so I lived in delusion, making excuses for her for years.

After three or four months of painful confusion, Dad suddenly appeared and woke me up in the middle of the night and told me to pack some clothes because we were going to Holland in a couple of hours.

Linda Owen from the Renault garage was meeting me in town the next day, Saturday, and there was some kind of exam at school next week, then there was my new little sister Lucy to miss. I'd no idea if I'd ever see them again.

When I told dad straight, "O'Leery's hitting me", dad just replied "Really? That doesn't sound like O'Leery". I told myself "You're on your own".

But I had to get away from O'Leery, so I packed quickly and we were soon on our way by train, boat and bus with dad's landlady, Alice, a very formidable half Dutch, half Israeli woman who had travelled with Dad from Arnhem.

As the train pulled out, the thought of never seeing my baby sister again had me in tears. A passenger lady said to me, "If you don't go to Holland now, you'll never know what you'll miss. This way, you won't miss out". True, I thought.

ARNHEM, HOLLAND; Brothel home.

After the boat, the coach. It pulled up to a service station petrol pump. "Where's the toilet?!" asked Alice. The driver pointed a hundred yards away at the cafe.

Alice muttered something, got off the coach, and right there on the forecourt, she hoisted up her skirt, pulled down her tights and pissed gallons all over the floor. In front of the windows of the coach passengers. Part of me died inside.

I'd given up being embarrassed on behalf of anyone else when I was a fourth year junior. It was a waste of emotion. How could I explain away Alice to the horrified Bible reading girl from Missouri sitting by me? I didn't bother.

The Missouri girl left the coach and an Afghan man sat next to me. He had a key-ring made out of a real baby crocodile's head. He explained that the crocs were bred in tanks until key-ring size, then decapitated. He gave it to me and I kept the croc head for ages, lest its short life be in vain.

We arrived in Spijker Straat, Arnhem where Alice and Dad lived with her two young sons Ronald and Harry. (Little Ronald was a 4 year old firecracker who went on to become a kick-boxing champion).

It was an elegant building with marble steps and a black wrought iron balcony on the first floor. Three storeys high. The ground floor was fire damaged and blackened which showed on the double front doors.

Directly at the top of the first staircase from the street, was an old style bathroom with a red light on and a brass bed. That was where the customers went with Alice.

Ali also ran it as a boarding house which is how my dad met her when he and his English mates moved in looking for Dutch or German work.

Ali would get ready for a night's work by painting her eyes in exaggerated strokes. I offered to help make her up, as I'd done so with my family and friends.

But dad explained that the men had to see her in the first floor window from the street, so she had to be theatrical in her application of silver and black eye make-up with her cleavage hoisted up. It was the late 70's, few women had tattoos and Alice was one of them. She was about 5ft tall in heels, fairly large, half Israeli with a fine featured face and tiny freckles on her olive complexion. "Much woman", as dad said.

When she was working we stayed out of the way, or out of the house. Dad said she was the best business woman he'd ever met and how she charged a set price for each breast, and more for sex.

OK... right...thanks.

One day I was staring at the Dutch city horizon from a top bedroom, oblivious to below, when a huge roar shook the place. "FUCK YOUR FUCKING DAUGHTER!!"

Alice had been working on the first floor and the men had been looking up at me, not Alice. I didn't know. It was an accident. Ali eventually calmed down but she wanted me gone.

Then one day a huge unshaven man in a dirty vest came storming into the kitchen upstairs. I was alone. "Where's Alice?" he yelled.

"She's out". Then he began lunging for me and managed to grab my top but I escaped his grip of my T-shirt and tore downstairs to the Gay Bar at the corner of Spijker street. No joy there. Five bars later I found dad and Alice and told them about the big guy.

"SONNY!" Alice said, looking at dad. Sonny was an ex-husband, fresh out of jail. Ali and dad took me to a Police Station and told me to say exactly what happened. I sat alone with an officer who listened to my memory and asked if Sonny had touched me inappropriately. "No, he just grabbed my T-shirt and I escaped". "OK, thank you", said the officer.

Outside, Dad and Alice interrogated me as to what I'd said to the policeman. "Ida!" dad said frustrated, "you could have lied and got him locked up!" Oh dear, how did I know I was suddenly supposed to lie? Alice was disgusted at me, shaking her head.

It's an urban legend that Alice went into town with a gun looking for a man who'd crossed her. She went into the bar with her gun ready, evacuated the place, except for a tall Dutch man at the bar. He looked down at her, five ft tall, nearly as wide, with tattoos and he laughed, "HA HA HA!"

"YOU!" Alice growled, "DANCE". He carried on laughing. So she shot him in the foot and said again, "DANCE", and he began hopping on one foot.

My father told that story and stated, "I'd rather have Ali on my side than an army!" Dad told of how Alice's phone broke which she needed for work. Instead of contacting the phone company, she took an axe and plunged it into the Police Chiefs desk. "Fix my phone!" And it was fixed.

Alice liked stiff drinks and when she got angry it took four Turks to hold her down. A Dutch TV personality wanted to write her colourful life story, but she said, "Write your OWN life!"

A woman approached dad, me and Ali in the street to ask the time. Alice growled, "GET YOUR OWN HUSBAND!"

People rarely turned up to the house without flowers for her, preferably twelve red roses. Every three days or so Alice would have a massive temper fit and the little boys and I found ourselves in the street below picking up the toaster and lamps etc that Alice would ritually throw off the balcony. My dad got tired of getting new glass and decided to put up bendy perspex windows to bounce the items back into the room. (Allegedly she once threw out a bread slab and hit a man below).

Alice went nuts again one day, holding a teaspoon with a bit of Rizla box wrapped round it,

SCREAMING as if unhinged, "THIS was in your daughters room! Geoffrey! NO MORE DRUGS in my house!!" I didn't know what a Rizla box on a spoon had to do with drugs. It wasn't mine.

Dad looked at me in disgust, "It's for heroin". I'd no idea. It was obviously a set-up to get me out.

SQUATS.

Dad took me to stay in a squat or 'KRACKHAUS' in nearby Prince Hendrix Straat. Oh my God it was beautiful. The floor was white painted, then swirled into black, it was like an Escher or Beardsley picture. The lights were cosy, the music was multifarious and EFFING AWESOME.

Young Bruce Springsteen, 'Baby we were Born to Run', Little Feat's album, 'Thanks I'll Eat It Here'. Talking Heads, 'Psycho Killer'. An Adonis looking blonde Dutch dude lived there with his stunning, blonde Dutch girlfriend. People arrived. Pot was smoked.

I slept soundly fumigated on the couch. No worries.

Somehow Dad got me my own bedroom in a squat in Ouver Straat, an old shop converted to a squat, with big shop windows either side of the door. On one side of the front door were loads of stolen bikes, on the other side, a big lounge kitchen with a massive trestle table, the window hung with coloured cloths and posters. There were loads of rooms upstairs and floors and I was given my own room.

Dad stuck around for about an hour then left me there. I only saw him occasionally from then on. One night he visited and slept across from me on my double futon thing. We were dressed. His hand reached for my tits briefly with a devilish cackle. Again, I thought "I'm on my own'.

(**John Cooper-Clarke the punk poet** stayed with me for a few of his B'ham gigs and he said, "Aww yer dad was just trying to cop a feel!"

If I don't get to finish PART 2 of this book chronologically, I'll say right here that Mr CooperClarke was/is a sharp suited cool and ageless man. Sharp brained too. His poem that features being brought up by an Alsatian dog transpired to be from his vivid imagination and observations, not autobiographical at all. He was a Grammar School boy from a pleasant home. John knows how to enjoy life and how to treat a woman. Great fun on and off stage. The brain is the sexiest organ and John is/was a gift to women. Always refreshingly direct and supportive of me. We sang Rat Pack songs into the night. No complaints.

ARNHEM

Men from all over Europe and America lived at Ouver Straat Arnhem Holland. Everybody living there was male except for Monique, a beautiful French hippy girl who used to visit.

Every single one of those men treated me with respect, fed me, took me out drinking and dancing until 6 a.m. They watched me throw up out of first floor windows, down the side of buildings. Even carried me home. Except once when I was dropped for being rude. I smoked weed in an upstairs room of the squat with a Leeds man, as I looked at him he became an old Rasta with a knitted beret, then Einstein. He was happy to know that. That was my first joint.

(Those were the days when no school friend could make me smoke a cigarette. I'd chew up peer pressure and spit it out).

In the Arnhem squat we'd sleep til 4 or 5pm, then I'd maybe go out stealing clothes and come back to eat food all together, hear the talk, get ready and go out until 6am. Repeat. For months.

School was forgotten.

Btw, I had a 'moral code' about stealing; never off an individual or small shop, only big shops.

THIEF!; All the time.

Thieving became a life-style as soon as I'd seen my dad in the supermarket with packs of bread and sugar down his jacket when we were desperado back at Highfields estate. I'd never seen stealing before. We'd been brought up not to steal and it shocked me a bit, but I reasoned that Dad was an enterprising person and was not about to let money dictate whether we ate. Good on him.

From then on, if there was a BIG shop with their guard down and something I wanted, I'd get it. Mum just said, "Don't get caught", when I gave her some stolen make-up.

In Holland they already had electronic tags, so I'd be cutting small holes in clothes to remove tags. When I finally got back to England all the estate neighbours were wearing expensive Dutch trousers with a tiny hole somewhere in each one that you couldn't notice. They liked the story of me cutting the holes.

I'd learned drinking whilst out in Dutch bars with my dad. It'd be day or night and we'd have cold ham and warm eggs from the bar and I was bought a bier. So I'd drink it then I'd want to go out and play or do something else.

But it turned out that grownups have another drink and stay where they are.

The taste didn't seem so bad after a bit. I began to look forward to it. I remember one shiny morning in a bar with dad. Bob Marley was sparkling the air with.......'three little birds'.... and... 'Could you be loved?' sunlight streaming into the dusty bar. It felt fantastic.

Arnhem is a wonderful place with decadent gorgeous people and sometimes weird. I spent a couple of afternoons with Dad and an apparently unemployed man whose wife was a high-flying lawyer, hence the book strewn des res he entertained us in. On leaving the house, Dad looked at me and said,

"That guy Mick just told me not to be surprised if my daughter kills three men". Clearly he was a madman.

What did they expect me to be like with brain damage from being hit by O'Leery and mum?? When I'd just been in an Arnhem bar and Ali burst in and started throwing me around? And when I had told dad, "O'Leery hits me".

Dad just replied, "Doesn't sound like him?"

End of subject. Sigh. I didn't bother telling him twice, I knew I was on my own.

AUSTRALIA; Easter Saturday.2018

A wonderful girl I know gave me a soupcon of weed and I'm giving it a go. Been months since I've had a bit, and not had it full time since 2004. (Just to prove I could stop after so many years of smoking weed).

I like it a lot. What a beautiful day! Look at my gorgeous brand new leather corner sofa that I pulled in off the road. GOD IS GOOD. (You can see why people take drugs). See you later. Where is this all going? You can see why people don't take drugs too.

ARNHEM; GREAT.

Met some kids my age on Spijker Straat. We played in derelict buildings and did ouija boards in the old ruins. Scaring ourselves when an old fridge flew open, running downstairs.

One guy had a little motorbike and we'd ride through flat, technicolor fields of blooms and towns. Helmets and just T-shirts and shorts in the sun. We never did anything more than be friends.

The Dutch kids were shocked and astounded when I told them that English kids sniffed toxic glue. Cannabis was legal in Holland. As it wasn't taboo they didn't bother with it much, but if they wanted to get stoned it was there. They certainly didn't sniff glue. But like the English kids, they too went into derelict buildings.

One night Dad offered me and Monique some cocaine. Monique said yes, I said no because I didn't trust my Dad. Lucky for me, as Monique threw up. Dad said it was because there hadn't been a sachet of crystals to absorb the moisture. I wouldn't try cocaine until my twenties. All my life I'd been around Dad's drugs, seeing all the people in the kitchen as Dad weighed dope on his electronic scales, so I wasn't impressed. Another time in an Amsterdam street he offered me an acid tab. Again I said no, as I didn't trust Dad not to leave me off my head in an Amsterdam alley aged 15.

I'd had magic mushrooms before, so I wasn't going to risk acid all by myself in the dark in the Red Light area. Glamorous naked women sitting in windows. One was oblivious to all the stares as she sat there engaged in a very animated telephone conversation. Or she was a good actress. Phones had curly leads in those days.

(When Jennifer Saunders show, ABSOLUTELY FABULOUS came out, I identified with the sensible daughter, Saffron,).

Back in Arnhem I got off with a nineteen year old Irish lad who'd moved into our squat and he decided my bottom was the tops. We never did it either.

This was good as I was in the 3rd year at school, the oldest in a class of fourteen year olds because of my September birthday.

A man in a bar asked me what I was doing at college? No, I was at school school! He said, "Well you said you had to go back to school, so I thought you were at college. Fifteen? OMG you'll get me locked up!!"

One day I was walking down Spijker straat and my heart stopped and I went into panic as up ahead I could see my father being dangled over the balcony above the street by his leg!

Ali was holding him there and yelling. Daddy was calmly pleading upside down. I was freaking out calling out to the Turks to help my dad.

They just smiled and said. "She never drops him".

"Well there's always a first time!" I replied! Alice pulled him back in.

I read books in Holland too, 'Jailbird' by Kurt Vonnegut and 'Mommy Dearest' by Christina Crawford.

(O'Leery screamed at me when I returned to Stafford that there's no such book by Kurt Vonnegut! He kept sneering and ranting for AGES. Weeks later Mum said they saw it in a bookshop and she said she told him he should apologise. He never did of course. But it was still a crumb of kindness from Mum for once, and it made me think that she must care really?!).

OUVERSTRAAT; JUNKIE

In that squat was a junkie who had his own room. He had such an air of authority about him when shoplifting that he could roll out an entire rail of clothes down the street. He reminded me of Snoopy. His room was a mess. I'd clean it up and the other guys said, "Don't waste your time".

They were right. In no time it would be filthy again. I gave up on the junkie's insanitary conditions.

VIDAL SASSOON; Leeds Hairdresser

In the Ouver Straat squat, I learned a trade from one of the two Mancunian hairdressers that were staying. The one that cut my hair was a very active stylist and I studied his cutting technique, learned at Vidal Sassoon. It was fool-proof hair sculpture that always looked good, clean or dirty. No hair talent or effort needed by the client to wear it well.

I'd always cut my sister's hair, but now I began emulating the techniques of Vidal Sassoon on the Dutch kids and transferred my skills to England when I went back to school in UK.

BACK IN SANDIFORD AND SCHOOL.

By this time, on opening my eyes in the morning in Stafford the first image that came to mind was a beer bottle. I knew it was wrong. But it wore off, and I was back with my homies on the estate but dreading O'Leery's vileness again.

Starting with my family I cut loads of hair, neighbours old and young, school friends, mum's friends, even 'O'Leery's hair.

I call him O'Leery because when I was cutting his hair he said:

"TO BOLDLY GO, WHERE NO MAN HAS GONE BEFORE!" Creepy much?! He got worse.

After school there would be a queue of school girls around my friend's bedroom as they watched me cut each one, waiting for their turn. I was Ida Scissorhands for real, a total perfectionist. A friend of mum had a haircut by me then went to 'Jim Jams' trendy hair salon for a shaggy perm. Francesco, the boss said it was a good cut. Mum's friend said it was by a fifteen year old girl and he said to send me in for a Saturday job. It was anathema for me to think of a salon on a Saturday, sweeping hair in the fumes. I was freelance thanks.

His salon would become the famed 'Francesco Group'.

SCHOOL; again, surely not??

All my family in England were given presents from me, somehow. At school, my hair was a talking point. I'd skilfully blow dry it to be the image of Stephanie Powers in 'Heart To Heart'. Younger girls stood and watched as I round-brushed it into place in the school toilets. Like it was an event. Roller-skates seemed a perfect way to get around the smooth corridors. They banned my skates before long.

In Holland I'd gone with Dad to see an unknown band called 'The Cure' at a big draughty empty place called Stockfish Hall. (English translation)

I wore their badge at school and people asked what it meant. Soon they were on TV with their first hit 'The Forest'. Great band.

I didn't want to go home at night after school. It comes to something when you prefer school to home. It was ultra violent towards me at home and nobody on Earth gave a shit.

At school I'd taken up with a boy from our estate and would go on his scooter and in his garden shed after school.

Mum yelled at me, "Are you screwing McKay?" I was speechless.

Then mum said, "Oh you better take these!" and THREW a packet of birth control pills across the room at me. End of sex education. No more 'advice' ever. I supposed the pill was a good thing?

My favourite thing was to go after school to a boys house whose dad was always out and he'd have a bunch of boys around. He had a video player. We'd dance to music videos of TALKING HEADS doing all the actions of David Byrne, "Same as it ever was!" and Adam Ant 'Killer In The Home'. Generally we had a wild time just bouncing around. I painted a big green Hulks fist smashing through the plaster on his bedroom wall. They all left me on our doorstep one night as I'd got very drunk. Sweet boys.

O'Leery cried out one night, "IDA FUCKS HER DAD". Utter nonsense. (It was brain damaging to me and the younger children. They weren't ever in the firing line but it was horrible for them to be around). O'Leery was the worst bully.

He'd scream repetitively, "I'M A FUCKING GENIUS!!!"

Then in a gross tableau, as mother mockingly leered at me, with O'Leery addressing me in the most repulsive way, he began playing with mum's tits right in front of me. Both staring at me sadistically. Nobody needs to see and hear that.

My sister broke down at school. On being asked why by a teacher, she replied, "It's the rows and shouting". Mrs Gordon, my Maths teacher wanted to talk to me about home and told me about my little sister crying at school.

I explained that O'Leery yells at me for hours a night and hits me. Mother does nothing. Mrs Gordon said that my mum was still young at 35.

Going home from school filled me with dread. I was punch drunk daily. (Years later in a stripping club a boxer and I smiled at each other and we had exactly the same smile).

Mother, on being asked by me, "Why are you with him? He breaks down the door instead of opening it, he spends all your money on drink, he screams and batters your daughter. Where's the attraction?" she replied, "He's got lovely blue eyes and long eyelashes. He's very insecure".

Oh well, don't mind me then, which vein would he like to open? The lights were on but mother wasn't home.

I couldn't imagine allowing any man to do that to a child of mine. And the best-looking man would be nothing to me if he beat my child's brains against the wall. OUT!!! ARRESTED!

Good idea!

As O'Leery started his nightly tirade as soon as I walked in from school, I ran up the steep hill to the phone-box and called Police and said,

"I'm getting beaten by an alcoholic Scot every night". The Police came to the house.

O'Leery did his best jovial greeting, "Good afternoon officers, just the people I wanted to see. Don't worry. Just a family argument. I don't want to keep you from your duties. Thank you, goodbye".

As they left, one policeman quietly told me to get more bruises. But I'd had bruises last week! And I was about to get it again.

As soon as the cops drove off, O'Leery began as usual, pinning me to the sofa yelling, "MORON!

MORON! MOOOORRRRRONNNNN!" X 50,000 or until he collapsed coughing, exhausted.

I eventually learned a technique of shutting myself down, waiting 'til it was over. I'd remain as BLANK as possible, bored looking throughout, as spit landed on me. I detested him.

The day after the police visit he went naked except for his hat in the back garden in broad daylight. The fence between us and the neighbouring quiet family was flimsy with puny wire, so they got an eyeful and an ear-bashing as he screamed at the top of his lungs, "I CAN'T EVEN BEAT UP IDA ANYMORE COS SHE CALLS THE PO-LICE!!!".

Inside, I went into my room to ignore him. The neighbours put up a 6ft solid wooden fence to protect themselves.

O'Leery was banned from every pub in town. Most visitors from my dads time stopped coming round because O'Leery was so verbally abusive to them.

When asked a question by mum and O'Leery one night, I answered, "Ida isn't here anymore, she's on a beautiful island". I was dislocating my brain.

One was heard to say to the other, "you better watch it, she's going mad". As if I was a specimen in their sick game and one of my legs was dropping off.

I had a box room, single bed, my own space. Lucky me. I got undressed one night and put on my nightie that tied up at the shoulders, a Christmas present.

Quietly reading in my room, when CRASH! O'LEERY WAS IN MY ROOM, SCREAMING AT ME, "WHERE IS IT?? You know exactly what I mean, WHERE IS IT??"

We both knew it was an act as I hadn't done anything, he'd just created a reason to BLAST into my room. I was genuinely bored and weary. But it quickly got worse.

He pushed me against the wall and ripped my nightie shoulder straps, but HA!!! It didn't show my tits because they held the nightie up! He then put his hand under my chin around my throat, with my head pressed against the wall, he took a mighty swing and punched my jaw and head repeatedly. I had to absorb the punches because a wall was behind my head! I SCREAMED and mum came running in, “IDA! WHAT HAVE YOU DONE NOW?”

Near hysterical I was saying, “Nothing, he just started hitting me”, when O’Leery suddenly reached directly to a certain place under my bed and thundered, “SHE STOLE THIS!!”

I looked and it was an Andrews Liver Salts tin. “I don’t even take liver salts”, I said. “NO!” He said, “It’s got my dope in it!” I didn’t even smoke cigarettes!

Despite my protests that it was obviously set-up as he knew where to reach, Mother was deaf to me, shook her head in disgust and walked out with O’Leery and his lies.

MADNESS

It came to me that night; The world was now mad. What kind of perverted inadequate breaks into an underage girls room and tries to rip off her gown, then punches her, then lies? And mother would still do nothing but blame me.. and dad doesn’t care. OK I’ll kill myself.

But quickly discounted that option as it would entail being one line on page seven of the local Newsletter;

’Unknown nobody kid commits suicide in nowheresville. Nobody knows why. No foul play’.

NO WAY was he going to get away with it. I’ll kill HIM!!

GOOD IDEA! I’ll get a carving knife from the kitchen and stab him in his bed as he sleeps next to mother! She’ll say I was driven to it of course....... Errr....nooo. on second thoughts I could no longer trust mother.

She may lie,

"Lock her up and throw away the key Officer! He was a lovely man and good to children, she's a psycho!" Instead of,

"He physically and mentally abused my daughter until she cracked!"

The thought of blood on my hands wasn't what I wanted in my life but it didn't bother me when it came to his.

SAMARITANS and S.S. What was I going to do?

I rang the Samaritans who asked me to come down and bring my biggest little sister with me. 15 months apart we were. She was called a, "Deliberate mistake"and I was the "mistake". Oh jolly japes.

The Samaritan heard me out then told us sisters that we both had the same "rueful smile". I asked, "So can you help us?" She replied that Derek would give us tea and biscuits.

Biscuits?

I proclaimed, "We need action! Please get him removed, locked up!". "But we just listen", said the Samaritans.

I didn't want to talk for nothing.

"Please stop him!"

The lady and Derek said they'd make an exception and drove us to the Social Services.

I told the S.S. lady behind the manager's desk exactly what O'Leery kept doing and she just stared.

Mother was fetched in and arrived in her posh 400 pounds apple green suede coat and high heels. Mum said in her most Mary Poppins voice that she was, “Terribly sorry about this, (rolls eyeballs), I just don’t know what to do with them sometimes!”.

The manager smiled at mum and we were filed out of her office into a taxi. Oh how ‘to the manor born’ my mother could be.

Doomed, my life was fear and worry with a few parties thrown in. On my way out one night O’Leery said something disgusting to me.

Usually I refused to give him the time of day or look at him unless contemptuously. But this time I went to kick the couch as I left. I accidently kicked Dave’s plaster cast covered leg instead. It was an accident.

O’Leery followed me outside where a group of party goers were waiting in the street. He stood in my face and tore off one sleeve of my best jacket and threw me in a puddle. He yelled abuse about me to the party people and Sheila Dunn shot back, “WE DON’T BELIEVE YOU! We believe IDA!”

We all walked to the empty house party of Gangsta, (it was the age of Ska beats), and his little sister. The house was always just bare. Seething to music.

Charlie’s Angels hairstyle no more. My life was a toilet. Punk and Ska were the way forward. I’d make-up my eyes to look like a cat’s. I hung out with punks who sniffed glue in a derelict building. There was no wall and I was on the first floor about to ‘step down’ like Inspector Gadget on my telescopic legs to the rubble below...when I suddenly jolted awake and stopped myself.

Oooh that was close. I didn’t try glue again.

My mates were shocked by the Wicked Wanda cartoons I had on my bedroom wall. I’d cut them out of some Penthouse magazines. Wicked Wanda and her friends were always half dressed with huge busoms and they tortured politician types in a dungeon. Vivid cartoons. I had so many images of all sorts on my wall.

I knew all the words to 'The River' album by Bruce Springsteen, The Pretenders album, 'Romeo and Juliet' by Dire Straits and I was their 'Roller Girl' song. Rod Stewart's 'Maggie May' was the first 45 single I ever bought with my factory money/ baby-sitting for neighbours money /haircutting money. Then I bought 'START ME UP' by The Rolling Stones'. I loved the 'Lodger' album by Bowie too. Always loved music.

DRAMA CLUB; Brilliant.

A guy named Sean Chapman in our Grade C maths class in the remedial hut, used to tell me how he'd played Mowgli on stage. He looked a bit like Mowgli crossed with Elvis. He eventually played Elvis in a professional play. He got me interested in going to his present drama group for teens called Sandiford Youth Theatre.

It was in another school's hall. LOVED IT! Great quirky people. Funny. Made good friends with whom I'd always hang out for years if in town. I loved the improvisations we did.

One day out of nowhere, I suddenly started sobbing uncontrollably in Drama Club. Our brilliant director, Julia, took me outside and I blubbed that mum's boyfriend keeps hitting me every night and I don't know what to do.

Julia told me to scream loudly. I did. God knows what the rest thought was happening. Julia said, "Oh Ida, you don't have much luck!".

I looked at her earnestly and said, "I've always thought I was very lucky".

Until I was 20, we performed Shakespeare, 'A Midsommers Night Dream', 'West Side Story', loads of shows culminating in a weeks run at the Edinburgh Fringe in a play specially written for the girls called

'The Other Island' based on 'Lord Of The Flies'. I played the one who yelled "KILL"!

READER, ARE YOU SICK OF ME LIVING AT HOME YET? I was desperate.

One Saturday afternoon when I was fifteen O'Leery blasted into my bedroom and started smashing my acoustic guitar repeatedly over my head.

It wasn't a loud electric guitar, I wasn't making a row. It was a Spanish beauty with inlaid mother-of-pearl around the hole.

I'd been softly strumming chords making up a tune. (Kurt Cobain stole my chords nearly two decades later). My lovely guitar from Dad was smashed into matchwood and my head pounded.

O'Leery must've hated me playing or doing any good thing for myself and decided to smash me. I LOVED playing that guitar.

A short while later he cheated his own death by hitting and beating me all the way down the stairs until I found myself running out the front door at nearly midnight, hysterically crying, bare feet all the way to dad's parents. Whom we hardly saw.

They owned a home opposite Rising Stream High School. I banged on the door and fell into my startled Grandad's arms. Granny tutted and said, "We knew this would happen, it's a madhouse up there".

They gave me the empty front bedroom and let me stay. I went to school from there. Mum came round to tell gran I was a no good thief. (She didn't mind when I gave her stuff!). She didn't want me to have any place to go. Gran threw her out.

Nelly and Tom Sputum were lovely folk. Nelly played piano and organ at the church, which I was never hassled into attending. So I only saw her play piano at home. She also played the ukulele and banjo and rang bells. She was a joyful woman who was the first person to pass the driving test in England. Her mother before her, my Great Grandmother, had played the cinema piano accompanying the old films and also played piano in pubs to feed her family. 82 Rising Stream was where I'd lived as a toddler in the garden caravan. Their home had elaborate Chinese dragon tea services in cabinets, electric blue giant butterflies pinned under glass (like me HA!), artefacts from all over the world, brought home by my father in his navy days.

Grandad, a Lancashire lad, had worked hard, cycling 46 miles a day to work and back at one point. He'd been a milkman too. The youngest of fourteen. Aged twelve he was given 6 weeks to live by the doctor. He was 80-something when he died. Tom and Nelly put my father through private school, a Jesuit place where dad had to call everyone "Brother". I think they were a lovely couple.

Grandad took me aside one day and said,

"Your dad's a waster, my dad was a waster, but you're alright and I am too, and your great great great great great ancestor discovered the circulation of blood!" Still don't know if it's true.

It was just the lack of stomach filling food. Grandad inquired, "DON'T THEY FEED YOU AT SCHOOL?" But I was trying to grow! And was starving again by evening. They were old and didn't eat much. Plenty for their little tummies, potted beef sandwiches. A bit of tomato and lettuce. Squidgy potatoes with soup on them. They were NOT getting paid to have me. God bless them both, they saved me from being put in a children's home

I'd try sleeping with my gurgling stomach touching my backbone. What was I going to do? I tried making chips out of the bendy spuds in the paper sack in gran's pantry..

Clueless, I'd only seen chips made in large family amounts, so I put stacks of chips in jugs of water around the draining board as if for a big family. But there was just me. I tried frying some in cold oil. Fail. At school I'd talk to friends about what they ate at night mmmmm, "chops, mash, peas".

I was allowed to visit my family once a week for Sunday lunch. With trepidation I'd climb up to the Highfields estate and quietly sit at the table, absolutely starving. O'Leery would stare at me. I plucked up the courage to ask,

"Please pass the peas".

O'Leery jumped up yelling. "She's upsetting me! She's upset me!" Mum just said, "You better go now! Go on Ida!".

I had to leave without eating a morsel. I cried, dragging down the hill. Sadistic bastards.

At school the free meal was a slice of pizza with tomato and cheese, beans and chips. But I was hungry again at night. Gran shipped me off to her daughter Denice's family in Wokingham for two weeks. I ATE FOR ENGLAND down there, three hearty meals a day. Trips out to Virginia Water and the Cutty Sark.

A GREAT TWO WEEKS with Denice, John and my two cousins Candida and Aiden. I was 3 pounds heavier on return, 8 stone 3lbs.

School was a mess. I'd been skiving off, listening to Rezillos records at Gerard Dodd's house instead. All my subjects except maths had been for O'Level exams.

Due to missing work whilst in Holland and skiving, only three subjects remained that I had any chance of getting O'Levels in; Art, English Lit and Eng Language.

Dad suddenly turned up at Grans and lay on the sofa in pain from eating a dodgy pork pie. He lied.

It was something serious and he was taken to hospital where he stayed a while, yellow coloured but in good spirits.

I'd won a bottle of fizzy plonk on the tombola and I wanted to take it to dad because he liked drink. "No no no, not in a hospital" said Aunty Kay, his sister.

When dad came out he was laid on the front room couch whilst I sat on the piano stool talking to him and drinking my first drink in a while. The fizzy plonk which we shared.

After a while I said, "Goodnight" and was leaving the room feeling quite peaceful FOR ONCE in ages, when dad said,

'Come here Ida, aren't you going to give your old dad a kiss?!" Alright then, and I leaned over to kiss him, and he grabbed my face and put his tongue IN MY MOUTH!

I left the room, in a state of shock, saying in my head. "Last straw. You're on your own". It's taken me until now to be at all level headed about that incident. It wrecked my sense of personal boundary for ages and I despised my dad for it, although I still thought he was an otherwise lovely person. 100% better than sadistic O'Leery.

So I cannot imagine the horror and mixed emotions that incestuous rape survivors endure. Rape is bad enough without it being a relative.

In the middle of everything, for no reason I was suspended from school completely. I'd handed in a note from Granny to say I was wearing jeans because my school skirt zip was broken. So after school I'd go to town, get a zip to fix it and would resume wearing said school skirt next day. My form teacher was fine about it.

An insane pterodactyl woman, Mrs Burrows, Head of Year stopped me in the corridor about the jeans. "Oh so your teacher said it's alright, well I don't agree. Fix the skirt now! Leave the school!" "But by the time I've travelled and fixed the skirt it will be the end of school and I'll miss a day". However she was unavailable to reason. So I did as asked and came back next day wearing the fixed skirt

The strict pterodactyl dressed in constricting 50's haute couture, accosted me and sent me to detention for taking a day off school.

I said nothing.

'Nah. Not happening' I thought and just carried on with my school day. The Art O' Level portfolio wouldn't paint itself, I went back to art class. Did the non-issue end there as it should have?

No, she trailed me from class to class. The French teacher said, "What's her problem? What does she want Ida cat?" I shrugged.

"Oh I suppose you better go with her...sigh", said the great Monsieur French teacher.

This was ridiculous. She was indeed corrupt and obsessed with me. She'd put me in a dark alcove to do physics which I wasn't taking. As soon as she was gone I returned to class.

A letter was sent to mother, whom I didn't live with, to say I was a disruptive influence, (only disruptive of corruption), and must be suspended from school. (On a rope?) Mother met me in the Principal's office.

"You complain when she's at school, you complain when she's not", said mum.

The Principal said I must be seen to be punished as an example to the rest. I replied, "Nobody cares. Nobody will notice. I won't be punished for something you ordered me to do. Please let me do art.".

Somehow I got A+ in Art O'level, again for photo realism in the exam, which was incinerated. A mainly impressionist portfolio, except for an extreme close up of Debbie Harry's face in coloured pencils. A teacher, Mr White, offered me 25 pounds sterling for it. No. I kept my portfolio.

I gave it to Dad in Holland for a wedding present on his marriage to Alice that year.

When dead dad turned up alive years later when I was 25, he said Alice had stabbed and slashed all my pictures, screaming,

"FUCK YOUR DAUGHTER!"

After school I used to draw whole pages of mouths and eyes. Just saying. I could never maintain a diary beyond day 1, if at all. But I'd suddenly find poems and songs tumbling out of my brain onto paper.

One was about women not being able to go out without their face make-up. 'CAN'T GO OUT WITHOUT YER FACE, MAGAZINES TELL YOU WHAT TO DO', or similar. A schoolgirl friend of my sister's wrote it out neatly.

Her name was Baby Jane. Her Asian friend was there too and said, "I always thought you were a dangerous tart, but you're nice and intelligent".

Another poem was about the nuclear bomb and ended, "When the last jewelled finger ceases to twitch".

Plus I did one about my teachers that went,

"So you want to be a rockstar, laid back on the stage? Not slaving for a minimal wage? Don't you think that's a trifle absurd? Craziest thing I've ever heard". You work your fingers to the bone to buy your wife a new phone, when you reach 65 are your dreams still alive? Do you even care?"

Fixated on the shallowness of society, I went out with a mud mask on my face, so the cars would beep when driving up behind me, then go quiet on seeing my monstrous face.

One day I asked a butcher for the dead pheasants' long tail feathers, hanging in his shop. He yanked and gave them to me. Same colour as my hair.

I created a bun on my head and wrapped it in a piece of batik silk. I then stuck a very long feather straight up the back of the bun, pointing skyward and forgot about it. Until I was stopped by a teacher who wanted to know the meaning of it.

Straight faced I improvised that I'd kept my religion in the closet up to then, but now wanted to come clean; the bun represents a temple and the feather points to Mecca when I kneel down each day at four o clock.

The teacher said "Oh" and for a while they played along with me. "We're doing pork in Home Economics today, is that alright with your religion Ida?" Or, "Do you want to sit outside the assembly because of your religion Ida?". Hardy ha ha. Funny teachers.

TWISTED UNCLE;

A twisted huntsman was related to me by marriage to mum's sister. He'd come up from the South to trap foxes to take back south for hunting with hounds.

He took all of us youngsters to the cinema once, then whispered to me to go to the back row with him. No thanks. Every time he'd visit he always offered me money for sex. I always said no.

Somehow the local art school had let me onto the Foundation Course with three 0'levels instead of five after seeing my pictures. Finally I caved in to my twisted Uncle's demands when I started Art School, as I was getting ZERO money from anywhere after being sacked by Props Winebar for being underage. Also for looking daggers at the middle-aged men who blocked my way when I was carrying a heavy tray. I'd yet to develop my Barbara Windsor impression. I wasn't on the dole.

VILE with my uncle the twisted huntsman, at least he wasn't blood related. My friend did it with the huntsman's friend, a rich farmer, and I did it with the twisted huntsman uncle at a hotel. Never again. Hey my stepmother did it, but it wasn't for me.

As I got the hang of how the foundation art course was run, I wasn't impressed. The teachers were always late and told us to do potato prints or draw a map outside in the rain. I wanted to try new things, like ceramics. Life was too short. After about two weeks, I went up to the lecturer who was showing films of cave drawings to us, and I calmly told him why I wouldn't be attending anymore. It was a polite spiel and made laser-beam sense.

Then I walked to the college refectory for food. After a while an adult student (21) approached me and said that Mr Osbourne, Head of Fine Art wanted me to go to his office. Oh gawd, what now. So I knocked on his door and a beardy wild man opened it, "Are you Ida?" "Yes, are you Mr Osbourne?"

"YES! COME IN IDA! I WANT TO SHAKE YOUR HAND! THAT FOUNDATION COURSE IS THE WORST IN ENGLAND! I HEARD WHAT YOU SAID, YOU'RE RIGHT!! I SPIT! I SPIT WHEN I GO PAST THAT COURSE! WE WANT BOLSHEVIKS LIKE YOU ON THE FINE ART COURSE! YOU KNOW SHIT WHEN YOU SEE IT!"

(I haven't accidentally got the caps lock stuck, he really was THAT ebullient. I told him that I hadn't got any A'Levels, would he like to see my work?.

"YOU DON'T NEED A' LEVELS AND I DON'T NEED TO SEE YOUR WORK, I WANT YOU ON MY COURSE!"

Fancy that. HOW LUCKY! I got a degree by the time the 6th formers at school were just starting theirs and I lived happily ever after?

Dream on.

Mr Osbourne sent his lovely student Joy Baines with me to the Education Dept of Sandiford Council to get me a Grant. (Money to live off).

The grant officer said

"NO. She's too young and must live at home until she's eighteen before she's eligible for a grant".

Mr Osbourne talked to the Ed Dept in person., "She can't live at home, it's violent. Can she sign on the dole and attend the course until she's eighteen?"

"NO"

"WHY?"

"Cos we're short-sighted sadistic petty tyrants". (I made that last line up).

So I decided to go to London.

Mr Osbourne wasn't happy with the system and asked if I would be a life model at the college until I was eighteen? After a moment's thought I realised I couldn't sit still everyday for that long and said, "No thank you". I needed a place to live. Couldn't stay at hellish home. My Grandad Tom had been a life model at that college because he looked like Bing Crosby in his hat. He told me that he'd said to the students, 'My granddaughter can do better and she's a child!' Couldn't see myself at Gran's anymore, putting her out, although she hadn't said anything.

The fact is I'd never see my Grandmother Nelly again, as I couldn't face her disappointment at my trying to stay in touch with my Mum and family and the terrible outcome that would bring. At Gran's one day my Aunt Kay and Gran were criticising my Mum. They were right but I couldn't stand hearing it and found myself saying,

"Please stop! She IS my Mum after all!"

Gran and Kay went quiet. I was so used to a large family that I couldn't conceive of not seeing them and couldn't face the hard truth of my Mum.

So as you'll see Dear Reader, I was eventually systematically destroyed by my mother and couldn't bear to show Gran the pathetic results. When I finally sent Granny a card in my mid 20s, Aunt Kay said she was dead.

I told Drama Club people that I was going down to London with a girl of eighteen that I'd met whilst working strawberry picking. Her name was Linda.

As I was just a chorus dancer/singer 'Shark' in the upcoming Drama Club production of Westside Story, I didn't think it mattered whether I stayed in Sandiford to do the shows or not.

Andrew Morton was a fantastic precocious 15 year old genius at Drama Club who loved comic books and music. Andrew earnestly gave me a message from our Director, Julia when we were sitting with some Drama Club people in St Mary's church yard. Andrew addressed the gang and said,

"Julia told us all that without Ida we may as well not do Westside Story because Ida IS Westside Story!".

Wow! Well I guessed I was more important than I thought.

So Linda and I hitched to London with our rucksacks AFTER the run of Westside Story at the local Theatre. Great show. My theatre friends met Linda after the show and said she spoke like Amy McDonald, a 70's actress. Well-spoken in a girlish way.

(LIONS. BTW, from age 16 to just turned 17 I went out with two of the most stunning lions of men on the planet, both estate boys, both hard workers from good families, both made the air shimmer as they walked through it. Both wanted to marry me and settle down. The first one, I treated appallingly, the second one I also left to go to London. Marriage hadn't kept my parents together, I had no home and both these young incredibly gorgeous men lived at home. Circumstances were against my settling down).

LONDON

Like a couple of Dick Wittingtons, Linda and I went to seek our fortunes. Some lovely musician guys picked us up and we stayed in their small Earls Court flat. From there we wandered lost until we met a man who took us to his Holland Park flat and made us laugh by coming out of his room in different crazy outfits.

Kindly he noted that my cotton glittery jacket was too thin for the Autumn weather, and he swapped it for a chestnut suede one, a bit too big but very dashing.

We decided to find hotel work as chambermaids. Wandering about, two teenage blondes with rucksacks we came to a most bizarre place with SEX signs everywhere and EROTIC DANCING signs. What on Earth was going on here in the middle of the day?

I asked a passing man, "Where are we? There's sex everywhere!"

He laughed, "Cor where you been, this is Soho mate!" Didn't mean anything to us.

A man stopped us in the road and offered us work at his club and said we could sleep in the flat upstairs. He took us to the 'club' and explained what we had to do.

It was upstairs, next to the Cambridge pub on Cambridge Circus. The place was called Nude Encounter. A desk at the top of the stairs is where one of us would sit and greet customers. We were then shown further stairs to booths, each with two doors and glass separating two seats. One seat for us and one for the clients. Our side of the booth had a lockable door.

There was a slit at the top of the glass for the customer to poke money through to us. We had to take an item of clothing off every time they put a note through, we could charge whatever. Simple.

Linda looked like a blonde Chrissie Hinde, everyone said so, same hairstyle too. I looked like me. We then were shown a grubby little room with a sink, sofa and kettle. That was the flat.

A massive flashing neon sign was right outside the window which looked onto Cambridge Circus.

(Where 'Les Miserables' played forever. We never saw it)

We took turns to do the desk and take the entrance fee. Alex, the Cockney man who had brought us there was the only other worker we'd see. It was just us three, Alex acted as a bouncer. He looked like Feargal Sharkey a bit. He told us to always say to the punters that there were "lots of girls to choose from". The clients always accepted one of us.

At first, when I was on the desk, the men would come in and ask what went on. I'd describe exactly what the booth was like, how they'd have to pay to get in and pay extra to see nudity and they'd walk back downstairs. Alex wanted to know what I was telling them.

He said, "BLIMEY! No bloody wonder they're leaving! You don't say that! You're not supposed to tell 'em the truth!" Then he took me around the corner in Soho to an older red-haired woman called Angela.

Alex said, "Angela, tell her what to say on the door for Gawd's sake!"

Angela spouted a smooth line of patter for me to say;

"Hello sir, you'll be all alone in a private room with a nude model, who will be happy to discuss any little quirks or fantasies you may have". Then the punters go in and SLAM they're in the booth with one of us locked in the other side, dressed. Business boomed after that. Linda and I were throwing all our paper money in the air in the flat.

We had every type of person coming to see us. People with bald heads and briefcases and suits, the kind I'd never considered as sexual beings. We had the son of the Prime minister of Rhodes who was studying to avoid conscription. He came all the time and took us to Ronnie Scott's Jazz Club. He asked what my hobbies were and I replied jokingly, "Hang-gliding, polo, water-skiing". But that was his real life, so he took it seriously.

A cagey looking man came in wearing a dark blue coat. I began sensing what people did for a living. "You're a policeman aren't you?" He defensively replied out of the side of his mouth, "I might be, I might not".' He was.

A bespectacled man gave me fifty pounds and asked me to force him to drink a glass of water with laxatives he supplied. He wanted me to stay dressed, as he said he was a very bad man to come into our establishment and deserved to be on the toilet for days.

I called Alex who got the water and said he'd make an exception about me going into the customers room. Alex stood by the door of the customers room while I had to say "Naughty man drink this!".

Another man arrived in the opposite booth who I swear was the young Boris Johnson, but I could be wrong! He was super posh voiced and spoke and looked exactly like Boris Johnson. He had friends in the hallway.

He said, 'Would you like to come to a kissy-come-dinner??" What's that?

"Don't you know about kissy-come-dinners!?" NO!

"Oh we all have dinner on a long table and you go underneath it and do the kissy-come-dinner!" No thank you.

He then said ebulliently, "Shall I press a ham for you?" Bewildered, I sat quietly.

"Oh look out I'm going to press a ham!" he shrieked! He then took his trousers down and pressed his large pink buttocks on the glass!

"Do you like that?"

A director /writer named Thomas K. and his friend came and took us out to the Cambridge pub next-door then to a stunningly spacious Mayfair flat belonging to the middle-aged writer. Mr Keyes started out raving about The Profumo Affair which I'd never heard of. Then he got Christine Keeler on the phone. I asked what he wanted from us as everyone seemed to want something in London. He said, "Cards on the table, I love bottoms and yours is the most beautiful I've ever seen".

"It serves its purpose" I replied, "And?"

"Come and see my bedroom, I want you to let me whack your bottom with a cane!"

I replied, "Oh no! I'll hit you with a stick though". He then told me that Marilyn Monroe did it and a list of other actresses, "They all slept their way to success".

I replied, "And they're all 6 ft under, DEAD!"

Trying to play me off against Linda he said I was 'The brains of the outfit' and he wanted a relationship with me. (Flattery).

I said, 'But Linda's 18 and has 'A' Levels!' He said it made no difference.

If I stayed with him, I quickly reasoned, then everyone would know I was only with him for what he could give, and I wanted to do EVERYTHING all by myself! I left with Linda in a cab.

We'd been having baths and showers at the municipal Victorian baths down the road. We now had enough for a proper flat. Sight unseen, I just picked a flat in Willesden Green from Flat Finder agency next-door. It worked.

We had so much money that I sent some home to my family, I thought I should be the provider now Dad wasn't there and O'Leery was useless.

Linda and I opened bank accounts with the Abbey National bank because we didn't want to lose our notes. Ha. When we went to get some money out, the bank wouldn't let us because we didn't have I.D. "But you know us!". Shabby National.

A Jewish New Yorker used to come to see Alex at Nude Encounter and he made us laugh at ourselves. He looked like Woody Allen/Sideshow Bob and he kept repeating in his NU YAWK accent,

"What kind of people ARE you?! You put the money in da bank and you can't get it out?! I never heard anything so dumb! You put your money in duh bank.....and you can't get it out??"

We had to trawl through the birth certificate section at St Catherines House and I couldn't find myself listed under Sept 1964. An attendant finally found me under December 1965.

Linda and I would always eat out at 'The Stockpot' around the corner and I'd see the actresses in their bold stage make-up and I thought, "I want to be a chorus girl too!" The only time I'd ever worn foundation make-up was to make myself brown to play a Puerto Rican Shark in West Side Story. In normal life just the thought of foundation was suffocating. Linda and I just wore eye make-up if anything. (Same all my life). We'd leave insanely large tips of notes for the waitresses.

One time we were having steak at the Angus Steakhouse in Leicester Square in our new leather biker jackets and started a food fight across the table at each other, laughing our heads off. The waiters thought we were going to do a runner, but we presented them with a ludicrously large tip instead.

By now I'd walked about a bit in Soho and found places that involved dancing and not talking to the customers. So I got a job at a Peep-show, dancing for letterbox eyes in a mirrored room while Linda stayed at Nude Encounter.

My strong gut feeling was to get out of London FAST.

I'd seen planes advertised to New York for ninety-nine pounds. Linda and I could easily afford it. Linda said, "No I want to see my family at Christmas first, January is soon enough to go".

"But you could send your family a postcard from L.A! Stuff Christmas! I can't see my family!" I urged.

I explained how I felt people looked harsh too soon in Soho, as if being eaten alive, they couldn't trust anyone. We'd seen some dead-headed girls with flat eyes and Linda agreed we had to quit while we were ahead. BUT she must see her family at Christmas. I reluctantly chose to wait for her just a few extra weeks. Sigh.

IT WAS A FAR CRY FROM THE STRAWBERRY PICKING FARM WHERE WE HAD MET.

November dragged and the bad feeling got worse in my gut..

AUSTRALIA; break.

Things are getting heavy in my memory again. Don't know how many times I've been raped. Going to bed now. Goodnight.

Hello, my P.H.a.M.s lady, Melanie, who looks like LuLu came round, as I was a successful candidate to receive their service. 'Personal Helpers and Mentors Program' - 'Justice, hope and opportunity for all'.

CAN YOU BELIEVE IT? HOW GREAT.

It was day one so we had a chat and a form to fill in and then next week we're going to the beach:-) Australia is the best country I've ever known.

LONDON; "IF I STAY THERE WILL BE TROUBLE", The Clash.

At my Peepshow job, you didn't know who was looking at you dancing. I didn't care too much. It was easy work. But in retrospect that's probably how Hash targeted me in the nearby Soho cafe. He came and sat in front of me across the table one morning. Chatty, friendly, hands clasped in front of himself on the table, a very intense air about him, always looking over his shoulder. He reminded me of John Cassavetes the actor, mixed with Ratzo Rizzo in Midnight Cowboy, except he had one freckle on the end of his nose. He was Iranian.

Don't remember saying much to him. Just, "Bye" as I had my shift to finish. He was waiting for me when I left work. (If you could call it work).

He was following me, dogging me as I walked. He insisted on taking me to a club, I was press ganged and went along with it. He introduced me to the owner or some manager, another Middle Eastern man. Ricardo Montalban, he looked like. Then after chatting with the owner, Hash left me there alone with him.

The owner spoke very charmingly and gave me a drink. He showed me into a harem looking room with drapes, soft lights and a heater. He asked me to undress so I did as if hypnotised. He sat me down and carried on talking calmly with a smile, but I couldn't tell what he was saying. I felt he was like a smiling snake and the room went blurry around him. Don't honestly know what happened after that. The next thing I remember is Hash walking outside with me and feeling strange.

Looking back now, I think he pimped me to the snake man and there was something in the drink. Made money by leaving me with that man. Probably. I dunno.

All I knew at the time was that Hash was freaking me out a bit. I just wanted to be on my own and he wouldn't leave me be. Then I went home on the train and didn't see him for a week or so and I forgot him.

Sunday night I was leaving work, walking across Leicester Square to catch the last 12.30 Jubilee Line tube and Hash appeared. Very urgently demanding to talk to me as I was walking to the train. I had my shopping that I wanted to put in the fridge at home. He insisted he had to talk to me and go with him to the Eros Hotel right there in Leicester Square.

I replied, "I can't, talk to me here now, I've got to go". He blocked me and insisted that it was alright, he just needed to talk in private. He was so insistent that I gave up and went to the hotel with him.

He said, "See I'll get the hotel to put your shopping in the fridge", and he took it off me. He made me pay for the room with my wages.

In the room I was standing in my winter mac, just waiting for him to speak to me. He came up to me and said,

"I have to tell you something... I am a prince in my country, I have land and a farm".

I said in a very genuine way, "That's lovely for you isn't it, I'm happy for you, but what's that got to do with me?".

He replied, "I want you to come there with me and marry me".

"Thank you, that's a nice thing to say but I don't want to get married and leave the country. Is that what you wanted to say to me? Well I've got to go now. Bye".

I went towards the door and he jumped in front of me. He pushed me onto the bed and I escaped and ran to the door. He grabbed me and started hitting me. I SCREAMED AND SCREAMED for HELP but nobody came.

I carried on screaming as loudly as I could and he knocked me back on the bed, sat on my chest with his knees pressing on my shoulders and started punching my head, one hand round my neck. I couldn't move, my arms were trapped. I was crying hysterically and STILL SCREAMED as he punched me. Smash after smash. Must've been 15 punches.

Then I heard a crack noise inside my own head and a PING! I didn't scream more. He kept punching me in the eye and my mind went very calm. "This is it, I'm going to die at 17. If I live I will be disfigured". BLACK. Passed out unconscious.

Who knows what time it was when I felt him shaking me awake, my head felt like a lead weight.

"I'm still here with him", I thought. He was saying repeatedly, (I shit you not),

"Love, love what happened to your head? Wake up now! What happened to your head love?" I knew he was trying to trick me that it wasn't him that did it. Alone with a psychopath.

"Here's your coat, put it on, I help you, come on love".

I couldn't see at all out of one eye. With my other eye I saw blood. He helped me stand and walked me out the door, down the hall to the lift. We came out in the foyer and the desk concierge was an old man. He looked at me across the marble hallway as if he'd seen Elephant man, shocked. He did NOTHING. He could've called the police. But I knew he was old and scared as Hash would maybe go for him too. I looked like a butcher's shop window.

Hash was saying to the old guy, "She hit her head on the sink, come on love". I walked like a zombie ghost to the hotel door steps down to Leicester Square, to where a car load of men were parked. All the time with the psycho Hash dogging me and nobody cared.

Hash opened the car door for me and ushered me in. I was frozen with fear. Were these guys also psychos?

Then they saw my face and started freaking out. "Hash man, what happened to this girl man? Fuck gotta get her to hospital".

(Phew!)

Hash replied, "This big black girl at a nightclub just smashed her, we go hospital now". I daren't tell them the truth with Hash in the car, I just wanted to get to hospital. I was bricking it. The men were fairly quiet and drove me to Charing Cross Hospital.

Hash followed me into the hospital. With one eye I had to write my address, terrified in case Hash could see it.

08.04.2018. PISS TOP UP IN BEAUTIFUL AUS!

Another log number with the police due to the return last night of the door pissers. I heard them in the night banging my bedroom window which is by the door, but I was too exhausted to get up, I stayed sleeping as I knew my doors were locked. As suspected, they'd drenched the porch again. Need more bleach now.

BACK TO SOHO

As soon as the nurses drew the screens round me, I hissed, "THAT MAN did this to me! Call the police!!" At that moment Hash stepped in front of the screens saying, "She's my girlfriend, she hit her head! She's gone crazy".

The nurses at this point could've sussed what had happened, called the Police unbeknownst to Hash, while detaining him and my life could have been simplified enormously.

Instead they said, "Could you leave please sir", while he was protesting and threw him out! My God, don't let him go!!! Freaking deep frustration.

He vamoosed and I was X-rayed. Fractured skull, orbital socket. Police were called, (AFTER the nurses had let him go!), and concluded, "G.B.H. Grievous bodily harm".

Then the Police station interview. "Are you on the game love? Nice girl like you?" I'd no knowledge of that expression, not being a Londoner, but I gathered that they were talking about prostitution.

"I'm a dancer, why do you ask? Is it OK to fracture prostitute's skulls? Why don't you ask if I'm a solicitor? Or a cobbler? What difference does it make?"

The Bow Street C.I.D. replied, "Now now, calm down love, just routine".

They drove me home. In the next few days I was sent to see the Middlesex Hospital eye specialist. I was navigating the Tube trains bandaged on one eye to get there and discovered I was a lousy invalid, "Out of my way! Can't you see I'm sick!" I yelled as I misjudged my footing and people knocked into me.

The eye specialist said that my eye was no longer facing in the same direction as the less harmed one. To fix it would involve an operation to cut the muscle, but the risk was that my eye would end up looking too far the other way, so he advised leaving it be. I concurred.

Ever since I've had one frown line from trying to line up my vision. When I relax my forehead I see double. He said the smashed eye was no longer round but rugby ball shaped.

I couldn't even walk to the Tube to get to Bow Street without some dirty old man trying to get me into his car. Three weeks later I was in Paris having been advised by Bow Street C.I.D. to stay out of London as Hash would get me again. There was no justice, I was repeatedly and strongly advised not to go to court.

Police said they'd been to Peckham where Hash had told me he lived but his mother hadn't seen him for fifteen years. I told them it was obviously a lie as he was always out touting in Soho, but the Police couldn't be bothered.

PARIS;

HOLD UP! BEFORE WE DO PARIS and BOB CRUMPTON, it's NOW JULY 2021. 3

YEARS since I wrote the above. I'm now 56 in 2021

AUSTRALIAN UPDATE. Since writing the above until my fractured skull in London; here in Australia I've successfully fought a war with the psychiatrist to get off the Flupenthixol injection and Sertraline pills.

Despite my 50 years of being FREE of all prescription drugs, and being hard against them, the psychiatrist insisted I'd be on them for life!

Insisted I was Bipolar and threatened me with hospital if I didn't comply.

Came to my house to inject me if I didn't show up. I told them I was classed as a VOLUNTARY patient. Terrified I was. But I wanted to keep the peace as I wanted to be a Citizen of Australia and couldn't stand the thought of being locked up.

I prayed to God a few months back to FREE ME and was immediately inspired to write an email that trod a fine polite line, ending it with,

"I am seeking legal aid to ensure my inalienable right to bodily integrity is protected".

Next day I was discharged from the clinic and was told I never need to take their drugs again.

YEAH! Thank you God. And my case manager left the clinic! She knew she'd been illegal.

People have said I should sue them for the last 3 lost years.

So mentally smashed I was that pulling the simple lever on the Reverse Osmosis water filter that Aidan set up in the laundry, was beyond me. I could only face drinking tap water and wine. That's why there must be life left in those filters.

Not got enough time to sue them now. Aidan has stood by me through 2 legal cases and an Immigration Tribunal. I won one legal case against a spiteful jealous landlady we rented a caravan from, who falsely took me to court to get me barred from Australia because she fancied Aidan, but lost a case against a rapist landlord, but he ended up in jail for paedophilia and more assaults on tenant women. We won the immigration Tribunal.

A month ago I also attended my Citizenship Ceremony and am now a proud Aussie. My support worker Sue Lambeth went away a couple of years ago to a different company. My new lovely worker, Jodie Mercer, helped me to get through it all. But as Jodie says, only I could take the citizenship test though.

Much occurred since I took this bungalow three years ago and started writing up to my fractured skull.

Sue Lambeth and I had checked this place out and agreed that it was gorgeous. At the end of a frangipani lined cul-de-sac of three properties. Enclosed garden, in a millionaires neighbourhood close to the sea. One thing was wrong.

On seeing the next neighbours dark red oily ragged bedroom curtain, I knew that the devil lived there. I said so to Sue. My Spidey sense and God told me. But as Sue said, I'd already turned one place down which was the size of an old UK telephone box and I would only get three choices, so to risk losing this place over a feeling wasn't on. (NEVER GO AGAINST YOUR GUT FEELING) I sighed and agreed and took this place, my first solid place since arriving in 2012.

My neighbour with the ragged curtain transpired to be a BIG meth addict. His name is Big Bill. He's very big and cannot hold his own weight on his knees. He struggles with a walking frame.

Everything he's ever done is big. He's from a big Cockney family who came here decades ago. He followed. But first he managed 20 London pubs at once, cooked thousands of meals as an oil rig chef and an army chef, was a massive coke addict, won martial arts awards as a big young man then came over here and became big in the underworld and big with the bikies and as a mechanic. He'd been taught from childhood to be a big bully with a big mouth. Still was one when I moved in three years ago.

He sent the street mad with his 72 hour benders awake on meth with 72 hours of techno BLASTING. The worst music ever, like a pneumatic drill.

Three years ago I was on an even stronger injection than Flupenthixol and for very complex reasons I was living on $25 a week.

Then I received $1000 compensation from a UK bank and wanted to buy a car for my birthday. I wanted to learn to drive.

My neighbour said, "They'll see you coming and sell you a lemon, give the money to me, I'm a mechanic and I'm going to look at a good car my mates got tonight".

So I did.

Gave him $1000. No proof that I'd given it. But like he said, he was my neighbour so he wouldn't nick it.

My birthday came and went. No car. He said he was getting the oil changed. A week went by and he invited me for a belated birthday drink with his friend.

I was given a card, a bottle of wine and some chocolate. It was promised I'd get the car or the money the next day. I hoped so!

Drunk off my head and on zombie medication, I sat comatosed. He'd got out the gin which in all my life I'd never had before. Then Big Bill got out his dick which he called Junior and told me to suck it.

I refused and said I did not feel comfortable. Only my money or my car kept me civil. I should've done a runner but I was heavily medicated and drunk.

Big Bill kept pestering me and so did his friend. Bill said his friend had never seen it in real life. As if that was a prerequisite of life, or as if it was my problem or business. I said that I only have sex inside marriage. They roared at me to do it. I thought of my fractured skull and I said, "This isn't about sex, it's about power". But on they nagged.

Eventually I rose up, decided to give it my best shot and get it over. GROSS. I threw up all over the place. Big Bill said, 'Oooh lucky you, I wish I could throw up".

Went home. Cried. Dropped my phone in my coffee. Next day, no money, no car, no proof. I went back several times asking for it and was lied to. Finally accepted the obvious, that Bill was in fact the devil and had spent it all on meth.

I'd been growing my hair out grey for gravitas and to deflect attention now that Aidan was away on the mines for months at a time, I was a spiritual woman, living alone on severely debilitating medication and Big Bill had wanted to feel like a big man to have power over me by robbing and degrading me. How very small and pathetic of him.

Big Bill admitted proudly that he'd "planned it!" To set me up. HOW vomit-worthy to be proud of such lowness.

No point going to the police as I well knew that even WITH proof they rarely do anything. Plus it was two people's words against my word.

For six months I trudged up and down the cul-de-sac past the sick neighbour's door, living on $25 a week, selling any possession I could.

ONLY ONE THING bad had happened to me from other men for all the years I was with Aidan, yet as soon as Aidan's invisible shield was gone....BOOM!

Managed to get Big Bill's deafening techno sound closed down with a petition signed by all my other brilliant neighbours.

Big Bill, according to other neighbours, had terrorised the previous woman who'd resided in my place, with his tons of visitors blocking the cul-de-sac so she couldn't get out. EVIL.

His cat spent all its time at my house from the moment I moved in. He accused me of stealing it.

I told Sue Lambert exactly what I'd done and how depressed I was. We tried to get me moved but it was denied. I wanted to slit Big Bill's gizzards. Alternating with just wanting to check out of the planet.

A lot of drinking and smoking on my part and praying to God.

I looked on Gumtree for a dog to chase off Big Bill's cat and saw an ad without a picture. Just the words "OLD SMALL DOG. FREE".

I rang and the surprise 15yr old dog was brought to my house. Her old owner had called her Mimi and he'd gone into seniors care where he couldn't have Mimi. She is now 18 and going strong, a 'champagne Shitzu Maltese cross' as it says on her paperwork. A little shaggy version of white Charlie girl, my only other pet whom I'd had so long ago.

The neighbour's cat just moved down the street instead of going back to him. It obviously hated Big Bill. I told Big Bill that he was EVIL. He said "Watch out!"

After six months of no money from Big Bill, a 20yr old African hit woman got in touch to say she'd got a flat. I'd met her in the psychiatric hostel. I invited her over and told her what Big Bill had done. She wanted to kill him. I said it's not worth it. She was a boxer and I used to hold up the practice pads in the hostel. She said I was good at it.

However, just from seeing her and her crazy Arab boyfriend coming down the cul-de-sac to see me, it might have influenced Big Bill into paying me back at $100 a fortnight. I don't think he expected me to know people like that. Anyone who underestimates me or God, is stupid. He eventually paid off the lot. Perhaps he has a conscience?

Aidan took me to buy an old car as a reward for not taking half of his money in our divorce. I learned to drive then banged a car in a car-park and Aidan sold my car. Now I've just got to pass my test.

Big Bill doesn't get meth anymore. Lockdown stopped all that. He is now very kind to me and cooks and washes up for me every night. He tells me that he is evil if I say how nice he is. I help him by putting out his rubbish. He can be very entertaining.

I've just finished doing all the painted illustrations for his children's story.

For his 60th birthday I gave him cookery books, a painting and a sketch I did of him as half a laughing cherub and half a horned satan. He loved it.

All I'd ever wanted was to be friends with him, just like 'The Flaming Groovies' song.

To turn that whole AWFUL situation around through the power of God is really, "True greatness", as Bob Crumpton probably STILL talks about but probably STILL does not understand.

Bill said, "If I wanted to get married again, you'd be top of my list".

MUCH LATER still in Aus.

Since the above I have cut Big Bill out of my life entirely. I did everything for him, even cut his hair and toenails and he repaid me by saying,

"Come here a minute". So I went over and he lunged at me, grabbed my head in his massive hands and stuck his tongue in my mouth, giving me stubble burn.

I left and felt gutted for ages. But AGAIN I forgave him cos Jesus said 'Love thy neighbour' and Bill could be a lovely funny man.

He refused to take accountability for what he did to me in robbing me and coercing me, instead he blamed those around him.

I said, "Don't pass the buck. Nobody but you was horrible to me. If you don't repent you won't go to heaven". He replied "I'll never be honest".

He then wanted me to get his washing in and I said "No. Because you wont be honest" and walked out. I ignored him from then on. I'd heaped coals on his head by being like Jesus and helping him get his fat feet in his shoes and helping him around the house. He texted me to come back for my dinner, but gave up eventually. He missed me. I missed him and his gifted cooking. But as Jesus said, we cannot live on bread alone. It had always driven me mad the way he called out to me EVERY time I went past his door. Now he was finally silent.

I said, 'Sorry Jesus' for my wicked thoughts against Bill because he wouldn't repent. I couldn't work for him anymore.

As a teenager I cried uncontrollably at a documentary about comedian TONY HANCOCK committing suicide in Sydney Australia. My address is Hancock Street and it seemed I'd die like Tony here for a while.

Now I can get on with my own book.

DAVE KUSWORTH R.I.P. 1960 - 2020

After getting the sad news that my best friend, musician Dave Kusworth died in September 2020, it wasn't until six months later that I could finally cry over losing him after escaping the zombifying meds. I was too much of a dead headed zombie to cry before that. (Also I'm back to normal size again since they stopped injecting me).

Dave's son Stevie, whom I'd known since he was at school, sent me a photo of Dave and I that he found in Dave's flat.

Dave was a very gentle, funny presence in my life from when I was 25 to the week before I left London in 2012 to come to Australia. His last words to me were "You'll fuck off again won't you?:" And a week later I was in Australia.

I only intended to be in Australia for 3 months to avoid the Olympics but stayed forever after meeting Aidan in August 2012.

Dave Kusworth was a lovely, funny gentle soul who was incredibly modest and rarely played his own music. Throughout all his girlfriends he stayed my good friend and saw me for who I am, had great conversations with me and we cracked up laughing together. We loved watching Martin Farrow the drummer's Laurel & Hardy collection. I was far more than just a sexy stripper to Dave. We never had sex in all those years. Except once but it doesn't count as we were hysterically laughing throughout. I will tell you more about Dave's antics later. I've only just discovered how good his music is even though I managed him for a while. Lockdown finished Dave.

Anyway last year Covid happened early 2020. I say a big NO to all of it. I made sure to be exempt from every mandate. Nothing more to add. Except that this is the longest I've ever been stationed since arriving in Aus and I'll happily get travelling again.

Reading back on my jaunty start to this book, I remember that I'd considered coming to Australia at age 15 after seeing a Judy Davis film and reading of the burgeoning Oz film industry.

I was also convinced a nuclear attack was coming to the UK after reading O'Leery's Guardian newspaper and took a petition to school to stop the Cruise Missiles at Greenham Common.

The teachers were very jaded and said it wouldn't help. I went with my theatre friends to Greenham Common and the feminists there said, "This is No Mans Land usually!" I replied that the men were helping and that the bomb wouldn't pick out only the men!

In the news was a huge dust cloud that drifted for thousands of miles across the USA. I imagined being in Australia and my family in the UK being nuked and thought maybe the nuclear fallout would travel like that dust cloud to Australia anyway. I didn't want to be alive if my family were dead. That's how much I loved them.

I'm mixing my Australian Update with the past story now, but the clues that my mother didn't like me were MASSIVE even to blind Freddie.

There was clearly something wrong with her from the way she scribbled her face out of a family studio photo with a pen, thus wrecking the portrait for us all.

Or we'd go with Dad on a lovely drive and she'd always wreck it by bemoaning that her house wasn't a detached country pile like the ones we drove by. Our house was brilliant! Thanks to my Dad's graft. We loved it.

She was like the old lady in a bottle story, moaning away until a fairy puts her into a house, but STILL she moans through successively bigger and bigger houses from the fairy.....until BANG!

The fairy puts her back in the council house she started from.

We had a great life with Dad around, taking us to eat out at fancy restaurants almost every week and sleeping in the back of his lorry to give us a broad grounding in life.

BIG CLUE.

A big clue that she wasn't the full deck was when O'Leery first started coming round. One night he arrived with a man named Mark.

A jolly enough evening. Then mother took me aside and asked if I'd sleep with Mark, because Mark had said to her that it wasn't fair that O'Leery would end the night shagging my mum but that he, Mark, wouldn't get to shag Ida.

"NO!" I replied aghast. I was 15, a virgin and still had over a year and a half left of compulsory school! I was just mortified as to where her head was at and went to bed. No clue as to the violence about to befall me.

While I was cutting the wheedling O'Leery's hair he opined in his sleazy Scottish accent, "To boldly go where no man has gone before!" Vile.

VIRGINITY THIEF

Then I went out on the night before my 16th birthday, with a full year of school yet to finish as I was the oldest in the class.

My old best friend Diana Wilson, the Head Girl of the juniors, took me out with her older male pals, Italian Paulo and Arab Ali. They took us back to Paulo's and we sat at the kitchen table getting drunker with each drink they poured. Until Diana's head was on the table and I was slumped. I felt Ali carrying me out of the room. He laid me on a bed and did something to me in the shadowy gloom that I assumed was sex. I felt nothing. I awoke, went home worried that I was pregnant. I quietly told my mum. Next thing I knew, O'Leery was screaming "IDA'S GOT A BUN IN THE OVEN!" LOUDLY over and over. There was zero sensitivity or respect for me at home.

AUSTRALIA 6th Feb 2022

World War 3 and people are locking themselves inside their own gas chambers. MASSIVE DEMO in Canberra against Parliament started yesterday (5th Feb 2022), and the masses of people are going to keep descending on the nation's capital, Canberra, until freedom from jab mandates and masks is restored. I'd be there but WA is closed at the fake new border, plus I've got animals. GO ON YOU BEAUTIES!! Here in Perth I've been on a rally per week for 3 weeks and more before.

Today is 22nd of Feb 2022. 22.02.2022.

NOW it's 13th of March 2022

Gutted that my Australian friend Marie, a senior from the op-shop, is in hospital with a heart attack after being jabbed.

Equally gutted that my 25yr old friend is now coughing up blood since she was coerced into being jabbed if she wanted to see her jabbed sick Granny. I did EVERYTHING to warn them!

Gutted also by the death of Aus Cricket legend, Shane Warne aged 52. He coughed up blood and had a heart attack. The mainstream media said he was on a strict diet. Yeah, a strict diet of JABS! I found Ivermectin in a local shop under a different name. Have given them both a link to it so it will hopefully flush their systems.

(Funnily enough, Aidan has been social distancing for years already. He'd stand at the bar and if anyone got too close he'd say "I need a metre! I need a metre!" and put his arms out. Such an eccentric! But he cannot stand the rest of it and left the mines due to jab coercion, which he refused. He's gone bush now near Esperance. I've never worn a mask and won't be jabbed unless it's in my cold dead body).

I BETTER HURRY UP with this book before there's nobody left alive to read it!

UK. BACK FROM LONDON to SANDIFORD

aged 17 with a bandaged eye. Like a mad fool to myself, on reaching Stafford at night, I went into the railway bridge pub toilet to check under the bandage. It was almost normal and I didn't want to scare the little siblings so I put eye make-up on it and went home to Highfields.

ZERO concern from anyone as usual. GBH? So what? I was obviously meant to take it and get on with it as usual.

The cops didn't tell me about compensation and mother said nothing. There were no ambulance chaser compo adverts in those days. Nobody had ever heard of counselling. Maybe if I'd left the bandage on I'd have garnered some comfort? Ah well, I didn't want to worry little sister Lucy.

I remember being at a party, asking a 25 year old how come they were still alive at 25? As they must be half dead from experiences by then? They said, it all evens out as you go. I hoped so, as my life was a series of head injuries and endlessly intense. I hoped for a break.

Less than 2 weeks later I was in Paris with a teacher called Ed Kite who was visiting his girlfriend who lived in Sarcelles with her lovely mother, Anike, and saxophonist brother. Anike and I both thought her son looked like Yves Montande. Forgotten his real name so I'll call him Yves. They gave me dark red raw horse meat to eat as I had a cold.

Next-door, a woman lived with her children in an entirely pink house with a pink van. Every item of clothing they all wore was a shade of pink. Like a blackberry yoghurt. Anike said, 'She lives La Vie En Rose'.

Beautiful Anike took me to a dancing club on the Champs Elysee. She tried to get me work teaching Arabs English but it didn't happen. All French workers seemed to be 18 or over. Or at school.

Yves wanted to marry me and said I'd be useful to him after I'd shown no fear and been charming in a rich house we visited. It transpired that Ed, his girlfriend and Yves had all been quiet because they'd been intimidated by the richness, as they afterwards confessed. They'd met the rich people while camping and hadn't expected them to have their own private lift into their marble floored Paris home, owned by their parents. I'd had a great night laughing and talking about music.

I said to his proposal of marriage, "Non merci Yves, je suis 17". He wouldn't let me come to his big gig in case I put him off.

He sent me to live with Katherine, an artist friend of theirs who lived in the forest with her little daughter.

Her toilet was called, 'Le Palais Du Glace'. Hundreds of shards of mirror embedded in white plaster walls in patterns. I saw myself pee from a hundred different angles.

A lovely woman.

Walking around, singing 'Lost In France' by Bonnie Tyler, I boarded a train to the Seine where Katherine's Art College was. A man with a wolf face and hair in a tight black leather bomber jacket and black skinny trousers started following me.

I tried to be clever and lose him by suddenly getting off the train. On going up the Metro steps to the street I was mortified to see him across the road leaning on a wall, staring and waiting for me. How had he got there so fast?

I ran to the big wooden gates of the college, went inside and found Katherine surrounded by art and forgot the man.

Hours later as we drove through the wooden gates by the Seine in her car, I shrieked! Wolfman was still waiting outside for me! I told Katherine I was so grateful for her voiture. Gosh! These freaks were everywhere.

Ed Kite had long since gone back to England, and it occurred to me that I'd been living libre for months, no money at all. Nada zip zilch. Anike gave me 20 francs to return to England. A debt that irked my conscience for years, but now I realise she probably didn't expect it back anyway. It's about the only debt I've ever not paid.

On arrival in Sandiford I moved into Sid's spare room. Again on credit until the dole came through. In the early Spring I'd sunbathe out the back and the other tenant, an Argentinian man, would look out of his back bedroom window every time I went out. The Argentine War was on, led by Prime Minister Thatcher.

At the nightclub the DJ would get the punters all chanting,

"WE'RE GONNA SMASH THE ARGIES!!!"

I appeared to be the only one who didn't join in. This is how easy it was for Hitler to get the people on his side, I mused.

Starving, I went into Sid's sliced white bread wrapper and took one slice. ONE. He returned home and said "There were 22 slices in this wrapper, there's now 21!". Unbelievable. I was starving Sid! There was no electricity in my room at all. No sockets and he begrudged me getting the extension lead to blow dry my hair. (I used a hairdryer in those days, because I was Kim Wilde, Rod Stewart and Ziggy Stardust).

Sid raised his fist to my head, I goaded him by staring defiantly at him.

After, I went to the phone-box and cried to the dole to hurry because I was starving, a cheque finally arrived.

I then tried to emulate the meals during my two week stay with Aunt Denise in Wokingham. Grapefruit, THEN cornflakes, THEN fried egg, beans and bacon for breakfast. A full lunch at the old people's 1950's cafe in Sandiford centre, 'The Brunswick'. Cabbage, meat, potatoes and for pudding, apple crumble and custard.

I dreamed of turning that cafe into a place for youngsters to hang out who loved music. The 1950's chrome fittings on the counter were curved and sumptuous. Soon I was back up to just over 8 stone. Not dead yet!

CARAVAN in town.

Sid moved me to a caravan at the back of a guest house right beside the town park. It was run by a big fat bearded man who told me his wife was jealous of me.

The caravan was in his yard next to big wooden closed double gates. There was no lock on the door, no catches or locks on the flap windows. I liked how close it was to the nightclub, just across the park.

I wouldn't be 18 for ages, and old enough to go back to Mr Osbourne's Fine Art degree with a grant.

All my friends lived at home with their families and went to school. A lonely feeling. So I hung out with Agz, the punk lead singer of Sensa Yuma band.

Agz would appear in my life like an angel several times. A car had ripped up his leg when he was a child, so he had one small boot and one normal one. His personality was so big that I only noticed it at 17, after knowing him since I was 15.

Also I went to the Valentine brothers' big house on Newport Road. Their Dad was a lecturer and their social worker mum lived in Stoke Newington, London. We had the whole house to ourselves to play in. Marcus played the keyboards and was studying science. Justin wanted to be a piano tuner.

We played Doors records on the record-player, played the piano, Marcus did photography. 'Private Eye' magazine and their Dad's Guardian newspaper were laughed at. They adored Monty Python.

These brothers, Marcus and Justin, were very academically clever. They were in the 6th form at their school. Their lovely Dad called me a "Funnical wordsmith".

Andrew Morton, the genius 15yr old son of a vicar also used to come around often and eventually his artist girlfriend, Debbie Sorrel.

Justin Valentine and Andrew Morton were in the great drama group with me. A couple of girls from drama group also used to visit and I thought they were friends until their small-minded jealousy surfaced. Bah!

I'd go up to Highfields to see little Lucy, my sister, to read stories and hope for the best from my Mum.

I knew she definitely wasn't motherly, but I hoped it was because she might just want me to be tough? Crikey I was delusional. Aged 8, I'd heard her tell my Dad, "I don't think she's beautiful, I think she's got a bland face, her teeth are alright". I'd just agreed with Mum's opinion, which she was entitled to.

If anyone said to her that I was pretty, she'd say, "Don't say that! They're all ok!". Fair enough I thought.

Aged 14 I'd overheard her say to Dad, "I can't stand her Geoffrey. I don't want her here. Put her in the shared house on Wolverhampton Rd."

Dad replied, "But she's never any action, come on!" The shared house was full of dodgy adults?!? Thank God for any small mercies from my Dad.

The sad truth which my brain refused to compute was that my Mum did not give a flying fig about me and I was just used to it as normal life. I'd block out all her past violence to me. On my return from London after my skull was fractured, I bought mum a very expensive black satin top by the designers Ghost. She wore it.

Kirsty, an artist girl who lived close by the Valentines told me, "Ida, your mother is jealous of you!" It was obvious to most.

But as it states in Desiderata *on my Mums wall,* "Don't compare yourself to others as you will become vain and bitter, there will always be greater and lesser persons than yourself", it was hard to believe that my own mum could read that and be jealous of me, her own averagely attractive child.

There were TONS of better looking people than me.

I just privately thought I must be no good somehow, as I knew my Mum had seen horrors happen to me and wouldn't want to be me.

That the emotion of jealousy was irrational, evaded me for too many years. If indeed she was jealous of her own child, it made me feel sorry for her to be so afflicted. Being ignored by her, I could stand.

Everything bad in my life was turned into a joke if I ever mentioned it, I never told the truth about the skull fracture in the Eros Hotel. (Eros, yes I see the irony). Even I believed my jokes about my eye instead of the truth. I was always UP, because nobody likes a sad sack sitting on a block of stone, weeping in the corner.

I resolutely decided to NOT let those bastards make me scared of all men, make me a victim or wreck my life.

STRANGENESS suddenly happened to me on the bus. I was sitting idly thinking of a ham sandwich, when SUDDENLY the image of a closed fist flying toward my head, shot into my mind's eye. My whole body physically jumped, jolted me in my seat. WOW, I thought. Oh well…. it will die off soon and not happen again I reasoned hopefully.

Nearly every night at the nightclub I'd dance out my neurosis to all the great music, or try to. A black boy said to me,

"Most people only dance to certain records, but you can dance to anything!" The DJ used to throw 45 singles on the floor by my feet for me to take home. I remember 'Banana Republic' Boomtown Rats.

I also loved Northern Soul and went to an all nighter session where Northern Soul Boys would do the most acrobatic moves and girls would trip the light fantastic in their long circle skirts and logroller shoes.

ALCOHOL

My friends used to say, “When I’ve had a drink, I will dance”. I thought, hold on a minute, I’m a dancer and do not need the crutch of alcohol corroding my system, costing loads and going down the toilet.

So I decided to stop drinking.

There wasn’t ONE adult I could think of in my immediate family that didn’t drink. I searched my brain for a non-drinking role model and came up with CLIFF RICHARD the evergreen singer! And ADAM ANT the pop star of the day! THANK YOU BOTH for being rebels!!! I danced on free water from then on.

I read an interview with Rod Stewart saying he used Oil Of Ulay and he always had sex at least once a week. I too used Oil Of Ulay and was strongly influenced to have sex as often as Rod. Such was the power of pop-stars on the young unguided and Godless.

“There were tears in her eyes as she kissed her little sister goodbye eye eye” sang Rod Stewart as if for me.

MASSIVE THANK YOU TO STEPHEN ‘TIN TIN’ DUFFY for delivering to my ears ‘Icing On The Cake’. What a perfect song for me to cheer me up. These songs were perfectly timed to often be my only comfort.

Sue Elphick, a very talented beauty from drama club, and Johnny, her best friend, were both adopted early and were really lovely. They both jumped in the river with me, in the park. We got covered in weeds and went through town, smearing our bodies on shop windows in protest at consumerism just for fun, (we enjoyed capitalism really). Then we all loudly sang down the road, ‘The Bucket Of Water Song’ from TISWAS TV show.

Johnny wanted to be a nurse. He once said quietly to me in private, 'Ida, you smile but it doesn't reach your eyes'. A very perceptive young man.

MY MODUS OPERANDI.

Why walk down the street under the tyranny of boring vertical perambulation when you can CARTWHEEL? Why laugh normally when you can do a Woody Woodpecker impersonation? Why walk on a pavement when you can BALANCE ON A WALL? I was a right proper case!

With Tanya Warburton and Sean Chapman, I'd been in a dance group called OUTRAGE, choreographed by Corrine from Sandiford School Of Dance. We practised in a big hall somewhere but the group dissipated with people's commitments.

SO I thought of all Sandiford's streets as my playground to dance in instead. It was so easy there compared to London and my past. Like Toy-town.

People often asked where I got my energy from. It was almost "superhuman" as Dave Kusworth would later say.

MEETING BOB CRUMPTON AT SANDIFORD NIGHT-CLUB aged nearly 17 and a half.

In the flashing disco lights, there was Adam Ant complete with curly dark hair with tiny plaits! It was Bob sitting with the Punky/retro-shop managers, Nate and Lurker. We had a conversation and Bob said he was Adam Ant's cousin. I had no reason to doubt him.

Then Lurker asked me to go with him somewhere, so I went with him to his flat where he did what he called 'Tantric Sex' to me. No drama, pleasant, not a bad experience.

A little while later I was out with Sarah who had a bright red Mohican haircut. She was known as Splodge the punk girl.

There was Bob in an army green parachute suit and carpet slippers, sitting on the floor against a wall of the nightclub. We said hello, and I think he came with us. Anyway, somehow he ended up with me at my caravan.

BOB LOSES HIS VIRGINITY

We talked happily together in my dilapidated 60s caravan. I'd tried to make it clean inside and homely, with bright coloured Japanese paper fish kites on the wall, like Hilda Ogden's famous flying ducks.

We were sitting together on the only seat, the double bed. We became kissy and close. Bob said he'd never had sex before. We got undressed and he had a circle on his bicep. I asked what it was. He said it was a tattoo with an 'A' for anarchy inside a red coloured circle. He showed me that his feet were webbed. Two toes on each foot were joined together. "Saves time on drying when you have a bath", I said. (I would call him 'The Crumpton From Atlantis')

Throughout my life I've consciously remained a kind person who can be gentle and tender. Animals, babies and children love me. All I can say is Bob was a very lucky man. It was special for both of us. Look what I and so many others endured when losing their virginity!

Next thing I know, I'm running down the road to get to The Grouse Pub where Bob had told me to come and see 'The Quartet', a jazz group he played with. Nate and Lurker played instruments, Joe Spain played double bass and Bob played a snare-drum with metal brushes.

Soon I was regularly with Bob. He was utterly fascinating to me.

He lived in one rented room with a shared bathroom. He was the first boyfriend I'd had who didn't live with his parents. ALL my other friends lived with their families, I was the only one on my own.

Band gig posters all over his walls and rows of cassette tapes, all with his handwritten unusually jagged little spaced out print on them. He loved to smoke hash. Loads of vinyl records.

A sofa ran parallel to the single bed, and his pals and I would sit facing each other. Jimmy James,

Captain, Joe Spain. Occasionally the brothers Babby and Daddy. They enjoyed saying their favourite catchphrase to each other, "Eat shit and die!" and saying, "Muwah muwah" archly. Captain drove a small van with 'SATAN'S MATES' spray painted on the side. Everyone was older than me, including Bob.

A lot of the time we were alone together listening to amazing music from Gong, Hawkwind, Frank Zappa, Alex Harvey and new stuff to me like Henry Badowski, Patrick Fitzgerald, The Fall, The Cardiacs and Wild Man Fisher.

I also discovered the funniest pop song through Bob, named 'LOVE LIES LIMP' by ATV. The greatest antidote to cock rock.

Here & Now band were new to me and Bob told me how he'd followed them to every gig since he was 15. Eventually they invited him onto their bus and allowed him to start performing as Bob Crumpton. He always wore a prison jacket on stage and was so shy that he talked with his head down in a funny voice.

At the beginning Bob said "Just because we've had sex doesn't mean you're my girlfriend". I replied "No. But I am a friend who is a girl". Bob was happy with that.

Soon he was telling me all about his gigs in places like Launceston and Torquay and how he recorded every single gig on a tape-recorder. All were carefully listed on lots of cassettes. He played lots of his gigs to me and I noticed they were all virtually the same every time.

He had about 5 jokes and bizarrely, the audience would call out the punchline in advance of Bob telling the body of the joke. Crazy. Not like anything I'd ever heard.

He said he only did his show to "Annoy people". And he didn't consider it a good gig unless people had hurled abuse at him. Such a weird character.

Daylight had revealed that what I thought were tiny plaits in his hair were actually tiny random dreadlocks. And his curls were all matted together in big blobby clumps.

He was the first white man I'd ever seen with dreadlocks. Not the uniform rows of locks that white people wear nowadays, but shapeless clods all over the place.

He said his hair washed itself and he never used shampoo. I believed him and liked it.

On examining his dick in daylight, there was a thick, congealed collar of old yellow gunk in a ring under the helmet.

"Why don't you wash it?" I asked. He replied, "It washes itself". Obviously it didn't do a very good job.

Bob said it was "SMEGMA". He had a T-shirt made by one of his friends with a cartoon mouse by a lump of cheese, saying "Aaah SMEGMA VALE!".

Smegma Vale was the name they used for the filthy cheese on a dick. He washed it off.

Bob broke it to me that he wasn't Adam Ants cousin. Told me I was "Gullible". I believed him that I was gullible. (Geddit?!)

We went everywhere together; to parties, to houses like hippy Les's shared house. Les was lovely and he was mocked for how like the character Neil from 'THE YOUNG ONES' TV show he was.

We, Bob and I, took magic mushrooms and the pair of us walked down town. Bob was freaking at the traffic. I had ribbons of colours coming off me, yet the business men didn't seem to notice and walked with their heads down.

That's when I learned that nobody can see what's inside your head.

We went into Bob's bank and I sat on the floor against the wall as the carpet came towards me like waves on a beach.

One day we were sitting on Bob's sofa and I drew a picture of a little eel with a quiff hairstyle.

I asked Bob, "What's this?" He didn't know. I answered "It's ELVER PRESLEY!" Bob didn't realise that baby eels were called elvers.

He asked me what I was doing with an ugly git like him? I said I liked him. I asked him what he was doing with me? He said I was, "Good fun".

LAST NIGHT IN CARAVAN

Bob went off to a gig one night and I went to sleep in my caravan. I dreamed I was at sea on a rocking boat. The rocking got worse and worse, then I opened my eyes and the actual van was rocking and male voices were calling "Ida!" One said, "It's me, Steve Palm!"

SHIT! I lay quiet and hoped nobody would realise that the flap window by the bed and the door had no locks! Damn. They said, "The windows open!"

Next thing Steve Palm rolled through it onto my bed in his Army uniform. He had sex with me and left.

(I'd met him once in a disco when I was 14 and he kissed me and nearly got me in trouble with his girlfriend who he hadn't mentioned. I was very moral in my dealings, never took other people's boyfriends and only dated one at a time consecutively).

Next day, gutted, I told the landlord what had happened! He gave me a screwdriver to thread through the door loops from the inside of the caravan. What about the window!?!?

I refused to sleep in there the next night and curled up on a chair in the shared lounge, indoors.

Bob came back and I don't think I even told him. I was always so consumed by the present moment and nobody had ever cared anyway.

(A photographer boy with round spectacles wanted to take pictures of me around Sandiford town. He said I was the female version of Dave Calvert, a Sandiford punk who stood so tall like a superhero. With his cheekbones and Mohican he was incredible. Older than me and we'd hang around, me usually speechless in his presence. It was a great compliment to be called the female version of Dave Calvert. I saw him years later in Notting Hill and his comic strip art work was so clever and brilliant. He's now in L.A.)

Bob would always cook Brunswick Cafe style dinners. Basic meat and veg which I loved. Also chips in his electric chip fryer with a metal basket inside.

I'd ask him if I could have a go at cooking. He always said "No! MY kitchen!".

I said "You're stunting my culinary education". He didn't care and I just consoled myself that if he could do it, I'd be bound to catch up one day. That day never came.

Bob told me he'd shared a house with a guy who didn't know how to wash-up a cup with a cloth. So Bob had told him how to do it properly and the guy had packed up his stuff immediately and left the house! Bob was amazed as he recalled it. "Don't you think that's weird?" he asked me. I thought I'd reserve judgement.

STONE HENGE

Bob said, "You'll love Stone Henge Ida, it's great". He went down there with the tent and sleeping bags in a truck of his mates and I was supposed to meet him down there.

Splodge/Sarah the devastatingly beautiful punk and I hitched down there. It was such a free time, we all hitchhiked everywhere. Sarah's RED MOHICAN started leaking red rivulets down her face in the rain.

We got there in the raining dark and were presented with a mediaeval scene of cooking pots on fires and higgledy piggledy tents and wig-wams. We could hear a band playing so we made our way to a big stage like a pyramid. HAWKWIND were playing.

After a bit we carried on walking and I said, "Don't look now Splodge but we're being followed by a vampire and a Red Indian".

They caught up with us and took us to their tee-pee. We sat on cushions in the lamp light. They gave us acid tabs and we talked until dawn.

As the sun arose we went outside and both of us began giggling uncontrollably at a big topless woman with pendulous tits, tidying up round her bender tent. She gave us a filthy look but we were rolling on the ground beside ourselves with joy.

We went and sat on the stones of StoneHenge, looking at the rising sun. In those days it was open to the public.

It was the penultimate StoneHenge festival. I feel lucky to have seen it. I took Andrew Morton to the final one and had a blast.

ANYWAY, Sarah and I were on a mission to find Bob who had our sleeping bags and tent. We met some bikers from Sandiford who said, "This will help you find Bob easily!" Handing us more acid. Splodge and I went to the port-o-cabin loos and did our eye make-up. Sarah asked "Does it look ok?" I laughed "NO! It looks terrible! But it's funny". We were tripping out of our gourds.

No sign of Bob yet as we lolloped around. Then we met some hippies who said, "This will help you!" and gave us some speed. By this time I could speak sentences but in the wrong order. Splodge was rendered silent.

A kind Indian lady from Sandiford gave me some grapefruit juice as she was concerned.

Eventually, minus my leather jacket, I found Bob whose eye pupils were tiny. He took me to sit in front of the Pyramid stage with the band The Cardiacs. Bob said, "They're like you, like little children!".

I remember one Cardiac being called Sarah and we sat there yelling, "WE WANT BOB! WE WANT BOB!", because Bob was meant to be performing on the big stage. But he didn't make it because he felt too muntered.

Bob took me to the tent and I lay there holding onto the floor that was tipping me off. Next day a lovely friend of Bob's took me on the back of a motorcycle to get a full English breakfast.

Don't know what happened to Sarah/Splodge.

BACK IN SANDIFORD.

Bob said he really wanted to just grow carrots on a Scottish island and have a baby. A vision of our baby came into my head, a beautiful girl like Bob, with dark brown wild curls.

But I had been on the pill since my Mum gave it to me two years earlier, and I believed she knew best. Although I knew I couldn't trust her. Confused. By all accounts I'm good with children and it's sad that I was never a mother.

Anyway, although the thought of growing carrots was lovely, my attention span was not held by carrots as there was a massive world to see.

Bob hadn't even known to wash his own willy so I didn't trust him with a baby. Also I wanted to dance in musicals!

Bob said he wanted me to dye my bleached blonde hair black because his mother had dreamed he'd marry a black haired girl.

"NO, I don't want to, your Mum should just accept this colour as it is!" But Bob was adamant, persisting with his request. Until I gave up arguing and dyed my blonde hair black.

His parents arrived at Bob's bedsit bearing gifts. They'd driven across the Midlands with a cooked meal for Bob in a hotpot. I was impressed by such kind parents. Mine had never visited me ever!

Mr Crumpton was a driving instructor but Bob crashed the car into the garage wall. I don't think Bob would ever drive again.

Mr and Mrs Crumpton were Catholics and very fond of Bob, as their only other son had been killed. Bob said that his mother was never the same after her other son died.

They invited us to their home, which was part of their job as hosts of a Religious Retreat in the luscious grounds of a monastery. They provided breakfast for the guests, sandwiches and an evening meal.

As I sat across from Bob in the retreat's massive kitchen, the sunlight streaming at him, I'd never seen such a beautiful man, with his hair all raggedy framing his face. Bob would blush bright red in those days.

We loved going to bed together and Bob would always ask to go to sleep, "in our special way". Which meant him inside me.

His little curls all over his body made it feel as if I was in a bubble bath when close to him. He said "I LOVE YOUR TOUCH!" About my magic touch. I'd never felt so secure and warm. Bob said we were a perfect fit, the way we snuggled up so effortlessly. We were both in love for the first time.

We used to hide our teeth behind our lips and pretend to kiss each other at 90 years old.

Bob said "I LOVE YOUR SMILE!" And his face looked so lovely that I knew he meant it.

I told him that a boy had called me Smiley at school, (punch drunk). Bob said it was a coincidence as he was also called Smiley at school because he looked miserable.

At the Sandiford bedsit, Bob suddenly went into a fit of temper over the state of his curtains. They hadn't been opened in the proper way. He went thundering ballistic.

I just sat with a frozen smile, staring straight ahead, thinking oh dear, that's nuts. But I let it go as I loved him. He'd continue to have little rages out of the blue but then he'd calm down

We were invited to a party in Birmingham by musical partners Nicky and Lara.

We hitched there. Lara and Nicky were very tall. Lara was having her 24th birthday I think, and she was the most elegant, beautiful woman I'd ever seen, and I've never seen a more beautiful one to this day. If I said Lara looked like Natalie Wood, it wouldn't do her justice as Natalie's nose was sharp. Lara was off the scale of natural beauty.

I met a musician couple, Toby and Zilla, a ginger long haired guy and the singer from a band called 'Dangerous Girls'. The people there were awe-inspiring and so grown up.

It was a lovely night. I was bumming fags and chatting merrily and everyone was most kind and gracious to this 17 year old punky, scrounging thing.

We stayed the night on the floor and left in the morning after I'd bummed another fag off the Dangerous Girls singer. Too much blood in my nicotine stream. I hadn't got into smoking long enough to get around to buying my own!

I'd started smoking in London when a guy took Linda and I to a porn cinema, which I wasn't impressed with. He offered us cigarettes then a week later I had another. Then in Paris I was smoking Katherine's menthol KOOL cigarettes. In UK, I went onto Golden Virginia tobacco like Bob. Nicotine is most insidious.

Bob would only allow me a cigarette when he rolled one for himself. He'd say, "Nyooo Babba". Somehow, Bob ran my life and I didn't mind that much.

Tania Warburton saw Bob and told me, "You can do better than him!" So did the actor, Steve Gittis. But NOTE I did not tell Bob.

I only note this because Bob told me about the night he'd first seen me. He asked Nate, "Who's that with Lurker?"

Nate had replied to him, "Oh someone cheap and nasty". When Bob said this to me I was crestfallen, dismayed and bewildered!

"But I've never even had a conversation with Nate!" I said. "I'm not cheap n nasty! I'M FREE AND SWEET!"

Bob said, "I know that. Nate doesn't know you like I do. He doesn't know you". What a mean way to speak of a young girl who was looking for love.

Never mind!

Rowan Atkinson and Stephen Fry made me laugh. But to Bob, all comedians were deemed "SHIT".

Every other comedian was "Shit" except Bob Monkhouse, whom he loved and Bernard Manning. He liked 'THE YOUNG ONES' TV show but hated Monty Python etc. It seemed quite a depressing outlook to me.

He thought it hilarious that it took me months to get one of his jokes. It was a phenomenon that unlike ordinary comedians who always used NEW material, Bob would happily stick to his same few jokes, over and over. Only the heckles might change and that's what Bob loved.

We'd talk about when Bob would be famous. There was no doubt in my mind about Bob's inevitable rise. He was so weird that fame was a given. I said I wanted to do musical theatre and Bob said, "You'll be famous and won't want to know me anymore!"

I replied emphatically, "The chances of that are as tiny as a grain of sand on the beach! I just love dancing and singing! In the chorus or wherever!"

Back then I didn't realise how easy it was to get on TV.

Drama group were doing 'Midsummer's Night Dream' by William Shakespeare at the local theatre. Unlike the original version, it was set in the 1920's.

My Flapper Girl costume was lycra and net, held up by one shoulder. In the dress rehearsal during a dance my boob popped out so they added an invisible strap. LOVED the show and the actors were excellent!

Bob and I went to see the movie 'E.T.' on its release at the Odeon Cinema. Afterwards I was filled with wonder, hoping to find an E.T. in a bush.

Bob was very cynical about it. Smilingly he said, "It pushed every emotional button, manipulating the audience's emotions".

WOW! I thought, this man is SO analytical!

Bob would come to Sunday lunch at my Mum's house. I was still visiting my siblings and felt as though I was hanging onto access there by my fingernails.

Bob was shy as usual and blushed bright red often. O'Leery was gobby as usual and I didn't feel able to talk as I hadn't been allowed to speak there in the past, thanks to O'Leery. Mum said that O'Leery reckoned Bob was "Wise beyond his years".

Bob said if it wasn't for his comedy act he would probably end up like O'Leery. A thought that made me shudder.

A big multi-band gig was arranged at a big hall in Sandiford. Nicky and Lara were invited along and came to stay the night in Bob's bedsit. The old sofa pulled down into a double bed. Cara and I got ready together in the big mirror while Bob went out with Mickey.

As I walked Lara through Sandiford I'd stop to introduce her to people I knew. "You're so civil and polite Ida!" said Cara. For a street kid, I really was.

I don't remember any of the bands except for Agz singing in Sensa Yuma. Agz gave me a gun and asked me to introduce his band with a bang and tell people to dance!

Back at the bedsit, Bob and I were there ahead of Nicky and Lara. Bob was creating a row out of nowhere as usual when Nicky and Lara knocked on the door. Emulating O'Leery I said brightly, "Just a family argument!". The couple smiled weakly.

Bob's rages were so mortifying to me and embarrassing. As life was too short for such nonsense!

Although young, I knew it was wrong.

Bob took me to a London pub to see Here & Now play. I said to one of them, "I really like your song 'Floating Out To Sea". He said "It's 'Floating Anarchy' mate!".

ITALY

In August, Bob's parents arrived with an offer we couldn't refuse. They'd been charged with the job of taking a camper-van full of Bibles and religious books to Italy. There were seats for four and two people had dropped out, so Bob and I could take those tickets.

Bob's parents took us for a meal at a very posh house full of art, with a super-posh ageing Catholic couple hosting the meal.

They chatted to Mr and Mrs Crumpton and told us about the proposed trip to Italy. They peppered their conversation with phrases like, "He was a first class bastard!"

Mr and Mrs Crumpton didn't swear, but later at home after the meal, mummy Crumpton supposed it was alright to swear because they were posh.

All the way across the continent Bob and I were in the back of the van full of stacks of Bibles. The van had pictures of Padre Pio all over the outside of it. Padre Pio is famous for bearing continuously bleeding stigmata in his hands. He's always pictured with blood soaked bandages around his hands, which were changed daily. Experts could not explain the holes in his hands like Jesus.

Mr Crumpton was practising his Italian as he drove, such a cheery fellow.

On the way we stopped off to say hello to Mrs Crumpton's younger sister who was working in a hotel in Baden Baden.

We found her happy face in the pokey servants quarters around the back of the amazing hotel. The pavements in Baden Baden looked as if they were made of marble. Cars purred by with the sound of great expense. A very rich place.

On we went through Switzerland. SO CLEAN! Bob and I noted a road sign saying 'Ferker Pass'. The cuckoo clock houses were in top condition. All the elites keep their gold in Switzerland. The service stations in Switzerland were immaculate with bubbly soft water. (As I type Switzerland has billions of President Putin's money). Onwards into Italy and suddenly in stark contrast we saw peeling painted shutters, creating gorgeous textures and flooded service stations from broken taps with litter abounding.

The countryside in Italy was ancient looking and marvellous, redolent of a Vincent Van Gogh painting. It was a long drive to the destination where the rich old couple met with Mr Crumpton.

The old posh man just came to the driver's window and waved on Mr Crumpton to go and park up. Bob thought this was rude after such a lengthy drive. I think Mr Crumpton wanted acknowledgement at least.

We were in paradise and I was grateful for it, yet Bob's temper tantrums were STILL in evidence every day! The phrase, "So near yet so far!" was in my mind.

It was excruciating to me to be on a FREE lovely holiday in a wonderful place with his kind parents, yet Bob was wrecking it for us all with his stroppy moods and niggling whining!

I begged him privately to think of his parents if not of me. He was selfishly destroying their time away! For what?

Bob insisted to me, "They love me and accept whatever I feel because they're my parents! THEY CARE ABOUT ME!"

Seriously!? I reasoned that although they were super tolerant, surely they deserved a break?!

Bob would often tell me, "You haven't been brought up properly, I'm your Mum now!" He had a point, but at least I hadn't grown up to be a spoiled brat!

AUSTRALIA UPDATE 27TH MARCH 2022. THIS BOOK HAS BEEN SERIOUSLY HARD TO WRITE. I hope it's easier to read.

UNLIKE the bloke in J.D.Salinger's 'Catcher In The Rye', I'd LOVE to be as thorough, detailed and measured as 'David Copperfield' by Charles Dickens. I enjoyed that book immensely. Time is my enemy as well as inadequacy.

I've cast my mind back to age 17 and know I did my utmost best to get on with Bob. Would his temper have been allayed if I'd not been on the birth control pill and had given him our baby and gone to the Outer Hebrides to grow veg with him?

It's unknowable, but I suspect he would have still made my life very hard, as he was a baby AND a bully in a grown man's body. BUT I'M JUMPING AHEAD with impatience as I know what he deteriorated into!

He hadn't fully started throwing me around yet. He still had his tender moments.

ITALY CONTINUED.

We went to San Giovanni where Padre Pio had lived in a monastery. A monk took us around the basilica to the monk's cell where Padre Pio had his famous physical fight with the devil. The devil had thrown him off his bed and knocked him unconscious onto the floor, giving him a head injury. The monks had found him laid there on the floor with a pillow under his head. Later, when Padre Pio came back to consciousness the monks asked him how the pillow had got onto the floor under his head? Padre Pio answered that Mary the Mother of Jesus had seen off the devil and placed the pillow under his head.

(We saw the same blood stained pillow wrapped in plastic for posterity in the cell). Next day after the satanic attack on Padre Pio, an old peasant woman visited the church and started talking like a rasping man.

She said, "I came for the old man last night but that bitch ruined it. I'll be back!" Or words VERY similar.

This story scared me alright. Especially as back in England, Bob and I had been invited to a newfangled video party at a lovely girls luxurious house, and the final film before we were shown to our room, was 'The Exorcist'.

In the guest bedroom afterwards we were laughing as Bob heavy breathed in the darkness, but the film so affected me that I was wary as I put my little sister to bed, as she had long blond hair with a fringe. I've never watched another horror film since.

In Assisi I was determined to get some enjoyment out of this wonderful trip and I went off walking by myself in the magical narrow cobbled streets, amongst the tourists in the early evening sun. WHY must Bob be so mardy all the time? ('Mardy' is a Sandiford word for brattish shit!).

FINALLY Mr Crumpton reached breaking point and had a few gruff words with Bob, who then sulked with his lip out like a huge toddler.

I don't recall all the places we stopped at but I know we did the Stations of The Cross set on a steep hillside with many steps, which meant nothing to me at the time. I still don't know what the Stations are as I have nothing to do with Catholicism.

We drove back through Germany, staying for a week at an army camp where another of Mrs Crumpton's sisters lived with her army husband and young son.

My 18th birthday came while we were there in Germany. Bob and I had sex in a German field.

Mummy Crumpton gave me a birthday cake and a book by Anthony Summer about Marilyn Monroe, entitled 'Goddess'. Very good book.

All Mrs Crumpton's presents lasted me for years. At Christmas she gave me a red trunk with brass corners and fittings that still has all my love-letters in it from Bob and others. It was left behind in London with all my photos of dready Bob. A Marks & Spencer eye-shadow set she gave me lasted for many years too, along with a tapestry bag that I kept my sleeping bag inside.

I have no truck with astrology anymore, but Bob's mum was/is a Virgo like me and it transpired that almost all Aquarian Bob's friends were Virgos; Nate, Lurker, Captain.

(In the year 2000 I met a world famous astrologer called Jonathan Cainer in a festival field. He computed my birthday to have 6 planets in Virgo. Virgo Sun, Virgo rising and all the rest.

I said "You must see plenty like that in your job".

He said "No, this is me excited, this is the type of chart I'd hand to my astrologer friends and say what do you think of this!"

Sorry Jonathan, but after being a slave to astrology for *years*, looking for answers regarding my mother etc., I now am inclined to think astrology is an Illuminati tool of division. Could be wrong but it only took me in a large circle and told me what I knew in the first place; that I am observant and that my devious mother got away with murder.

Chinese astrology told me that I am a Wood Dragon and that Bob is a Metal Ox due to his early January birthday. He cut me like a metal axe alright and I didn't need astrology to confirm it. Now I never look at astrology, I just go straight to God, the Most High).

Bob called me "Babba" or his "wife". He liked hearing his own voice saying, "Nyooo Babba!" at requests I made for cigarettes or whatever.

He would breast feed me on his pretend milk and sometimes be so gentle and exquisitely sensuous. If marriage was only about sex I would never have left. He even said my wonky eye was "Distinctive".

I have to buffer my brain with happier memories as I get to the sad facts that drove me to leave Bob. He excessively freaked out and went into a mad flap at wasps or dogs. Very ridiculous behaviour.

I remember being 11 at a hippy commune in Pontrilas on the Hereford border of Wales, running in fields with an Irish WolfHound, much bigger than me. We came to a field of wild grey horses who stampeded towards us with the sun behind them. In a millisecond I decided that if I ran, I'd be trampled, but if I stood like a post they would run around me, as they're not stupid. So like a knife thrower's assistant, I stood as the wild horses thundered by me, creating a breeze. Bob would've been dead.

BOB'S HAIRCUT

Bob noticed seeds and gunk from his hair on the pillow and decided I should wash his hair. We shampooed it over his communal bathtub one bright day and we both looked at each other in horror as the water ran dark blackish purple and green! Gross. His hair went into the texture of a dead crow on his head.

He decided I must cut off his dreadlocks. I left soft short curls all over his head. He hadn't gone full skinhead yet.

As I cut into the locks all manner of foreign bodies popped out, having been entrapped for years in the matted maze. It's sometimes a blessing that I cannot smell.

On my return to the room I saw a massive tarantula on the sofa and squealed! Bob had put his dreadlocks on the sofa and said to me, "I could sell them to the fans!"

"UGH! Why don't you sell your klinkers as well?" I retorted! (A klinker is the English term for an Australian dag, the turd particles stuck in fur around a bumhole)

Then I broke into the Russian folk song in my clearest carrying voice, "KALINKA KALINKA KALINKA MY DEAR! YOUR NAME IN THE WHISPER OF PINES I CAN HEAR!"

At 18, marriage was fresh in my memory as being full of infidelity, rows, violence and my Mum ripping off my Dad's new silk purple and blue shirt that looked like a Tolkien illustration, so it hung in shredded ribbons off his body.

I'd rather be faithfully unmarried than unfaithfully married and screaming. The pilgrims in Italy had called Bob my "fiance" and I protested that we were not getting married!

Back in Sandiford Bob was an angry man most of the time. I saw a tiny blue flower like a Forget-me-not peeping its head out between the bars of a grid in the street. Amazed, I bent down to look through the grid bars to see how it managed this feat. Its skinny stalk was at least 7 feet tall! It had grown towards the light from the bottom of a filthy dark sewer. Bob said, "GET UP off the floor!"

Bob would tell me, "You've got too high an opinion of yourself!" and he'd throw me across the room then get me by the throat against the wall, his face twisted with rage up against mine. I'd cry because;

A) It hurt and I hadn't done anything to him. My opinion of myself was non-existent. Isaac Newton said, "The more I learn the more I realise I am like a small boy paddling on the edge of a vast ocean". So that made me feel like an amoeba!

But I knew that I had a God-given right not to have any more violence against me. Like it said in Desiderata, 'You have a right to be here, no less than the trees or the stars' I needed a BREAK from viciousness.

B) I loved him

C) It was a waste of life.

Then I'd go off and tell my friends that he was Jekyll and Hide.

Like the nursery rhyme, he had a little curl in the middle of his forehead and when he was good, he was very, very good and when he was bad he was horrid.

I went to my caravan……and it was GONE! I asked the landlord where my home and possessions were. He said "I sold the caravan. Your stuff is in the coal bunker". I looked in the coal bunker and all my record albums were strewn haphazardly in the coal, along with my clothes and whatever else.

TINA SLATER

Next thing I knew, I was given a new home in Rowley Grove, just over the railway bridge from Bob.

Tina Slater aged 32 was the landlady, who turned out to be a real diamond of a lady. My stuff was put in the back bedroom and I rented it from her. The house was minimalist Victoriana, or maybe 1930's. I loved it.

Tina was an Oxford or Cambridge graduate, (can't recall which), and she worked in computing I think.

She owned the house and was a Tory. I'd been on marches for the miners as a very young child with my parents, as they carried the bed-sheet sized banner Dad had painted in the kitchen. Forgetting to put wind slits in it so it took off like a sail in the wind.

Tina and I had good natured rows about politics. She reckoned in the 1800's I'd have been a maid. I replied, "I'd have been a dancer and you're forgetting that women weren't educated back then, nor could they vote". Also re: miners strike I stated that all the tins in her cupboard were made by coal power. (In reality I had no idea and made it up).

Now I believe in free-market capitalism and decentralised government.

All Tina's food jars on the shelves had 'Mine' written on them, which amused Andrew Morton. Tina had orange wavy, silky hair and the biggest most friendly smile that anyone has seen. Tina was known by all for her cheerful smile. She played squash after work and would have a half hour "power nap" before meeting her colleagues down the pub.

She even taught me how to make a roux sauce from scratch. Amazingly kind.

I had really landed on my feet there.

With Bob the same cycle of aggressive behaviour continued, then the making up, until I was so weary and realised I was spending too much of my life crying in despair.

"You don't love me!" he'd say. I'd reply 'YES I DO! But you want me to totally adore you and you're not totally adorable! I'm not your mother!"

It hit me that Bob was a textbook case of what happens when parents lavish love on their only child. (Like the 'Little Emperor Syndrome' which occurred after the one child policy in China). He was an emotionally immature brat.

In their grief over losing their youngest child, Bob**'s parents had unwittingly created a monster!!**

Whether it was by nature or by nurture that Bob was a vicious brat, I cannot know. But he was ultimately responsible for himself.

One day at Bob's parents' new Walsall home, Bob complained that his toe hurt. His mother spent the evening watching TV with Bob's big foot in her lap, massaging his toe. He acted as if to the manor born, as if it was completely normal.

The sight of Bob being molly-coddled by his Mum made me feel unwell. Queasy.

Another time at his parents place Bob lunged at me, pushing me backwards and I landed on the sofa, as he came at me I put my knees to my chest with my feet out and his stomach was grazed on my stiletto heel.

He looked at his tummy and there was just a tiny scuff of skin, no blood. If I'd have kicked him there would've been a lot of blood! He went to his Mum and said, "Mum look what she did to me!" like a completely embarrassing brat. He'd done it to himself by coming at me!! Bah!

What about Eric Fromm?

I told Bob about the first two pages I'd read of Eric Fromm's 'The Art Of Loving'. It described a boy who found a butterfly which he loved, so he took it to pieces to see how it worked, then it died! It said you have to love someone without taking them to pieces! What about Khalil Gibran, 'The Prophet' and his recipe for a relationship being two equal pillars holding up a temple?

Bob was never satisfied until he saw my tears come.

Tina had a party at her house and Bob sat on the stairs crying, stabbing his forehead with a felt-tip pen saying,

"LOOK WHAT YOU'RE MAKING ME DO! THIS IS YOUR FAULT!" A couple of tiny lines of felt-tip colour were on his head.

I had no words. Nobody but himself chose to be repeatedly vicious and drive me away.

It all clicked FINALLY in my head. I weighed up the good against the bad on the old fashioned balancing scales in my head: the bad times outweighed the good times with Bob.

Then I made a very calm and matter of fact statement to Bob.

"As a good friend of yours, I will have to go. Otherwise I will be guilty of perpetuating your delusion that you can treat me like shit, and I will end up as a vegetable and you will become a worse tyrant, a lose lose situation. So as a good friend I have no choice but to say goodbye".

(WHAT A COOL HEADED 18 year old!!! FFS! BANG ON THE MONEY! I wish he had stayed away for the rest of my life!!!)

He didn't take my goodbye very well. It dragged on a while. He moved to a flat overlooking the same railway lines which my house backed onto on the other side. His new flat had slugs in the kitchen. He played me a recording of himself bashing the strings of a guitar, singing mournfully, "You don't love me but I love you", over and over.

I BELIEVED HE LOVED ME IN HIS OWN HEAD! But that wasn't safe to live with in real life!

I recall him being in a bookshop with me and he chose a very good book for Lucy's Christmas present entitled 'Eric The Punk Cat'.

By Spring I had TOTALLY cut him off. ENOUGH CRAP!

One dark night, I was doing the washing up in Tina's kitchen, looking at the reflection of the lit up kitchen in the dark window. I looked at the reflection of my own eyes. Strangely I could see four eyes in the window, my own eyes......and BOB'S! I walked swiftly to the back door and turned the key. Locked. Standing in the dark, staring at me like that. Coming down the entry passageway to the closed back garden. Creep.

The housemate Bob had told me about, who left the moment Bob told him the ONLY way to wash a cup, had the right idea!

I ought to have left the moment Bob first raged about his curtains which overlooked a walled backyard. GET OUT FAST KIDS! If I'd had anywhere safer to go back then, I probably would have.

FLUFFY PEACE AT TINA SLATER'S

About time eh? Holidays at festivals, like the Elephant Fayre in St. Germain with Ed Kite. Dancing all night right in front of the band in a tent, following the rhythms then creating new rhythms within the rhythms and melodies with my moves, which the band would follow. We went on until way past dawn, like a spiritual experience.

Going with my theatre friends to a cottage in Devon. Driven down there by James who had played Bottom in Midsummer's Night Dream. What a happy, joyful larger than life character he was/is.

StoneHenge with Andrew Morton where we made a hair salon that was out of this world, with a mobile hanging from the roof for clients to stare at.

"Hello Sir/Madam, you look well balanced and a fine upstanding character, BUT OH MY GOD! THAT HAIR! I CAN HELP YOU! WOMEN WILL FLOCK!"

I did the make-up for the little theatre kids for their production of 'Dracula Spectacular'. Every little boy wanted a Magnum P.I. moustache! All these little blonde cherubs with huge thick black moustaches like TV actor Tom Sellick!

Jack Kerouac and William Burroughs were read and I learned the words 'paregoric' and 'jissom' respectively. Also the chilling book '1984' by George Orwell. (Here we all are then!)

The young singer Charmaine Baines would come over to Tina's in the day and hear records with me. Vincent came over too and Andrew Morton.

Then Andrew would say, "Ok I'm off to have a conversation with my mother!" He'd do that every day. She was a vicar's wife.

I remember day-dreaming one day wistfully that I should put myself up for adoption by a family that wouldn't be a threat to my physical safety. But I didn't know how to do it and I guessed I was too old at 18.

Years later I read that actor Neil Morrisey had put himself up for adoption somehow at a similar age and it had been successful.

Tina NEVER got angry or aggressive. She was amazing. She'd say, "This house is Ida-fied in the day and Tina-fied at night!" I will always adore that cheery benevolent woman.

I'd occasionally venture up to Highfields estate to see Lucy. I never spoke in that house if O'Leery was around. Still traumatised from being banned from speaking by him.

One day he rambled in with a champagne bottle and fell onto the sofa after a row with Mum. He asked if I'd have a drink with him as it was his birthday. I answered,

"I only drink champagne when there's something to celebrate". It was the most I ever said to him.

I DESPISED that man for the abuse he'd put me through.

Somebody told me that Bob had left town to go down South. This info meant very little to me.

Captain stopped me in the street to pass on a message from Zilla and Toby, the musician couple I'd met at Lara's birthday party in B'ham.

The message was their phone number and for me to get in touch if I wanted to get involved in creativity with them. I thanked Captain.

Zilla and Toby's connection with Bob Crumpton put me off, as I knew I wouldn't be able to keep quiet about his viciousness and I was dragged up to not tell tales. I didn't think anyone would believe me. I didn't ring them. A great opportunity missed.

Oh FRABJOUS DAY! CALLOOH! CALLAY! The auditions were being held for the next production, and I was actually around to attend! It was the musical 'CABARET'.

I sang in the audition and was awarded the lead part of Sally Bowles! WOW! James played the theatre compere character who sings 'Money Makes The World Go Round' with Sally.

James and I had such a lot of fun rehearsing the song at Tina's. I learned all the songs and would rehearse them with the group.

But not everybody was happy. The girl who usually played the lead roles said, "I won't be in it if I'm not the lead". She dismissed my getting the role as "Typecasting".

So much for the camaraderie of a small town production! Saddening to think I'd always been happy for her to play the lead in show after show. Bah!

Then she said something that made as much sense and was as surprising as if she'd put a Purple Amazonian Tree Frog in my hand.

She said "We've always been rivals".

Incredible! We were nothing like each other! Curry is not a rival of Chinese food! It's a different dish! In HER mind ONLY were we rivals!

Andrew Morton had argued with her boyfriend that Snidey Falters, (for that was her name), looked "Horrible!" when the boyfriend had called her beautiful.

Andrew repeated it, "Absolutely HORRIBLE". I could now see why and noticed for the first time that even the corners of her mouth pointed downwards.

I would meet a few like Snidey in my life. Pea-brained, tight-hearted, irrational women who hadn't evolved above their lower traits. Snidey was born in the year of the Snake, very jealous creatures. If she ever grew beyond her base nature I will never know.

At that time I certainly hadn't evolved beyond my basic Dragon nature of thinking the best of wankers! Until dismally disappointed by reality.

Having said that, Jason, one of my best ever friends, was a Snake and a sweeter man I've never known. There's always the odd exceptions to every rule. Meeting Jason while living at Tina's was so romantic. We lay in the snow and made angels, we ran in slow motion towards each other across a motorway bridge into an impassioned slo-mo embrace. We were married in the service station shop with CCTV as the wedding video and the cash register woman was our registrar. We danced in the nightclub and wanted to join in with the young Staffordians dancing around their handbags, but we didn't have handbags so we danced around our Tesco plastic shopping bags instead. We reenacted the Olympic ice-skaters Torville and Dean's 'Bolero' dance at the disco, with me dragging Jason across the floor in a mighty way. Then we'd mime beating each other up in time to the music. We camped on Cannock Chase and sang made up cowboy songs and invented animal calls. We stayed up all night writing creative notes and poems to the milkman, who said they were put on a special display shelf at his work. I made a bouncing red paper arrow that pointed at the bottle. "Milk is good, it's better than wood. Milk is white, it's never red! You can pour it on your head! You can pour it in your bed but it begins to smell after a few weeks or so".

We saw a sign in a Sandiford centre pub for an 'Australian Night' and we were the only pair with Aboriginal patterns painted on our faces.

Tina went away for a weekend and Jason and I invited every youth faction in town to a party there. Punks, Rastas, theatre kids, feminists, and everybody else. An audience track was played to cheer and whistle and applaud as people arrived. It was a superb party and Johnny from Drama Club helped me clear up.

A shocking turn up for the books was seeing my Mum and O'Leery sat on the sofa in the front room of the party! They must have heard about it. I was stunned and went into another room and ignored them.

(Looking back now, I should have THROWN THEM OUT!)

The kids who went to the Valentine's house called themselves 'The Clique' and I was one of them.

They stuck only to themselves, never went anywhere. When a lovely Clique person called Po walked through town with me he found it bizarre that I said "Hello" to everyone. (Like an Australian!)

I thought, "What do you expect? I've been out since the late 70's!"

They said they only needed 'The Clique' as friends. They were very sheltered sixth formers, living at home.

Being aloof was a luxury I couldn't afford and didn't want.

Andrew Morton took me to meet his special friend Steve the tall punk who was 25. Steve played 'THE CRAMPS' records and I was bowled over by them. It was my new favourite music, I LOVED music with a KICK!

Andrew said he wouldn't take the rest of The Clique to Steve's flat as only I would "get it".

Amazingly, without any mobile phones or internet I met Linda from the strawberry fields in a Sandiford pub for the first time since my skull fracture. She was living in Hackney with the drummer of a band named 'Furniture'. Her father had hung himself in her family's kitchen. Shocking. Linda told me that Hash, the rapist skull fracturing maniac, had hassled her to find out where I was. She said that she got a friend of a friend from Brixton to break his legs. I do hope so. He'd be hobbling about, madder than ever. There was no other form of justice available.

She said that Patrick Fitzgerald had stayed at her Hackney squat (which I visited), and laid in a bath of baked beans for days. Bob used to play Patrick Fitzgerald's album to me, 'Grubby Stories'.

My Dad turned up at Tina Slater's briefly. He'd come to see his parents. He was wearing a cigarette lighter on a cord around his neck with a skull on it and over the skull's eyes he'd put a thick elastic band as a blindfold. He told me he was now a guru in Holland and that, like the skull who could see nothing, he himself knew nothing. "I know nothing!" he said.

He lived in a tent inside a large squat for a while and claimed guru status as a ring of listeners would sit outside his tent. Then he moved to another squat and slept in a coffin with a face hole to breathe, so that the drunk punks who fell on him when he was sleeping wouldn't squash him. He said he'd built an adventure playground for rats. Dad was bald on top, so instead of a Mohican hairstyle he said he'd had a horizontal Mohican, like the rings of Saturn. When he heard I'd been prohibited by Police from London in case Hash fractured my skull again, he said "You're a cool customer! You never told me that". (As if I had a choice).

I replied, "What was the point? It was done and you couldn't change it".

He'd never listened to me about O'Leery beating me up, so why tell him anything? He went back to Holland to resume guru-ing.

I always had the feeling that I could not trust either of my parents. They were children and I was the adult. A dour feeling.

AUSTRALIAN UPDATE. 2nd April 2022

Mimi was fed some dog food from the food bank and directly upon finishing her bowl she had a seizure. It was awful.

I cried so much as my front neighbour drove me to the 24hr vet. That little old dog Mimi rules me! I'm her butler. The vet gave her a Valium injection and charged $162. RIP OFF BASTARDS. I rang the food bank and told them to desist from giving out dodgy dog food. I'd shared some with my other neighbour who looked for reviews online. All reviews were of animals vomiting and getting ill. We threw it all in the bin.

The Sandiford Tory council had it in for me personally, and yet again put the kibosh on my artistic ventures. Cabaret was cut. Not enough budget. Oh well, I was ever resilient.

I had decided not to go back to art college to do the Fine Art degree course, reasoning that I could do art on the side and when I was old. However, I must dance and show off when young, so I applied for the only drama school I could find that had a Musical Theatre course, Guildford Academy of Drama Dance Education.

'A Streetcar Named Desire' by Tennessee Williams had deeply affected me when I saw the Vivienne Leigh and Marlon Brando movie on TV when I was 14.

So I went to the vinyl record library and took out a recording of Rosemary Harris in a Broadway production of Streetcar. (Seemed sensible as I didn't know how a 40+ Southern belle sounded and I wanted to get into the course).

For the audition I had to choose a modern play and a Shakespeare play and two contrasting songs. For the Shakespeare selection I impersonated my friend James's Bottom from Midsummer's Night Dream.

For the songs I chose 'Cabaret' that I knew well and the sad, 'Another Suitcase Another Hall' by Andrew Lloyd Webber.

EVERY DAY I exercised my voice until I could reach the back of a big hall without a microphone and could effortlessly hit the highest and lowest notes. EVERYDAY I learned my play lines from Rosemary Harris. Physically I was fit as a flea for the dancing.

As the big audition day drew close, Tina said, "You've worked very hard for this, I'm going to take you to the dancewear shop and get you the right clothes". She did! A black leotard with thin shoulder straps and a pair of shiny black footless leggings. I LOOKED GREAT IN THEM! Tina was a fairy Godmother.

Nick, a very handsome platonic friend, drove me to Guildford and paid for me to stay overnight in a guesthouse ready for the morning audition.

A lovely bearded young man who spoke like Oliver Reed said he'd show me where to get changed. A gorgeous older girl told him to stop perving and go away.

The other auditionees were queued up to go in and were talking about OTHER auditions they'd got lined up.

Shit, I thought, I've only got THIS ONE shot!

I could only afford one audition as they cost ten pounds or more each. AND it had stated that 'A' Levels were required unless in exceptional cases. I better be a bloody good exceptional case!

First we all danced in front of the panel and it went like a dream. Then we went in separately for our play renditions and songs.

For the songs I could not have done better. I said I'd sing without accompaniment as I didn't have a piano at home.

For my Blanche Dubois piece I found myself crying real tears on cue as all my pain and despair built up inside me.

Then I went straight into comedy Shakespeare and did James's interpretation. "Tongue not word! Come trusty swerd!"

They laughed.

An existing student boy saw me out of the room and said, "You were very good" (I would later see him on TV).

In my interview with Michael Gaunt the Principal, he said, "If we let you in, will you try really hard to get a grant?" "Yes" I replied wiping a tear.

I thought to myself, well that was the very best audition I could do, so if I don't get in I must be crap.

I didn't believe I'd been accepted until I opened the reply letter downtown after I'd cashed my dole cheque to buoy me up against disappointment.

WE ARE DELIGHTED TO OFFER YOU A PLACE ON THE MUSICAL THEATRE COURSE!!!

I screamed and ran through town giving all my money away to children. Then I physically picked up a man named Dodd, who later told Kirsty that he was going to marry me.

As I write this I am in floods of tears, as I know what happens next.

For a minute I thought I was all set.

But Sandiford Tory council refused my application for a discretionary grant. I appealed. NO.

I went to the local paper, Sandiford Newsletter to appeal further. The one page story had a headline something like 'CURTAINS ON Standiford girls stage dreams'. I'd wanted them to take a dynamic smiley physical shot of me in the standing splits or something, but they insisted on a big close-up of my face looking sad.

STILL NO GRANT.

My twisted Uncle was a millionaire so I asked him, selling it to him that I was very employable and would soon repay him, and he could see me on TV and take the credit.

"OH NO! I could never get it past Auntie Betty" he whined. "Ask her!"
"Oh nooo, my dear, why don't you sell your body? You're sitting on a goldmine!"

"Because I'd be too dead to spend the money!! How long would I last? Whereas with theatre I can do it until I'm old!"

Betty was Mum's sister. Mum was zero help, true to form. I had no idea what to do next to get the fees.

James and some theatre kids were at Props Winebar with me. Snidey was talking about her 20,000 pound inheritance that she just didn't know what to do with.

James piped up, "Why don't you loan some to Ida for drama school?" She said, "Mmmm no". "You're holding back talent!" implored James.

No.

On reflection, what was Snidey doing bragging about a large sum of money that she didn't know what to do with? It's only dawning on me now. She really was horrible. Thank you James.

A playwright wrote 'The Other Island' for the girls in, a female version of Lord Of The Flies. We took it to the Edinburgh Fringe Festival. When I had to yell "Kill!", it was bloodcurdling.

BRAIN ALERT

In the Edinburgh Fringe Club we were sitting around a long table and I was at the head. The girls started talking about rape. I thrust forward my heartfelt belief that, "You cannot allow one wanker out of millions to dictate your emotions and life. You cannot allow them to turn you into a victim!" As I trotted out my fully believed spiel, the weirdest thing happened. As I spoke tears started coming out of my eyes!

I apologised, surprised at my tears and went to the toilet, facing the realisation that my heartfelt beliefs didn't match my own leaking eyes. Something was very wrong. Then I wiped my face and carried on regardless.

My Mum actually spoke to me, saying, "I was in a taxi the other day and the driver said, that girl in the paper could have put Sandiford on the map. I said, that's my daughter".

This gave me some small idea that Mum was on my side deep down.

In a vivid dream of a sunny, sandy lane there was a parking attendant with a metre stick poking it into the sand. He said, "The sand stops here!".

THEN as it states in the Bible; "LIKE A DOG RETURNS ITS VOMIT", I WENT BACK TO LONDON with Jason to try and get an elusive equity card through stripping. This was very misguided, but I had zero guidance and believed an equity card was crucial to getting theatre work.

Jason was bi-sexual and worked as a stripper in a gay club. (I tried being bi-sexual a couple of times but ultimately it wasn't a choice I wanted to take. We don't have to take every choice available to us. Now I'm a Christian I'm convicted of that).

At first I worked in a few places, including a place where I was sat on the reception desk looking out onto the street attracting customers in my de rigeur Sam Fox blonde long feather cut and my jumper and leather jacket in the winter chill like a Polish girl; some European academic types arrived and I took their money and they went down into the bar/stage room downstairs, then I'd have to quickly change behind the scenes and run downstairs to do the strip-show as well! One cultured bloke laughed good naturedly to see that it was me again on stage as well as on the door. Instead of laughing along I gave him my killer death glare as if to say "You try it buster!" and he straightened his face.

Then I worked in a place that played Tina Turner's 'Private Dancer' on repeat. Unlike the lyrics, I definitely thought of the men as human, but I tried to focus on the dancing, as if I were in a field or anywhere but there. 'When Doves Cry' by Prince was on a lot too.

I ended up working at The Swedish Strip next to Raymond's Revue Bar.

It was with sadness that I stripped again. But that was lost on the boss who kept increasing my workload, from three nights, to four nights to six nights a week. The other strippers weren't happy. The hostesses loved me though because I hated hostessing. It was less money per night to be a stripper, but that was fine by me if I didn't have to talk to customers.

On busy Fridays and Saturdays the boss would insist I hostessed as there weren't enough girls to go around.

"My wife doesn't understand me!" said a punter. I replied, "Neither do I. Talk to her then instead of spending the family money in this shit-hole". I hated hostessing.

Jason and I were walking through Leicester Square when I gripped Jason and said, "There's Hash!" He was staring at me from a hundred yards away, touting outside a club. We walked on. Nothing else for it.

Overwork and lack of sunlight was sending me insane. I felt like going on stage limping and slurping like Elephant Man, saying, "I'm not an animal! I'm a human being!" Why didn't they go home, get undressed and look in the mirror at a naked body for FREE?

The boss would get other bosses to come to the club and they'd nod at me and point. "Look what I've got on my stage".

I realised the manager had no regard for my health or well-being and would take me into the ground. He could have spread the workload between a few strippers, that way everyone would be employed and nobody would get sick.

But no.

For the millionth time they played The Cars 'Who's Gonna Drive You Home?'

The Swedish Strip had a Christmas party for all the hostesses and strippers etc in the area. I remember seeing the German hostess who was paying for her Monster Make-Up course and a French one who was funding her new business, and a stranger hostess who said to me "I've heard nothing but good about you, your stripping, your personality". I was dying in the club.

In the end the boss came to the dressing room one night and said, "Come on, it's full out there!" I was bent double on the floor with knitting needles stabbing my stomach inside me. A taxi was called and I was sent home.

What with closing down a male strip joint in the daytime, then clubbing with Jason at The Pink Panther club after work, I was breaking down.

Jason and I had a tape recorder on which we'd listen to David Bowie's 'Heroes' and Lou Reed's 'Perfect Day' and try to drift away.

One of the clubs Jason worked in was run by a tall gay black man. When I went to collect Jason the tall black gay boss would say "I smell fish".

I witnessed that boss brandish a large fence pike at my Scouse friend who pleaded with him.

I always totally blanked the boss and wore Terminator dark shades at night. The boys who worked there were often heroin addicts, and runaways.

They told me that their sadistic boss hit them with the stick and said, "Tough, if you don't like it there's plenty more out there".

Of course he was right, there always were more. I galvanised ALL the boys to leave AT ONCE. NEVER go back. Rent was high and the boss would be fucked.

ALL OF THEM LEFT. By magic another club opened up around the corner and every boy got employment immediately. It was called 'The Colt'.

The flyer was gross. 'Boys so young, so warm, so tight. Boys to keep you awake at night!'

We all walked down Brewer street on the opposite side of the street to the black mans club. He was standing in the doorway saying, "Boys! Hellooo boys!" wringing his hands.

We walked past, our noses in the air, blanking him entirely.

A couple of those boys died soon afterwards, so I heard from Jason. May they rest in peace.

After leaving The Swedish Strip in a black cab, I was back at the shitty B&B in Paddington and had time to actually see it.

I'd always been out or asleep and never around for breakfast. The breakfast in the basement was poor. There were bugs everywhere. Guests had red bites on their faces.

I went to the boss of Devon House Hotel, Sussex Gardens, Mrs Kukielka and told her to deal with the bugs.

She said in a wheedling voice, "I have a contract with the bug man". "Well it obviously isn't being fulfilled!" I replied.

She came around the hotel rooms with a spray can of PARAFFIN!! Spraying where the children lived, several to a room including their parents! The Yale door locks were way too high for tiny children to reach. Fire death imminent!

Little John had already burned his neck on a kettle on the floor of his crowded room, and had to have operations to remove the webbed skin on his neck!

An American passing through was at breakfast saying, "Omg! This place is gross!"

I thought, you're ok, you can go, these families live here with no place to go. Somebody has got to do something!

So I rang up Westminster Council Environmental Health from the payphone. A man with a briefcase perused the building and said it had Legionnaires disease and was a death trap.

Mrs Kukielka was totally CLOSED DOWN!

But all the guests were moved two doors down to an identical B&B. The Italian room cleaner girls invited me to their squat in Brixton, it was full of Italians. I was stunned to find acres of empty council houses! With yards and gardens!

So why was Prime Minister Thatcher paying B&B bosses 100s of quid per family per week to live in one room, nowhere to play except the service road where the garbage skips and prostitutes were?

WHEN THERE WERE LOADS OF CHEAPER EMPTY HOUSES????

Why was Thatcher paying me to live in a shit-hole instead of going to Drama School??? She seemed to hate artists. She was a chemist who didn't like people with original thoughts 'outside the box'.

In a long crocodile, I led the children with Jason, along Sussex Gardens, across the road to Hyde Park (or whatever its name is). The children went loony, leaping with excitement! "GRASS! It's grass!"

I thought of a way the guests could publicly complain. A way that wouldn't involve any bus fare or expenditure of any kind. GET ALL THE BUG RIDDEN SHEETS AND BLOCK OFF THE EDGWARE ROAD JUNCTION AT THE TOP OF THE STREET. I'LL GET THE TV CAMERAS!

There was a Goth couple sharing a room in the hotel. The boy was a bisexual who shared a room with his girlfriend. One night at the top of the hotel stairs on my way out, I saw him groping Jason. An almighty ROAR emitted from me from upstairs. GET YOUR HANDS OFF HIM! The boy was on acid. It transpired and said he was so shocked that he shat himself. I told Jason that he could do what he liked but our sex life was over.

In the Pink Panther Club, (or was it called The Pink Pussycat?), just diagonally opposite The Marquee, a very gay man friend of mine, dressed in a royal blue silk toga, put me against the wall and put his tongue in my mouth. "He's breaking the trades description act!" I thought.

Is nobody safe?

A Liverpudlian gay boy from the strip-club who'd been beaten with the stick by the boss, said to me, "You are the most beautiful creature I've ever seen", and kissed my hand.

In 'TIME OUT' magazine it described the Pink Panther Club as being for, "Good time girls and boys who just don't want to go home". CAN'T go home more like!

There wasn't much laughter in that club and I would get lost in music. A hairy massive man would sit against the wall each night, never speaking. He held a tiny handbag on his knee and was dressed in a tight pink miniskirt revealing his thick hairy legs with a strappy ladies top over his huge hairy body.

All of us strippers were offered a massive house by a black bouncer we knew. Each floor was a separate flat. We all paid him 60 pounds and moved into this huge house opposite Le Beat Route club, by Soho Square Park.

Scouse Billy with his amazing technicolor dreadlocks and his confused friend had the flat above Jason and I. We cleaned it and thought we were lucky. Then the front door got boarded up with a sleeping girl inside on the top floor. The bouncer said it was owned by the mafia and they'd boarded it up. The bouncer jimmied open the wooden boards enough to crawl through to get the girl. None of us got our money back. I heard Billy died. He was thrilled to be offered the chance to sing 'Somewhere Over The Rainbow' before a band went on at the Rainbow venue.

One night in our hotel room on the top floor, strangeness happened.

Ghostly white amorphous shapes, frilly tendrils waving softly appeared on the ceiling in the corner of the room.

They spoke to me, "Come up here with us. It's paradise here. It's hell down there!" I wondered if it was a trick?

What if I went with them and it was only nice for a while, then I'd be trapped in black hell and unable to get back to the nice bit, and end up locked in a different dimension, unable to recognise my own family? Like those mad people picking up rubbish in the street, talking to themselves? In their minds they may be picking up vestiges of a lost society, but to everyone else they were mad. I verbally argued with the white ghostly shapes, "No! Go away! I don't want to go with you!"

Jason had started crying. The effort needed to get away from the shapes drove me to climb naked out of the window! Jason saved my life and pulled me back.

How many people accidentally jump off buildings and get impaled on the basement railings below through trying to LIVE and be free from ghosts???

Next day we bought some herbal Kalm tablets. I held onto the railings as the pavement was waving about.

Jason said we MUST get out of London.

We went back to Sandiford. I cried a lot for the trapped children. Down at Props Winebar I saw Linda Owen who took one look at me and burst into tears, saying, "It's like a film!"

A couple of months went by and O'Leery wasn't around much. So I got to know my new brother James, who'd been born when I was 19. I was improving all the time.

Suddenly I came into the dining room to see BOB CRUMPTON

What was he doing there? He said his Mother had shown him the newspaper with my story of not getting the drama school grant.

Oh yes? He said he'd recorded a 45 single. Oh yes?

"Well we knew you would, and?" He gave me a copy of the single.

I asked him if he'd use his platform to help the B&B children in Paddington? He said, "It doesn't work like that".

(Not long afterwards LIVE AID happened, proving that, YES Bob it DOES WORK LIKE THAT! 'Who's gonna Drive You Home' by The Cars was played over starving children pictures)

Bob said he'd changed and wanted to help me. He asked me to come to his new B'ham flat to make a video.

Jason said, "Well if he's changed and wants to help you now, that's good. But you know what he's like so be careful".

In B'ham I waited and waited for this video to start and after 3 days I realised it wasn't happening.

There was a photo of me in a frame by Bob's bed, it was a candid shot of me in the street saying goodbye to his parents who were out of shot. I didn't know he'd taken this shot of me. Didn't read much into it. Couldn't possibly imagine that it was a VOODOO photo!

Bob said he wanted to go back out with me and I replied the sanest reply a girl could ever say.

"Do you have an 80 room mansion, 40 rooms each and we see each other every 2nd Thursday for half an hour under supervision?

No? Well we cannot be together then as you and me in one room does not go".

God knows I was bang on. Wish I'd stayed that cool.

In the time I spent waiting at Bob's for this elusive video, I ascertained that he now actually owned 2 books. 'Bernard Manning's Joke Book' and '1000 Facts About Elvis'. He'd also discovered a comedian he liked, Lenny Bruce. Listening to Lenny Bruce I felt he sounded very self piteous and whiny. Bob said Lenny had a stripper girlfriend called Kitty.

I returned to Sandiford after 3 days away and Jason had gone!!! I rang every police station, hotel, hospital, and his parents. NO CLUES.

All I could do was pray he was OK. Well I HOPED, I didn't know about praying then.

Jason considered cutting his face to stop people from propositioning him. I dissuaded him, saying, "Then you'll get freaks who love scars. It's not worth it". Jason was extraordinarily beautiful. Continually harassed. When we met I protested that we were only talking to each other because of our looks. Jason insisted it was also my personality. I said, "That girl over there might have the cure for cancer, but you won't know because superficially she doesn't attract you". He concurred. I was right, the world was a shallow fascist.

17th APRIL 2022. AUS UPDATE. EASTER SUNDAY.

Aidan sent me a photo of his latest meal cooked on a BBQ as the frying pan wasn't big enough. Rustic potatoes all herby with veg and chunks of meat. It looks delicious. I miss Aidan and cannot cook for myself.

Aidan also texted; ROMANS 6:13

And do not present your members as instruments of unrighteousness to sin, but present yourselves to God as being alive from the dead, and your members as instruments of righteousness to God.

HOW APPROPRIATE. Aidan is amazing.

Have finally banned my mate Shayne whom I sang with to his computer keyboards. We left a BBQ recently and returned to my house late afternoon where I passed out on the couch. I was awoken by something alien up my dress, poking around my nether regions!

Looking round I saw Shayne with his dick out! He'd tried to poke it in me as I lay face down unconscious! Gross betrayer of trust! Power mad!

I said "That's so bad, that's attempted rape!" He replied, "I didn't though did I?". Effing scum. He left and I fell back unconscious.

Because he didn't actually rape me I forgave him for a while. He'd always called me 'bro' and I'd thought of him as family. He'd been trained from the start that our relationship must be platonic and I thought I could trust him. I knew he was spoiled and both his parents doted on him, sending him to the most expensive private school, but we had music in common, though I hated some of his own efforts and told him so. We also both disagreed with the government.

After he'd betrayed my trust so grossly, all his selfish creepy traits were no longer bearable. Any man who is nearly 50 and plays computer games is pathetic but it was bearable prior to him assaulting me. I kicked him up the ass and pushed him out of my house.

Nobody is more disappointed than me that Australians gave up their guns due to a false flag Govt attack in Port Arthur. I seriously want to cut off Shaynes cock and shoot him. My entire life would've been so much easier if I'd been able to get a gun out. Yes it would've opened up another can of worms, like maybe prison, or bad karma but at least I wouldn't have had to be so insanely mentally strong. Knowing that scum walk amongst us without punishment. God has the last laugh though and I know a few that hurt me have faced dire karma.

Let's face it, I only knew Shayne due to him stealing my number out of his landlady's phone. He also stole my lighter to bring to my house, as he knew where I lived when he saw his landlady drop me home. Red flag from the start!

What a pretentious way to spell the name Shane anyway! 'Snake' is more fitting for him.

It transpires that the pharmaceutical companies are putting snake venom in the mandated jabs as well as nanotechnology cyborg ingredients. Shayne's already a snake.

Chinese people are throwing themselves off tower block balconies because their government has locked them inside for weeks without food!

SHEFFIELD ENGLAND, CITY ON SEVEN HILLS. GLORIOUS COLOURS.

After staying with friends in Bristol a while, I went to Sheffield in time for my 21st birthday. University student Helen Onion was my hostess, who lived in a little cottage adjoining another cottage of more students with one big shared back garden. Next-door lived unicyclists Tao and co. My 21st birthday was divine, trying to unicycle in the back garden. It was my favourite ever birthday.

Helen Onion was/is a beautiful generous hearted, clever girl with long hippy curly hair whom I met through her being a friend of some kids.

The idea was to get 'A' Levels so I could study drama at University for free. If I'd been a few years older I wouldn't have needed 'A' Levels, but I was 21 so I enrolled at Granville College Sheffield to do English and Art.

Helen introduced me to the loveliest people I'd ever met in my life, Artist John, Richard the hippy and Tim the hippy. Sheltered but not spoilt. Gentlemen. All platonic good friends. John did succulently insane paintings of dried up cracking mud riverbeds and plenty more. Tim was studying Chinese and Richard was studying literature and could cook and grow anything!

(On meeting them I had no idea that they would become witnesses to a vicious crime of Bob Crumpton. The first witness died. Muz was his name and he was a taxi driver associate of Bob. But 3 remain Bob! You didn't know about them did you?)

At first, as I walked around Sheffield with Helen visiting hippy student house after hippy student house, it was impossible to keep my temper at the luxury that many university students haven't got the good sense to enjoy.

One student had a huge room in a 100 yr old big house with a garden, free grant and his dad was a dentist. His biggest problem was going to the launderette.

I yelled, "Just down the motorway two or three whole families are living in the size of your bedroom in the B&B's! All you do is moan! You don't know you're born!"

Then I reasoned that I couldn't shout at the entire student population of Sheffield as I'd get exhausted. Be thankful they're not trying to stab me for a cigarette. Everything is relative, they just haven't seen what I've seen.

So I enjoyed their company immensely with scintillating conversations and four way stereo sound systems, sitting in circles of hippies, often on magic mushrooms, hash and homegrown weed. Also I got involved with the Anarchy Centre and their malarkey.

Oh Sheffield! A little pocket of time where I was a free woman in a beautiful place, beholden to no man, my brain just about intact. I still had access to my family, if tenuous and because of that I still had my innate personality.

Dancing at the Leadmill nightclub with Helen Onion and co. Me in my stripes and red and black lace edged tutu that I'd bought in Kensington Market. Kirsty noted that I was wearing that long before Madonna turned up in a movie wearing one. I'd stolen the idea from the Monty Python men.

Kirsty sweetly said, "Madonna's an old hag of 24! You're loads better Ida!"

Mid-week on an empty night at the Leadmill, we saw a man sitting alone against the wall with his leg in plaster. A boy told me, "That's Jarvis". Allegedly he'd fallen out of a window at a party and broken his leg. He had a band called Pulp. A boy gave me a record by Jarvis which could have been written for me;

"You're just a little girl with blue eyes, everybody looks at you. You've got a hole in your heart and one between your legs, and I know which one he's going to fill".

It was sung in a rich and beautiful classic crooner style. I was raving about Pulp years before anyone had heard of them.

Helen, artist Chris and his girlfriend Gabby all drove up to the Edinburgh festival to stay in a rich Scottish student's mansion house. Ali was the female student's name. She mistakenly said, "Ida's never got any problems!" Wtf?

I'd had SO MANY MASSIVE traumas that I just didn't dwell on trivial non-issues.

Chris took his guitar and he and I busked, me singing, 'You aint nothin' but a hound dog'. And I cut hair too.

We saw a play called 'Stevie' about the woman Stevie Smith who wrote the poem, "Not waving but drowning". I read her work and was very moved.

At the Fringe Club I saw 'Decadence' by Steven Berkoff. The acting and script blew my mind.

In my bedsit on Crookesmoor Rd, I read Fyodor Dostoyesvky's 'Crime and Punishment' and 'The Idiot'

An image that haunted me was Dostoyevsky's description of a mare pulling a cruelly heavy cart, being beaten and flogged as she strained to move the cart through mud, until she died in agony. Horrendous.

I drew a close-up portrait of Katherine Hepburn in a skull cap without make-up with an unusual dramatic expression, with her hand to her head like Edvard Muntz's 'The Scream'. It was from a black n white photo and I did it silky smooth and like a laser beam. Chris the artist said "I didn't know you could do that!"

(I gave that picture to Jonathan Cainer 15 years later for safe keeping whilst I was briefly living with a snakey jealous Countess in Holland Park. She was horrible and knocked my pic off a table and stepped on it deliberately).

At Granville college aged 21 I was learning the Metaphysical Poets work. I could see where Mick Jagger may have lifted an idea or two from Andrew Marvell's 'To His Coy Mistress'. "The grave's a fine and pleasant place, but none I fear do there embrace".

Mick sang, about telling a girls that when she's old nobody will know that she was a beauty, but so cold.

Maybe it's just an ancient universal ploy that men have used throughout time.

Amazing to study, John Donne's poem, 'The Sun Rising', especially as I had lovely boyfriends and my room became the world.

One night doing my homework in my bedsit, listening to Janice Long on Radio 1 talking about homeless people in London, I was suddenly HIT by the realisation that a few short months earlier I'd been in the middle of all that in Soho. What a contrast!

Crying I scrawled a poem about the streets of London which contained the lines,

"Centrepoint points you nowhere, Piccadilly sell your willy, on the 'Meat Rack' in the cold.

McTell 'em Ralph! I ain't bragging Billy!"

Bob would come up to visit me in my bedsit and we attended a party at Helen's cottage. An unknown hippy took me aside and said, "There's a light aura around you, but that guy (Bob) is very dark and heavy". How right he turned out to be.

Bob was crying again and Helen said, "Ida's making a popstar cry!" I said, "It's not like that, he does it to himself and he's not my boyfriend, Jason is but he's gone AWOL".

EVERYBODY knew that Jason was my love, my best friend but he'd gone missing, possibly dead. Bob was someone I knew, who visited.

A spooky boy called Sean Ring Willy was in my class. I called him that due to the Prince Albert ring on his willy.

He'd help me manage my homework until I understood the format expected for essays. I had never owned a TV throughout my life to that point and in Sheffield it was no different. I loved doing my homework about 'The Dubliners' by James Joyce etc.

Sean did the artwork for Genesis P. Orridge of Psychic TV band. Sean was into Aleister Crowley Sex Magick and he showed me where my clitoris was and what it was for. What had he unleashed!?

(Sean's Satanic leanings soon transpired to be too dark for me. Psychic TV's 'Godstar' record about Brian Jones of the Rolling Stones wasn't anything I could get behind. I couldn't worship Brian Jones. It was funny that Sean put stickers around Sheffield bearing the words 'Oh Brian!').

Sean played The Smiths band to me and I loved Morrisey's lyrics. Sean made me some great compilation tapes. He fully knew that Jason was my lost love. In the bath together, Sean looked heavenward and said, "Take me now Lord, take me now!" How lovely.

(16 years later I was in a Brighton cinema watching The Simpsons Movie and Sean called out to me! He recognized me! He'd become a tattoo artist).

Bob Crumpton came to the window of my ground floor bedsit as I was astride Sean, sitting on his tummy.

Dressed.

I let Bob in as Sean left and it felt farcical. Bob had a ghetto blaster with him so I'd have music in my bedsit and could hear my compilations from Sean. Also so Bob could play his gigs and music of course.

Bob was as good as gold at that time, but I really didn't trust him yet and was happy to be free in cobbled Sheffield, in the foggy streets and sunlit hills. The monolithic elongated block of council dwellings called Kelvin Flats nestled against a hill at the perimeter of the city centre looked almost beautiful in the bright sun.

An excellent country and western band came from Sheffield and I saw them in the Anarchist Centre. Their name was DON VALLEY & THE ROTHERHIDES. All the band members were named after places around Sheffield; Don Valley, Kelvin Flats, Red Mires, Thorpe Hesley and others I cannot recall. Funny and TOP ENTERTAINMENT.

Of course I had sex with Bob as Jason might be dead.

Bob was trained in knowledge of the clitoris and I'd want him to go on and on rubbing it even when his arm was dropping off.

Sean had led me to become a terribly demanding wanker by proxy. I didn't know that a tiny touch on a wet clitoris was all that was needed. Didn't know that for years. I just copied Sean.

Bob invited me to his Birmingham flat in Strensham Hill Road and we went boating in Cannon Hill Park. Bob was improving with age I thought.

I went to his Sheffield University gigs and he was friendly when he stayed with me. But I didn't fully trust him.

Edward Rowe of Silverdale, Middlesborough or 'Eddie The Writer' as I called him, was in my college class for English.

He wore a battered grey suit without a tie, braces and boots and a trilby hat, just a year older than me and very charismatic and handsome. He moved so brilliantly, loping and bouncing down the road like a punk writer. The Pogues came to mind around him.

He loved the author Henry Miller and gave me his books, 'Tropic of Cancer' and 'Tropic of Capricorn'.

Eddie wanted to go to Paris like Henry Miller had. He made me smile when he said he wanted to find pain and suffering.

"If you can escape pain it's not pain if you can get out of it! It's only pain when you're stuck in it!" I said.

He left for Paris and gave me his vinyl records and record player. 2 weeks later he was back after running out of money.

Eddie wanted to be a nurse who also wrote. He was very good to me, very funny and he knew the genius kid Andrew Morton who had lived in Sheffield before I arrived there.

Eddie The Writer said to me "You're very warm and very brave". It made me think, as I didn't realise I was brave as I'd not felt I had any choice. And at times I felt freezing. Especially when my landlord just opened my door with his key without knocking and emptied my gas meter full of 50 pence coins. He'd rigged it so that every 20 minutes my gas would run out and I'd freeze in the cold climate. That meter ate 50's so fast it nearly took my arm off!

The heroine addicts in the back flat were very fair. They'd knock on my door to hand me any of my giro cheques that the corner post office had refused to cash for them.

A lot of letters were written between Eddie The Writer and I. Also Bob wrote to me as there was no social media, mobile phones or any technology back in the 80's. All my letters went in the trunk given to me by Bob's Mum.

I left Eddie The Writer to go to my family house for Christmas. Going home was a very mixed experience; exciting to see the little ones, intensely wary of seeing O'Leery, and Mum was just unfathomable. It always had the feeling of going behind enemy lines.

At the family house my sister called upstairs to me that a letter had arrived for me. Staggering downstairs I opened it in the hall in front of my sister. Eddie The Writer had begun the letter with, "Get up lazy bones! It's 2pm!" We looked at the clock and it was exactly 2pm. He also wrote "Even though you never wear perfume you smell sweet".

My sister said, "ACRID Ida! The word is ACRID! You smell ACRID!" As I cannot smell, I didn't know anything for sure.

Always I laughed at the family jibes, never realising how seriously behind enemy lines I really was.

Bob stayed over at my family house for whatever reason and we were both in a rarely available spare single bed.

In the morning my mother burst through the bedroom door wearing a short T-shirt and very tiny pants, nothing else.

She began yelling at me about something unintelligible, "IDA! BLAH BLAH BLAH! IDA! BLAH BLAH BLAH!"

Bob looked shocked and embarrassed, I was just stunned. What kind of mother does that? Wearing effing tiny pants!?

Typical of what I'd always had to tolerate I guessed. She was/is a terrible woman and a mother in name only to me.

January (86?) arrived and the prodigal JASON was on my Sheffield doorstep! I said "I've got 6 months worth of dinner in the oven for you!"

EVERYONE was happy for me except Bob! Everyone could now see that Jason was real!

Not a figment of my mind!

Jason had been living in the New Forest on wild potatoes, (frantic spuds). Jason moved in to my Sheffield bedsit and joined the local circus, so did I. Until whilst I was upside-down a snakey girl trod on my fingers deliberately. I couldn't trust her not to cut the rope when I was high up so I left the circus.

Because Jason knew he had disappeared into the New Forest on his motorbike, perhaps never to be seen again, he couldn't argue when Bob kept turning up. So Jason would leave when Bob arrived.

Jason told me that he'd returned to the B&B where the little children John and Karen lived, and had punched John's dad in the face, saying, "That's for John". John's awful dad had said, "I hope you drown!" when Jason and I had taken them swimming. John's dad was a horrible man. Jason said he'd seen little John in a documentary on TV. It really had been bad enough for a TV crew. I wasn't mad!

(20 years later I was working briefly as a street magician's assistant in Torquay.

We were at a cafe when little John's mum called out,

"Ida! Oh she used to take my kids for me! How is Jason?". She recognised me and told me little John was now in the Navy and Karen was a care-worker.

Their horrible dad was jailed for paedophilia against little Karen and the Mum said she'd gone on to have 10 more children with a good man in Torquay. She was Irish Catholic. She sent me photos of them all to my Little Venice flat.

IT WAS SUCH A RELIEF TO ME! As I was living near to Paddington and couldn't bear to look at Sussex Gardens B&Bs, hadn't been able to look at Sussex Gardens for 20 years, but knowing all was well was a weight off.)

Jason went on a tour of France and Spain with the circus for 6 weeks and sent me a postcard from Toulon. I was happy if he was happy and vice versa because we were sane positive people.

All the time Bob would be visiting and I entertained the idea of how great it would be if he'd really evolved beyond his viciousness, as we often had the most sparkling best fun together and the sex was truly gorgeous.

But even though Jason had been away a lot, he ended up getting sad that Bob was around in Sheffield.

Jason left me notes saying "You give him EVERYTHING and give me nothing", and he eventually moved on.

In London Jason had asked me to sign my name on some paper with my trademark flower picture at the end of my signature. He returned to the hotel with my signature and the flower tattooed on his bicep. He kept it for years until a new girlfriend demanded he cover it.

In Sheffield Bob threw something at my head and I flinched as it whizzed past. Bob sneered,

"What are you flinching for? Didn't hit you did I?"

He raised his fist in front of my face and said the same thing, "What are you flinching for? Didn't hit you did I?"

I innocently explained that even if you don't hit an animal, but just raise your hand to an animal that has been hit in the past, it will flinch. Why did I bother?

Picking up a balled up pair of socks I threw the soft socks towards Bob's head and he flinched! "What are you flinching for? Never hit you did I?" said I.

Proving anybody would flinch and anybody could be stupidly nasty like Bob but I had better things to do.

Lara had got a job as the keyboardist for the band **'Everything But The Girl'.** Bob and I saw her in concert at the old Birmingham Odeon, I think that was the venue. Lara and the whole band were magnificent.

BOB INVITED ME TO BE ON HIS ALBUM.

He told me roughly what he wanted me to say. The song is set in the North West of England. As a very conscientious girl I asked a pretty

Liverpudlian girl in my class how to phrase the words in Liverpudlian. (She was a stunning girl who wanted to be a nurse).

I went to Bob's Birmingham flat armed with my genuine Liverpudlian phrasing to record the song.

Goodness knows why but Bob kept being nasty until I cried. I said, "You're supposed to be a miserable git, I'm not! How can I do it if I'm crying?"

Eventually I did a really good impression of a Brookside soap opera character. Really earthy.

Back in Sheffield, Bob told me he'd "LOST" the take I liked but he'd used a "better one". How could you lose something all on the same tape?

Oh well, whatever.

Nicky and Lara had holidayed at Xenon Cove at Lands End, Cornwall and had recommended it to Bob, so we went there on a long train ride.

At the guest house Bob was very stroppy, whining through the walls so the owners could hear. He wouldn't stop. In the local pub the regulars looked at him with suspicion.

A boat mender on the beach said "Not to worry, I've been here for 20 years and I'm still called the new boy".

On the harbour wall Bob bought some take-away fish and chips. I was so hungry and looking forward to eating it but Bob snatched it out of my hands and threw it into the sea. Oh dear, I might have enjoyed that meal and Ted couldn't allow that! Why must he wreck every trip we ever took?

When it was time to leave, the guesthouse owners said they'd drop us off at a bus stop. They dropped us in the middle of nowhere. I wasn't surprised after Bob's behaviour, but Bob was pissed off about it.

Half my brain almost thought vicious abuse was par for the course of life, based on all I'd experienced since childhood, but also part of me knew from Desiderata to "avoid aggressive people as they are vexatious to the spirit".

I just knew life could be better and hoped Bob would realise it too.

Then a radio DJ started playing my song on his afternoon show so I was told. No other songs from the album, just the one with me on it.

I was a lone customer in a Sheffield retro shop when I heard myself coming out of their radio and I was crying over the airways. I said "That's me!" The manager said, "Oooh".

Bob had used the recording where I was crying! Crying on vinyl. A snuff record! A record for sale of a woman being abused in a Brummie bedsit.

Nobody could tell I was crying on the record and nobody cared. I just forgot about it. Nobody would hear it anyway.

VIDEO

One night in Sheffield, Helen Onion, artist Chris, Gabby and others were at my bedsit when Bob arrived and asked if I'd come with him to make a video for the song.

All the students were excited and I was thinking maybe Bob really has changed? He didn't have to invite me, it was his choice. (I was tricked into believing it was his choice).

I went ahead with Bob. In Birmingham we were picked up by a couple of camera men and driven to Liverpool.

Watching the camera man frame the shot he was doing, I said "That's perfect!" It turned out that of course it was perfect, he was a TV pro.

The director instructed me to walk along the street and kick a metal grill on a shop.

Bob was taking me aside and hissing and spitting at me, being nasty until I cried in confusion. I'd done everything he said, I was wearing his old stage costume of a prison jacket and my old baggy decorators dungarees, NO PROBLEM, it was his video and I was happy to help.

The camera man even asked Bob to, "Leave her alone Bob!".

I did the walk down the street and seriously kicked the metal grill. Bob laughed at making me so aggressively upset. They told me to do it again less aggressively. Done, finished.

That night in Birmingham after the pub closed I had to be drinking a pint at the bar and miming the record as I spoke to Bob at the bar. Done finished.

Bob and I went to bed tired at 2.30 am with the direction to be up again at 5am to complete the filming.

Bob's record company had talked to a Radio 1 DJ and asked if he'd keep playing the song if they released it as a single. The DJ said yes he would play a single of the song.

I was washed and snuggling away to sleep when Bob started rowing at me. Mentally I could not be riled and sweetly told him to calm down as we had to wake up again soon to film the rest and he'd only regret it.

But Bob's anger continued, on and on, worse and worse. IT MADE NO SENSE.

Then Bob pinned my shoulders to the bed and turned his head on an angle, brought his face close to mine **AND CLAMPED HIS TEETH SHUT AROUND MY NOSE! BLOOD EVERYWHERE.**

PAIN. Like a demonic attack. (It still gives me nightmares).

I went into shock, he threw furniture at me and I dressed and ran into the street. He was psycho out of nowhere! WHY?

WHY ASK ME TO BE IN HIS VIDEO if this was how he felt about it?

As I stumbled exhausted down the road at dawn, not knowing my way around, a car pulled up and offered me a lift. It was Muz, a taxi driver friend of Bob who lived opposite the pub we'd filmed in the night before.

I got in and asked him to take me to the railway station.

He asked what had happened and I told him straight that Bob had bitten my nose, knowing we were meant to finish a video today.

He took me to his house for some tea. I rang the pub we'd filmed in to ask for the camera man's number. I told the video maker that I couldn't film today as Bob had bitten my nose.

"He bit your nose?!" he answered incredulously. Yes, I answered matter of factly.

The video maker said, "Well you know we can't wait as this video has to be out this week!". I sighed resignedly, "Yes I know".

Muz dropped me at the train station.

Back in Sheffield, Tim, John and Richard saw Bob's blood-soaked gappy tombstone front teeth prints in my poorly bruised swollen nose.

They were shocked. I was dumbfounded as to WHY BOB EVEN ASKED ME to be in his vid in the first place?!

I thought maybe he had initially good intentions, but then his jealousy kicked in and he couldn't stand it?! WHO KNEW?

Well, I thought, that video will never see the light of day.

A week later I was in Sheffield Library doing my homework and I rang my sister about a book.

Suddenly they were screaming down the phone that I was on telly. They said they'd recorded it. Next day at college the students had seen me on TV too and described what I'd done and it was indeed Bobs video. After a few days I saw the vid myself at someone's house on a TV music show.

Bah!

Bitter sweet. The only good aspect was that I'd told my evil teacher that I'd be on TV by age 21.

Bingo. And I'd forgotten all about that promise. Really it was an abusive video until the scene where (despite his jibes all day), I'd managed to be composed in the bar, which had obviously flipped psycho Bob out and incited him to bite my nose.

Bob came up to Sheffield to my bedsit and said, "My mate Muz isn't talking to me anymore because of you!"

Incredulously I just looked at him. He was blaming ME for Muz by chance picking me up in a wrecked state on Strensham Hill road and me telling Muz the truth about my nose!?

INSANE.

Months later Bob returned to my bedsit and said, "You know Muz's baby? Well I got him walking!" He said it pointedly, as if to drive home that Muz now was talking to him again and trusted him with the baby.

I didn't care anyway! Never asked for any of it. How petty and unspeakable.

What a tosser Bob was and still is. As you will see.

(Babies walk by themselves when ready anyway! You can't make a baby walk. But Bob's point was that nobody will take my side over him, no matter what).

Bob was a petty minded ghoul.

I said to him, "**YOU HAVEN'T CHANGED AT ALL HAVE YOU?!**"

Bob replied, **"I DIDN'T *NEED* TO CHANGE! YOU SHOULD NEVER HAVE LEFT ME!!"**

He honestly believed that I should have stayed with him while he abused me and that he'd been fine all along!!

It was fair enough of me to believe that Bob had genuinely grown up in the 2 years we were apart. He was older than me too.

He'd spent 7 months visiting me in Sheffield, behaving as good as gold to give me reason to trust him…..only in order to revert to his original viciousness. I WAS ASTOUNDED.

It was rational to believe that Bob **must've realised** *he'd driven me away with his viciousness when I was 18 and that it wasn't socially acceptable, so why not evolve, grow up, stop being vicious?.*

BUT NO.

Bob had NOTHING better to do in the day than visit me for months, *putting on an act, knowing that his viciousness was socially unacceptable to me and everyone*……but instead of Genuinely evolving beyond it into a good man, he HID IT very successfully, only to strike when I was softened up!! HOW DARE I NOT TAKE HIS ABUSE!?

MIND BOGGLING.

We went to see SID 'N' NANCY the film. Afterwards we staggered out punky style and went in a pub with a pool table.

The players there all had Pool Team uniform shirts on and took themselves very seriously.

Me and Bob vs The Pool Team. Game on!

A freakish thing happened, EVERY ball that Bob and I hit went down a hole, several times taking 2 other balls out with one hit. At least once 3 balls went down in one hit!

I was doing trick shots with no idea how! Bob and I were CRACKING UP LAUGHING, we could not miss! The Pool Team were missing loads! WE WON!

Yet we never practised. INSANE.

Why couldn't it always be like that? Equals, laughing at our supernatural skills from nowhere. No aggression and domination. It was a golden hour in a sea of shit. (OK, our supernatural skills were God given to teach the priggish Pool Team a lesson!)

Bob invited me to his new shared B'ham house. I forget the name of the young man he was living with. I WENT THERE! Like a zombie!!

I was losing my grip on reality yet was dressed superbly like a Cossack with a Russian fur hat with a metal filigree silver star on the front and a large pearl at its centre, a black cape flung over my skinny black jeans and skinny black leather jacket that Jason had bought. Tight low stiletto black boots. An awesome look with my tumbling dark red curls, though I say it myself.

(At the Sheffield Uni launderette a student was doing a project on student style and asked to photo me. "But I'm not at University" I said as I sprawled provocatively across a dryer).

Bob said he was doing his own version of an old pop song. He'd got so far but didn't know what to say next.

I gave him a funny line. Bob liked it and used it in his song.

Later we watched Elvis in his '68 Come-back Special' with his friends. All I could say was, "Elvis looks like a caged beast".

I felt caged and was wary of anyone Bob knew as maybe they were like him? Like in the film, 'Rosemary's Baby' where everyone is psycho except Rosemary. Maybe they were different? I didn't know.

They seemed like good, friendly people. But then so did Bob when they arrived. Yet he'd just been bullying me the minute before! How did he switch so fast?

On the other hand they might be great and I would've loved the opportunity to meet them on a level playing field, not hobbled by Bob's outbursts.

I'd be in a chirpy, fresh and frisky mental state, excited to be expecting company, and Bob would thoroughly kibosh me. Accusing me of manufactured crimes out of nowhere, annihilate me, then greet his guests affably as if all was fine. I'd try to rise above the recent oppression to sparkle but I was strained, utterly browbeaten, confused and always under a cloud of despondence.

Time and again this pattern occurred. Awful. I couldn't say anything about Bob's behaviour as I didn't want it to be true as I loved Bob and couldn't tell tales. Bob was the most solid person in my life.

One time we were in some small dingy Balsall Heath lounge with a group of Bob's mates and Bob had been suddenly bullying me out of the blue on our way there. In the dour lounge Bob decided to put his hand on me and I couldn't help but shrug him off. As we left I heard a bloke say, "What's her problem?"

Bob had asked me to sign some paper so that his record album could be played on the radio. It was for the Musicians Union or something.

They sent me a small book with 'Diary' written on it and I wrote one thing in it.

"Being with you, going with you is like one foot nailed to the floor and a mouth full of glue. You've got barbed wire round your heart and machine guns in your brain, being with you is sending me insane".

Bob read it.

AUSTRALIAN UPDATE. 26th April 2022

I HAVE to give you **IDA'S TIP FOR SUPER STARDOM >>>>MILO McCABE<<<<<**

A couple of years ago, before LOCKDOWN, I went to Perth Fringe Festival to see Milo Mc Cabes show, 'TILES OF THE UNEXPECTED'. His self-penned character of **TROY HAWKE**, a Scrabble player who sports a mid 19th century silk smoking jacket and was home-schooled, taking his gap year in the conservatory, made me laugh so hard that drops of wee came out! I had to see that show a second time! Even though I was severely 'medicated' on the monstrous Flupenthixol injection, his genius performance could rouse the dead.

Milo McCabe brought TROY HAWKE back to Perth the year after with his new show 'SIGMUND TROYD'. Again I was slain! And amazingly Milo McCabe remembered my name from the year before. What a pro! Milo is also a boxer in his spare time. I'm very impressed.

Back to the past; Bob had a fit at seeing my writing in my Musicians Union diary and was very horrible to me at length, so I left B'ham next morning with tears in my eyes as usual.

Thankfully I made the effort to wipe my face in the train's toilet before taking a seat in my Russian Countess finery.

Across from me sat an intriguing older man who looked like actor Ed Harris. He was looking at venues for his show of skiing on stage! He also asked me about pantomimes as they didn't have them in America.

I wrongly assumed his show was a comedy type Edinburgh Fringe style show like 'The Smallest Show On Earth'. So I told him about Edinburgh and the Leadmill and various venues around and about pantomimes.

He asked about Sheffield's Crucible Theatre. "Only snooker tournaments and opera singers go there I think", said I.

But he got off the train at Sheffield and asked for a hotel, so I directed him at the one across the road with a Tudor style. He took my number and said he'd meet me at The Crucible that night.

I was now living in a shared house with a pianist and a guitarist. The skier rang to say he'd found the hotel to be a dive and was in a better one. I met him at The Crucible and saw a pantomime, 'Jack and The Beanstalk'.

Afterwards we were having a drink and he said he'd been the Olympic Bronze medallist for ballet skiing. He'd been brought up on the ski slopes of Vermont. His show was a spectacular revolving stage with dry ice and somehow he skied on stage. Just before he'd got on the train in Birmingham he'd been looking at the National Indoor Arena. His name was and hopefully still is Alan Schoenburger, meaning beautiful mountain.

Being a gauche 21 year old I said, "That doesn't mean I'm going to have sex with you". He said, "Of course not, it's a terrible reflection on society that you would have to say that".

We left the theatre to go to a pub and he left a tip on the bar. The barman said, "Hey you've left your change!" Alan said, "Doesn't anyone tip here?" I told him that in recession Sheffield the only reason people leave money on a bar is by accident.

At The Pace Hotel it was gorgeous, very white with a birds-eye view of the city through plate glass windows. Alan spread out a map of a harbour and told me top secret squirrel things that I cannot repeat. He said he didn't mind me smoking but worried for me. Alan invited me to America and said I'd do well in New York as I had a good face. He let me go to sleep sweetly and said he'd be gone when I awoke and that I should stay until 12pm the next day. A far cry from being browbeaten by Bob!

The next night Alan phoned and asked me to send him my pantomime program.

From then on I was determined to quit smoking so I'd keep my looks. I went to an acupuncturist. The acupuncturist Dr asked me about my life. "I just want the needles to stop smoking, I don't want to go into my life", I replied. The Dr said it was necessary for the treatment that he know about my life. So I gave him a potted brief history. "NO WONDER you smoke!" he exclaimed and directed me to lay on the gurney. He stuck needles everywhere and said I may feel emotional for a while.

I left in tears and the tears didn't stop for a week! At home I'd be washing up and the men who lived there would see sheets of water running down my face. An endless flood! Unstoppable tears. "Poor Ida" they said.

Somehow I HAD to get to America! So I went to a BUNAC CAMP open day at the university, determined to be a summer camp leader. They gave you a return ticket and 6 weeks to travel around after you'd worked on the summer camp. That way I could see Alan and not owe him a penny.

All the time Bob was visiting like an insane demon. Apropos of nothing, he announced, "You won't get any money for that record you know, ONLY what I choose to give you". Where was his head at? I was so weary.

It transpired that he was wrong anyway. The paper he'd asked me to sign must have been responsible for a cheque for just over a hundred pounds arriving for me, regardless of Bob's wishes. I bought snow boots to walk in the freezing Sheffield snow.

I've no idea if any more cheques came for me ever again, as I moved house and terrible things happened. It didn't occur to me to tell whoever sent the cheques that I'd moved, and would keep moving. Still don't know to this day if any more money came after that initial cheque. It would have been damages and danger money.

I got a job from the newspaper ads, selling insurance. Before I began it I had to answer a series of multiple choice questions. Then I was summoned into the manager's office. She said without shame,

"Out of 100 applicants only 5 of you have the correct graphs from your personality tests. It is the personality profile of a FOOTBALL HOOLIGAN.

You all have 2 graphs each. As you can see, these applicant's graphs are the same. One of your graphs is the same but what about the other one?"

I replied that I cannot sell anything I don't believe in. She said, "Well you like acting so where's the problem?"

I answered,

"Acting is an agreed lie with the audience, they know you're pretending, it's what they expect and pay for. I can't just lie to unsuspecting people, and say something is good when it isn't".

The manager then explained to me that insurance was good and I agreed to do the job.

On day one I looked around at these sharp suited sharky people that I was supposed to be like and the scoreboard on the wall with the champagne bottle prize for the most sales and thought, "Is this me?"

Then after a couple more days everybody CHEERED wildly at some political move by Margaret Thatcher. I could not cheer her after seeing those kids in the B&Bs in Paddington and knowing she was a chemist who did not fund artists who thought outside the box. I left knowing I was a hooligan with a heart.

Bob at some vague point took me to see 'Hey Luciani' a theatre show by Mark E Smith of The Fall. Bob left me alone as he went without me to say hello to Mark E Smith. I sat elegantly and dramatically on a table top and Brix Smith stared at me from a distance. I wasn't mad keen on Mark E Smith anyway. I loved him really! 'Totally Wired' could've been written for me.

It appeared that Bob was happy for me to be ostensibly an attractive shell, as long as I was a numb wreck emotionally and he made sure of it.

If on occasion I gave him a smart answer, he retorted, "Oh*aren't you so together!*", in a sneering way.

At Hallam University I was doing an evening class on a post-graduate drama course called 'The Arts Of The Theatre'. How I got on it, not being a graduate, I don't know. We were doing Ibsen's play 'The Dolls House'.

I cannot recall the entirety of the play but I know I related to feeling like a doll in my relationship with Bob. A rag doll, thrown around.

Asking Bob to read it was a waste of my time. He only attempted to read 'God's Banker' due to Mark E Smith's show, 'Hey Luciani' being loosely about the banker found hanging under Black Friars Bridge.

Bob bought me a dress and I chose a 1950's white cotton sleeveless, with a gathered skirt and big red roses all over.

Eventually it was time for me to go to America and I dared go to my family home to say goodbye to the little ones.

STUPIDEST MISTAKE I EVER MADE. CATASTROPHIC MENTALLY.

I weighed up the pros and cons of daring to visit 'home'; O'Leery was in Cairo, so Mum would be alright with me surely?

As it was all O'Leery's influence on her? Right?

It should be O.K. and I'd enjoy time with my siblings.

Then if I really tried, I'd have just enough strength left to manage summer camp, then collapse and peg out in America. Away from God forsaken Britain and its knock backs.

"Peg out" were the words in my head. Lay down in the sun, meet Alan and take it from there.

On arrival 'home' I was wary as usual but all seemed fine enough. Then Lucy my youngest sister said she was sad to see her Dad kissing a girl. (She saw O'Leery as her father as she'd never really known her blood Dad before he went to Holland).

Mum said "Oh Lucy don't tell HER!" As if I was Mum's enemy. Nothing O'Leery did was a surprise to me.

Then Mum started sniping at me about when I'd gone to the Social Services about O'Leery when I was at school. It was *years ago and I'd had no choice.*

I thought I must be dreaming. Mum couldn't be serious, it had to be a joke, a wind up. Surely? I was tortured nightly/daily by that man O'Leery!

What else could I have done? Die by suicide? Go to child's jail for murder?

Inconveniently my brain was still blanking the fact that my mother had hated me since birth. I only focused on O'Leery's influence on her.

I did NOT have the mental energy or time to spare for this utter bullshit, and was looking for my mother to go back to her coldish neutral behaviour, which was the best I'd ever known from her.

She surely had to stop this unfair tirade? Right?

DREAM ON.

I was crying after several hours of it. She took me to a GP surgery and told him I was sick. Totally baffled and quite scared, I explained that I wasn't sick, just tired. The doctor sent her away.

Surely, if she had my best interests at heart, this would calm her down, right? Wrong.

Stunned, I watched her call Social Services to the house to see me.

As I spoke to the officer who came into my bedroom, I felt like I was talking for my life, when all I wanted to do was scream;

"Thank you for coming, I have no idea why my mother has called you. There must be people all over town that require your services but I'm not one of them. I simply returned 'home' to say goodbye to my family before going to America. I'm fine, just extremely tired".

Again, the Social Service worker told Mum that I was entirely rational and just needed rest. Phew!

So Mum would be happy now right? Whatever fears for me that she may have, must be allayed by now?! Surely!

Mum's reaction as the Social worker left was NOT one of relief at all. She looked vexed. I honestly couldn't fathom it.

As I lay troubled in bed that night at my Mums house, my sleep eventually came like a cosh.

Deep in my sleep I felt a sharp pain in my body. Then another in my thigh and another whack and my eyes opened to see my mother standing over me with the buckle end of a leather belt raised over her head, her eyes glinting like steel, raining blow after blow on me with my bed covers ripped off me. I tried to curl up to avoid the blows and pull my nightie down but there was no escape.

She then departed from the room. I lay completely stunned in shock and pain..

3 minutes later a couple of policemen entered the bedroom and said, "You've got 2 minutes to collect your stuff and leave. We've had a report that you've been disturbing the peace and the householder wants you removed".

All I could say was "But I was asleep.... That's my Mum". The policemen repeated that I had 2 minutes to leave.

I got up and dressed in this nightmare alarm call from hell at around 7.00am. I left the building with no time to collect anything.

Police took me away to the bus station. I was decimated emotionally. Somehow I got back to Sheffield on the 4+ hour bus ride and made it to my drama class that night.

People later said that I walked into class looking as if I'd just seen a bomb explosion. I was unable to follow proceedings. I was in zombie automatic pilot mode. But I showed up.

In a world of catatonic mental trauma and physical pain I phoned my Mum and asked if I could get my clothes etc. She said, "Yes I suppose so".

Like a dead person I made the interminable bus journey again, through the shire of Derby, the place of my birth.

On arrival Mum just stared coldly in disgust. I went to get my things from the bedroom, came downstairs and my mother said,

"Why don't you kill yourself Ida? Go on, just kill yourself!"

Unable to take anymore I grabbed a knife and in tears fell to the ground. Next thing I recall is a family friend, Denise standing over me in the hallway. Mum was telling her to take me to the mental hospital that's across the road from the house I grew up in on Corporation Street. Oh no!

Denise drove me there and we were taken into a room with several workers there including a beefy crew cut male student nurse with glinting piggy eyes.

The doctor talked to me and I babbled very coherently that I was supposed to be on a plane to a summer camp job in America and had gone to say goodbye to my siblings when my mother attacked me with a buckle-belt.

He asked about my family life and I told the truth that my father was in Holland and my mother's boyfriend used to beat me up when I was at school and nobody helped me.

Denise said "I didn't know any of this". Well she did now. My mother was a great con artist at presenting the 'posh' Mum.

I said, "I shouldn't be here! My mother should! I'm not mad, I don't belong in a mental hospital".

Denise was shown out and I was given drugs to swallow the size of rugby balls. I'd seen 'One Flew Over The Cuckoo's Nest' and was hard against hospital drugs.

I was put on a ward with a cupboard by the bed. The ward was full of very sick looking people. My brain went foggy.

A cleaner was going through some double-doors and I asked her to let me through. I found a pay telephone and reversed the charges to Eddie The Writer, telling him I was incarcerated in a mental hospital by my mother and was not happy, it was fucking nuts! I think Eddie was shocked.

Planes flew overhead without me.

My intellect remains as the tattered rags of a beggar, cobbled together like a patchwork holey cloak.

But in my early twenties on reading 'Candide' by Voltaire, I realised I was very much like Voltaire's character, Candide, believing the very best of people in the best of all possible worlds, and so for too many years I valiantly tried to believe the very best of my so called Mother. I wished I had a mother, although I was very resourceful and 'no action' to my mother as Dad had said, I still wanted to feel basic neutrality if not love. Just not active hatred. I didn't know love from a bar of soap.

As I sat on my bed in hospital, drugged, Mum arrived and made a disgusted face at the old skinny woman with no teeth and a sunken face who was walking about the ward.

Mum then had the audacious nerve to say to me, "Well if you want to spend your life in a mental hospital, that's your fault!"

A patient on a neighbouring bed called out to my mother, "You're going to lose your daughter!"

At that time I couldn't imagine a time when I did not care about my mum. It seemed an alien concept.

But after her further cataclysmic disgusting cruelty to me over several years, I finally understood what it means to not care if Mum rots in eternal hell with burning tongues of fire and rabid pestilence.

The old toothless woman couldn't talk in sentences, but just made sounds. She was nice. I took her outside into the grounds and went skipping with her and she smiled.

At night a drugs trolley came around into the large day room where people sat slumped. Drugs were administered.

Then it was time for the old toothless woman to be taken to her own separate room, away from the general ward I was on. Each night the big beefy crew-cut pig eyed student male nurse would usher her out of the day room and the old toothless one would shake her head and put up her hands defensively, managing to say the words, "Nooo No No No No No!"

A female fat nurse looked at me and said, "Ignore her she's senile". Every night, the same routine. I took all this in, not making sense of it.

Then one day as I sat in the day room, the double doors were open onto the corridor and I beheld a dreadful sight in the corridor.

The beefy male piggy eyed nurse smashed the old toothless woman so hard with his hand that her feet lifted off the ground and she flew across the opening of the double doors and landed in a heap on the floor.

I could not move, I did nothing. The night-time pleading of "No no noo!" was explained. God only knows what he did to her in her private room when he took her to bed, if he could do that to her in public.

All I could think was that I had to get out. The old toothless one had family that would visit her and she'd make happy sounds, but I felt as though I was underwater and couldn't move to tell them she was being battered. It felt like a thousand miles to move across the empty space between the chairs set in a ring on the edge of the room. It haunts me still.

Elton John wouldn't have to deal with this, I mused. He'd be in a 5 star hotel in Switzerland relaxing.

Alexandra Gribbin from school came to see me with a bunch of yellow daffodils, we were in the grounds outside. She must have heard I was there from my mother.

I opened my wrap skirt and showed Alexandra the blue welts on my thighs and broken skin that were STILL there a week later from the dents caused by the corners of the square buckle.

"Mum beat me with a buckle belt", was all I could say.

Suddenly mum appeared, all smiles and fakery, showing an attitude of concern about me to Alex, who to her credit said bluntly to Mum, "Ida says you beat her with a belt".

Mum just rolled her eyes, never missing a beat, she continued her fakery. (Munchausens Syndrome By Proxy). But Alex knew and had seen the proof.

The drugs were strong and rendered me pretty speechless.

Fucking Bob turned up at the hospital one day in his trademark long navy bookies coat over black clothes. He said things to me that made no sense. I could see his mouth opening and closing but the sound was distorted, just a drone.

Artist Kirsty arrived one day as we sat indoors and she cried, saying "You shouldn't be in here!" As if I'd had a say in it.

A couple of years earlier, I'd visited Kirsty in that same hospital and she wrote to me later saying that I'd saved her as she walked the razors edge. I'd smoked in the non-smoking area and acted loudly, talking about Vincent Van Gogh. They convinced her that she had a 'chemical imbalance', and she believed them. (I do love Kirsty, she was great fun and often very supportive. Many an ale was quaffed with her on Sunday nights in Props Winebar).

2 of my mum's brothers arrived and told jokes. I was glad to see John and Tommy as they always reminded me of Western movies and rock 'n' roll. I couldn't tell them about their sister, my mum, as that'd be telling tales, even if I could have spoken.

The only good thing in hospital was Parachute Therapy. Once a week the parachute woman would pop her head around the day room doors and say "Parachute Therapy in five minutes in the big room". She'd only mention it for 5 seconds and be gone.

For me to move off my chair felt like fighting the weight of an ocean on top of me. It took every ounce of strength, but I'd grip the arms of the chair and force myself to my feet and go to whatever room where a silk parachute was laid on the floor. We'd stand in a circle round it and hold the edge and billow it up until it was so high we could walk underneath it, crossing to the other side.

I noticed that most people in the day room couldn't move in time to catch the parachute woman. I was 22 years old and fit and it was very hard for me to fight the drugs to get up, and for the rest of the patients it was near impossible.

So when Parachute woman popped her head in briefly I would pull the others up off their chairs by their hands and say "Come on!" Dragging them to their feet to come with me.

(I wish hospital staff cared enough to get the patients moving. To give them a chance to fight the ocean of drugs on top of them).

After 5 long weeks I was finally released and the Doctor instructed my mother to, "Give your daughter a restful supportive environment". Mum agreed politely. Sounded nice, but would my mother actually heed him? I didn't know but could only hope.

In the taxi as we left the hospital grounds Mum said, "Now FUCK OFF Ida!" I had to collect my stuff and go.

At 'home' Bob Crumpton was there!

Mum and Bob were talking at me, blocking the doorway of the lounge. The sadistic look in their eyes was palpable but they'd got the wrong girl!

I was NOT a masochist! My instinct had me leap over the sofa and climb out of the living room window!

The two people I should be able to trust the most, my mum and my boyfriend, were actively out to get me.

In Sheffield the landlord had chucked everyone out and a woman called Izzey, 10 years my senior, from my drama class had given me a room in her large Broomhall ghetto house, which was shared with a bunch of men, all at least 10 years older than me.

Izzy was very dramatic and well spoken with cropped red dyed hair. She sent the males in the house mad with her wailing. I was very taciturn from the drugs, pretty much a zombie.

A pool hustler called Bernadette came around a fair bit with a Mimms Medical Directory. She saw my drugs and looked them up.

"UGH!" she exclaimed, "Optimax! These are highly addictive, toxic and not even fun! They're going in the bin!" Straight away she threw them away. Bernadette saved me from being a vegetable.

A party was happening in the afternoon next door and I went round to join in. Before I left I looked in a mirror and was stunned at how fresh I looked! Like a young Irish girl with blue eyes and little freckles and wavy brown hair. TOTALLY belying the state of my brain inside that shell.

A youth kept saying, "You're giving me the raging horn". I left the party and went home and he followed me, pushing me into my room and although I pleaded for him to stop, he raped me and left.

So much for the "Supportive restful environment" prescribed by the doctor.

I lay thinking HOW am I going to get my head around this rape in time for my dance audition in Manchester tomorrow?

It was hard enough already to be getting my head around the fact that my 'mother' could assault me viciously while I slept when I was 22 years old! It'd been dehumanising and a tad degrading! (It was actually a crime but I didn't think to get her arrested as nobody had ever cared and Mum had then called police to ME!)

Some say stripping is degrading, but compared to my life it was a breeze! It was definitely not the musical theatre of my dreams and capabilities but at least I was paid to dance!

I dragged myself to the Manchester audition the next day and after dancing solidly to just ONE record I nearly passed out on the ground with my heart pounding so hard in my chest, I thought I was going to die. Parachute therapy once a week on drugs had rendered me less fit than usual.

Bob turned up to my new Broomhall house bearing gifts from his American tour. A gold plastic bottle with a dreamy painting of Elvis in white on the label and the words, 'Elvisly Yours, Love Me Tender Moisturising Milk Bath' and a black n white country & western shirt with silver ric-rac braid.

Also a black T-shirt with a skull wearing a Red Beret and crossed swords, emblazoned with the motto, KILL 'EM ALL! LET GOD SORT 'EM OUT!

Bob and I were in the upstairs lounge and Izzy was heard to scream from downstairs "IDA!!! GET HERE!" With a stricken face I looked at Bob and he said, "Is that your mum?" Sure sounded like it.

AAAAAAGH!!! DEMONIC POSSESSION!!! IS ALL I CAN SAY FOR THE NEXT BIT

At night we lay in my bedroom on the first floor and Bob was rolling a joint, laying on his side staring at me. The lamp was shining on the long shelf next to us, which served as a headboard.

AS SURE AS I'M TYPING THESE WORDS, Bob's face changed before my eyes into the scariest thing I'd ever seen.

His eye pupils went into vertical slits with bobbles on the top and and bottom like a goat's: his mouth turned into the Joker's leer with corners up high, his tongue hung down long with a forward curl at the tip like a butcher's hook and gently bounced up and down whilst hanging. To top it all there was a FLY on the tip of it!

I turned my head away and tried to calm my thumping heart and in my mind I whistled to keep up my spirit, remembering a Carlos Castaneda book, "Just gaze, don't look or it will feed off the fear and you'll die of a heart attack".

I dared turn to face him and his face had resumed its normal features. FFS! He's possessed by the devil I thought!

(20 years later on reading about David Icke's lizard people, I was convinced that I'd gone out with a shape-shifting lizard in Bob. The webbed feet! The long bouncing curled tongue with the fly on the end hanging from the leering Joker grin! The vertical slit pupils!)

Izzy actually chased the male inhabitants with boiling water in the kettle and was thrown out by the landlord who lived next-door.

Her white painted, massive, top floor, wooden floored room was given to me. It was the best room I'd ever had, with a sloping roof and a massive skylight that could open, and a blackout blind. One thin corner window looked into the backs of the houses. It was awesome, with wooden pallets to hold the mattress.

For 50 pounds I skint myself to buy a baby Olympic drum kit with a Limpet practise pad that I rarely used, preferring to bang the drums. The previous owner had shown me how to play with my limbs all moving at different times.

Bob actually said I was good and he showed me the drum rhythm for 'Bournemouth Runner' by The Fall.

Playing the drums was great!

I taught myself all the rhythms for the Elvis Presley 'Sun Sessions' and Adam Ant records and anything I could think of.

It was time for my practical exam for the drama class and we had to learn a section of play that involved 3 characters interacting, so I trained with a ginger haired male visitor called Neil (I think), a really nice friend of the house men. I got Distinction in the exam!

A young 17 year old called Johnny moved in and took Izzy's place. He laughed and said I had grey streaks on top of my head, I smiled at the joke. He must be joking cos I was 22. Another day, he said it again. Then again.

There were no good mirrors in the house, so I'd thought it was light shining on my hair. Then one day I saw my hair in a good mirror somewhere and WOW! It was true! I had white streaks on top of my head.

My mum had traumatised me so much I'd gone grey in streaks on top of my head overnight! The rest was long brown curls.

Eventually I stopped picking them off my head and dyed my natural hair again, just as I had as a teen. What a bummer. I liked being natural. I just looked too young to be grey. The grey was too incongruous with my face to leave natural.

The men in the house used to send me down the street to buy weed for them from down in a cellar filled with smoke and black men. They sent me because after the first time I went, they were amazed at what a good deal I got.

Those were the high-lights of my time in Broomhall.

A lot of the time I was crying about by 'mother' not noticing all my sterling efforts towards her over the years, the money I'd sent her from London when just turned 17, the presents, the stoic acceptance that I must be old enough to live my own life and allow her the choice of a psycho boyfriend over me, her own daughter. Surviving horror all alone, thinking I must be able to take it and must be expected to or somebody would stop it. The fact that I'd lived a lie until aged 22, that my mother MUST care really. All just a figment of wishful thinking. I had to get my head around it.

As Albert Finney in 'Gumshoe' said, "It was an ordinary day all over the city, but me? I had to get used to living without the family". In my case, without even the tenuous delusion of family.

Then crying more when Bob came round with his sniping, whining and manufactured rows. I'd play him 'If I Can Dream' sung by Elvis and hope he'd be inspired by Elvis's imploring to live as one, in hope and love! I'd play 'Thanks I'll Eat It Here' album by Little Feat, with Lowell George beseeching 'What Do You Want The Girl To Do?' But Bob was deaf.

Bob said, **"Your mother treats you like a dog! I'm all you've got!"** I replied in a measured tone, **"Then I have nobody".**

Bob had yet again yelled at ME when I told him I'd been raped AGAIN whilst living at that house. Good job I didn't tell him about the earlier ones.

This time I'd gone to a party up the hill at Crookesmoor Rd at a house where a girl in my English class lived with all males, same as my house.

(I was re-taking English A level, having failed the year before due to running around with Bob and not reading all the books; it was a long-shot to even sit the exam, clueless to what the questions were about. Just as it was insane to turn up to the art exam having run all the way from the train station after being late coming back from Bob's in Birmingham with only 15 minutes of the exam left!

I arrived panting and emotional to a room packed with easels of beautiful pictures all set around a naked woman, whose skin was concrete coloured and hair was like a Brillo pad with a nose like Concorde. There was no good position left available to view her from, and no easel, so I sat on a chair with a pad on my knee in the only viewing position available looking right up her crotch with her legs fore-shortened into just thighs and feet due to the perspective. My paper was a dreadful scratchy mess of indecision. Do I risk painting this child of God realistically? What if the examiners hadn't seen her and think I've gone wrong to do her concrete coloured etc?. Then the exam was over. Miraculously I got grade E for the Effort of showing up).

I was setting off down the hill from the party to go home, when a guy whose name I've blanked from my brain, said,

"You can't walk down there on your own, you'll get into trouble, come back to my house with me and you can have your own room because the house lads are away climbing this weekend". He wasn't some random bloke on the street telling me this.

He often came to my house and sat around our kitchen table chatting to the men who lived there and I. He was writing a politics novel and was a graduate who wore little John Lennon glasses with curly brown hair and looked like a typical boffin.

Thinking about what he said, I mused that if anything did happen to me walking home, I'd get the blame for walking by myself. So I thought, OK, what could be wrong with having a room on my own and walking back in the daylight next day? I trusted the guy because he was a friend of my house.

We went into his house and had toast and I wanted to go to sleep. He said, "Actually, on second thoughts, the lads might come back so you better sleep in my room as there's a spare bed".

Mmmmm..... alright. The spare bed was across the other side of the room from his bed, so no worries.

I fell into the bed and was drifting off to sleep in the dark in my clothes. When I became aware of something on my feet under the covers in my bed!? I was so tired and kicked him off and said,

"What are you doing? Get off! Get in your own bed!"

He weaselled his way from the bottom of the bed to the top and held me down with a manic grin on his face visible in the street lamp light. I pleaded with him to NOT force me. BUT HE RAPED ME.

Next day I didn't even know where I was geographically, but I got home and told all the men in my house that their 'friend' was a RAPIST!! They seemed surprised.

Bob asked me how big the rapist was. "He's a little weasel" I replied. But Bob just yelled at me and was zero support as ever. No wonder I'd never told him about the other rapes. Fucking useless. As if I needed to be yelled at on top of being violated! I despaired.

Another day a while later I came back to the house through the wide open front door to find a strong looking black man sitting at the kitchen table. None of the men were home and I asked who he was looking for. He said nobody, he'd just walked in off the street. He then kept me captive with the front door closed and took great delight in my desperately trying to talk him out of raping me. AFTER AN HOUR that lasted forever, the front door opened and all the men arrived and the strange black man shot out past them and down the street.

Again, I yelled at the men for leaving the front door wide open so that strangers could get in and take me hostage! He could have killed me! The shit you deal with when you don't have a gun.

NEVER "a restful supportive environment" for me. NEVER except for my time at Tina Slater's place.

TRAPPED IN A MOVIE. 'Blue Velvet'.

Eddie 'The Writer' Rowe was just about the only friend from before my hospitalisation who knew where I now lived.

He decided to visit one Saturday and that sunny afternoon we went to the 567 Cinema to see the matinee of 'Blue Velvet'.

The cinema was a very atmospheric old building. As the film unfolded and Isabella Rosselini was assaulted by Dennis Hopper who was playing Frank, I found myself leaking from the eyeballs again. I'd suddenly realised that my life now consisted of a man named Frank who came to my house and made me cry. Bob's real name is Frank.

I went to the toilet. It was dimly lit by a red light and I thought, "When does the film stop? Even the toilet looks like the film".

At the end of the film there is a stuffed animated bird on a windowsill.

As we got back to my house I noticed the incongruous white picket fence with red roses across the street, totally at odds with the ghetto it was in. At the start of 'Blue Velvet' there is a beautiful white picket fence filling the screen, decked with red roses against the blue sky. In my room was a red stuffed bird on the window sash in the middle of my window! I thought 'Blue Velvet' would never end!

A while later I was in the bath when the men called up that someone was at the front door for me. Bob ran downstairs.

I asked Bob who it was and he said "Eddie, I told him to go away!". I was so fed up as Eddie was my best friend and the only person in my life I could talk to!

All the students had probably gone back to their families after getting their degrees. They had a different world. I'd be at a student shared house when parents would roll up in a car with their student child, (who was my age), the car would be laden with all the goodies their old child might need.

There was no rucksack and hitching or a bus ticket for these students.

I'd always known that those students would never be able to solve any problem I may ever have.

They'd often sit with me telling me their idea of woes. I could solve everything they asked me about.

I solved everything for myself. If I ever faced a crisis in future, I knew it was because it would be unsolvable.

Bloody mother only told me on the phone that I could never see my little siblings again!

Major crisis. How could I solve it?

I did all I could to assimilate this horrendous info. I rationalised that if they were dead in war time, then I couldn't see them. If they'd never been born, same thing.

But there was NO WAR. And they were ALIVE! And I DID KNOW them and we HAD A GREAT TIME TOGETHER! They were my

ONLY decent family!!! Why should it end due to one maniacal power abuser!?

I woke up from a nightmare in which I was in a court and the judge announced that I must be imprisoned for 2 years!! I was led down some steps and along a metal verandah inside a prison and put in a dark cell. "Oh I'll be ok as long as you write to me", I said to whoever. Then I saw my legs in jeans and red boots doing the heel together, toes together sideways shuffle, then the image of Elvis's lip curl in a dark mirror. Then I was sat in the cell and the gravity hit me! I screamed out loud, **"TWO YEARS!!!"** It woke me up in a panic!

Then I said, "Phew! It was just a dream!"

Then I realised that I was sentenced to a psychological prison of pain by my mother which could take me ten years to get over, if ever!

So I had to solve it!

My brain needed to be a bank canvas so that I could play every emotion on stage, NOT be stuck in permanent pain mode!

I booked into a Hypnotist's office and asked him to hypnotise me that I'd NEVER MET MY FAMILY!

He said it was not possible. Absolutely no way.

But how could I live with it?

I decided that I just wasn't going to accept my mother's word and went on the hellish long bus journey back to Sandiford, which stops about 18 times!

Mother let me in then told me she'd recorded the snooker over my only video to be on TV, at a time when there were only 4 TV channels and zero internet. Recorded sweetly by my siblings. God forbid! Verboten! NOT her eldest child on the TV idiot lantern! Ida must DIE!

I surreptitiously stole some childhood photos out of the family photo box that feature in this book. As I couldn't trust 'mum' not to destroy all evidence of my life.

(On leaving Blighty for Oz I scanned them onto a memory stick. Damn I wish I'd bothered to do the same with my young Bob Crompton photos! But I left them behind along with the vinyl records that I'd avoided like the plague since they were minted.

In 2021 a young cousin by marriage of his mum to Uncle John got in touch with me via social media. I'd not seen cousin Stephen Turner since a Christmas party at Uncle John's when he was he was 9 and I was 14. He said he'd also seen me in a play in Sandiford with his mum, Marie. He went to London to pick up my photos from the actress Zoe Zak who was leaving my flat. If he finds any Bob Crompton pics they will be in this book. But it's going to be difficult as he's no idea what Bob looks like. Update; Stephen found Bob pics but the publisher said I'm not allowed to include any.).

I told Mum with sad stoicism that I supposed I must accept that she really doesn't want to see me, which is awful, but that nothing was going to stop me seeing my little siblings who meant the world to me.

Mum then called the Police to remove me from her house when all I'd been doing was reading to the children! I wasn't trying to usurp her position as mother, I hardly ever saw them. Every few months I'd call in. I just wanted to be what I was, their big sister! What's wrong with that?

Mum totally abused the law which states that a householder can remove anyone they choose. I was their blood sister who had never harmed a hair on their heads! Yet O'Leery who wasn't blood, who was a child abuser, had completely free rein to visit! It was insane and heart-breaking.

Mum said, **"It doesn't matter if you NEVER see them again! It doesn't matter if they NEVER see you!"**

Police put me on the hard shoulder of the slip road to the motorway to hitchhike. They would do so many times, no matter how dark and rainy.

Mum got a lawyer/solicitor to send me a cold typewritten letter telling me I was banned from her house and would be arrested if I tried to see my siblings who lived there.

I went to a solicitor to see if there was any access law that could help me. There was no law to help a sibling see siblings that were under the jurisdiction of a parent, without that parent's consent. The householder had complete rights over who was in their house. I would have to wait until the children were 16 and legally allowed to see me on their own.

This destroyed my heart more than anything ever had. What if the children were abused by O'Leery and told their mother and she just ignored them, as she had done to me? It killed me.

By telling Mum that the children meant everything to me, I'd played into her sadistic hands and she capitalised on this one weakness in me, (which should have been seen as a strength). She actively wanted to destroy me and always had.

Only then did it become apparent to me that I must have annoyed her intensely by rising above onslaught after onslaught. Yet I had dumbly thought she must be proud of my resilience and deep down loved me.

I realise that any good thing that ever happened to me or that I'd achieved, had pissed her off and infuriated her in her sick world view.

On telling her that I'd met Alan Schoenberger the Olympic skier and was going to America to escape again from violent Bob, ...again I'd played into her hands and she decided to try and get me put away somewhere by taking me to a doctor and then phoned the Social Services.

When those attempts failed, she beat me up as I slept, lied to Police and had her friend hospitalise me. And she must have called Bob as if she was his henchman.

How dare Ida aspire to escape from violence!? NO WAY!

My 'mother' is a fucking evil obsessed psycho. Mum went to see mediums when we were young children and she said that one old psychic told her that one child would know deep sorrow. Mum made 100% certain it would be me, by taking EVERYONE I loved. I was the happiest child who loved family.

AUS UPDATE. Sad news. Amy Saunders Carter passed on 12th May 2022. A very talented singer songwriter and guitarist, a close friend for years in Birmingham. R.I.P. my beautiful young friend. Gutted. Amy and her family were very close to me.

Aus Update 12th May 2022

After Shayne touched my privates with his dick when I was unconscious, I started itching around my crotch. Have reported him to Police but it's a painfully slow process as they decide whether to prosecute him. I have next to zero hope. The GP did a blood test on me and I have 3 viruses down there. On antibiotics. The itching is excruciating. Shayne KNEW I've been a born again virgin for almost 20 years and would only be with my husband.

<u>BAY CITY ROLLERS!</u>

Bob came up to my Broomhall house and we saw in the newspaper that the BAY CITY ROLLERS band from the 70's was playing in a Sheffield working-mans-club. We HAD to go!

On arrival it was sold out, full up and we were barred from entry by the bouncers. Bob said, "Oh well, that's that".

I said, "Come with me" and led him by the hand around to the back of the club. I checked out a high window. No good. Then I saw a fire-door opening and said "Come on!" Next thing we knew we were right by the stage looking directly at the last remaining Bay City Roller, the guitarist. Bob looked at me with such pride.

An awesome 'shang-a-lang' time was had and we slipped back out of the fire doors before the fighting.

GENIUS

Some writer for the NME or some such music paper had called Bob "a genius" and he overly loved it. We were in my top floor bedroom. I had 2 keys and had to figure out which one was for my bedroom and which was for the front door down two flights of stairs.

Bob took the keys and set off downstairs. I stopped him and said "Just try them both in this door".

He looked at me and said "You're a genius!" I'd only done the obvious thing.

I told him that idiot savants can be geniuses; excellent at one thing but rubbish at everything else and emotionally retarded; and that I would rather be with a bin-man who was a great person and knew about love than be with an idiot savant.

BEEHIVE ROAD

Paula and I decided to live in our own house away from our respective houses full of men who leave the buildings insecure and hang out with rapists.

Beehive road was near the top of a cul-de-sac not far from my first Crookesmoor Rd bedsit.

From the way Paula put a doll in a big dress over the toilet paper, I knew we weren't on the same page.

As we sat by the fire doing our homework, we felt drowsy and headachey. Paula complained that the gas fire was full blast but not giving out much heat. After a while she called the gas board who came to the house and slapped 'OBSOLETE. DANGER. DO NOT TURN ON' stickers on both heaters.

The landlord went mad at the expense of getting new fires, saying we shouldn't have gone to the gasboard but gone to him. Paula said it's illegal not to report a gas leak.

It appeared he would rather have the expense of 2 dead tenants and half the street blown apart. ***(What do you call a bomb in a French kitchen? Linoleum Blownapart)***

Paula saved us from death. I can't smell and was so gone from loss and trauma that I'd have just been gassed.

Paula then attacked me, accusing me of fancying her boyfriend who still lived in the house of men that she'd left. I was sitting and she came up behind me and whacked my head with a hardback book. Her boyfriend was Plug ugly but I couldn't tell her that or she'd go even madder.

Totally weary from onslaughts, I ran crying to the phone box and begged my mother to let me go 'home' for Christmas. "NO!"

THEN A MIRACLE HAPPENED. A man knocked on the front door holding mail for Paula. I cried, "She's out and she's a nutter who attacked me for nothing".

He said, "I'm her ex-landlord. Oh Paula is no angel, leave it with me". He then moved all her stuff and I never saw Paula again! BRILLIANT.

Alone in that house I listened to the radio and learned all the words to the 'Bing Sings' vinyl album I bought because it's black n white cover was such a good photo of Bing's head in his homburg like my Granddad.

'Don't Fence Me In' sung by Bing and The Andrews Sisters remains a favourite and I played it a hundred times. I also played free cassettes I got with music magazines.

Craig, the bleached punk Paul Newman look-a-like motorcyclist heroine addict used to take me on his bike and I didn't care if I died. He rode under a moving juggernaut once and we lived. We'd lay side by side on his bed, never having sex. I shot down all his bullshit complaints about his 'sugar mummy' lady who gave him gifts, telling him he wouldn't accept the stuff if he didn't like it, so he cannot complain. He was just silent from then on. Better.

Craig was smart enough to realise that my outer appearance did not reflect how utterly wasted and wounded I was inside and that I had zero time for pretence.

(In retrospect I had become my false idol, Winter Steele, the animation character on Liquid TV that I'd watched when I had access to TV at Tina Slater's house. TV shit is too powerful for impressionable minds).

But I was alone a lot with Bing in between vicious and incomprehensible visits from Bob. Who even was he?

Bob would suggest I move to Birmingham and I'd look askance at him. Why on earth would I do that?

I told him that once on a summer's day waiting for a train in the Birmingham Bullring, I'd sat on a small quadrangle of grass with flyovers above me, thundering traffic, surrounded by hot-dogs and obesity in man-made fibres and I'd said to myself calmly, "I am in hell".

Birmingham was the last place on Earth I'd want to live in. And Britain was unanimous in a poll that B'ham also had the stupidest accent known to man. No way!

(Sorry Brummies but that's how I felt and I wasn't alone in that. Never in my wildest dreams did I imagine that I'd one day have the occasional Brummie lilt to my own voice and actually grow to love the Bullring even BEFORE it was remodelled, and that I would love the Rag Market where my friend Patti Bell the famous punk designer sold her self-made wild designs).

A letter written to me by Lucy, my little sister, invited me to her birthday party. Stabbed through the heart.

OF COURSE I'D LOVE TO GO! There's nowhere I'd love to be more! I wrote to her telling her so. BUT had to add that it was up to 'mother'.

My reply had to tread a minefield to get across the fact that I didn't want Police to ruin her day, without scaring Lucy that her mother was a PSYCHO who wrecks all our lives for NO REASON other than treacherous wicked spite!

The family, to my mind, was like an octopus. With the parents as the head and all the children were the different limbs doing different things, but all joined together as one body. I couldn't be a one legged octopus, it was psychologically a step too far for even me with my record of survival.

I took to writing inveigling begging letters to 'mum' and rational letters, pleading letters. I recalled my dad following mum around the kitchen whilst she ignored him, as he read her a story he'd written for her called 'Fortress'. She shrugged him off.

She shrugged *HIM* off but surely she wouldn't shrug off her own daughter? She COULD NOT!

Life with my siblings depended on it!

Surely MY letters would work and we'd all play again and I could lie on my back and balance them on my feet saying, "FLY TO FREEDOM

LITTLE BIRDIE! FLY TO FREEDOM!" as they put their arms out just resting on their tummies.

All my creative energy that I DEARLY WANTED to be spending on other ventures, all went in the black hole that is my mother.

I wrote poems,

"That bee! That hive! Buzzing alive! "I'll fetch the honey" says he! If you break my jug I'm just a bug and that's no way to bee!"

Imploring, reasoning letters to BREAK THE CYCLE, if indeed she'd been abused as a child.

Telling her that I'm on her side and that her past is NOT my fault!

I knew it was hoping against hope as I'd been a battered child myself and had never resorted to attacking children or adults and I was 23, not 43.

Telling her that I'd be more vulnerable to rapists if I couldn't go home.

ALL WASTED EFFORT.

I took the Mogadon bus from Sheffield and trudged to her council house in Milton Grove on Highfields estate.

Mum went crazy ape-shit and ran to her neighbours house. I followed her and looked through the window at her shaking her head, telling them how bad I was. The neighbours saw and heard me saying to mum, "I just want to talk to you, please mum".

The neighbours, who obviously treated their own children in a sane manner, said, "There she is, she just wants to talk to you! Off you go".

Mum returned to her house and sat on the sofa. I thought, "I've got a live one here!" And hoped that she'd relent and let me see my own flesh and blood when they came home from school.

But mum's face looked vexed and thoroughly pissed off. She left the room and made a phone call.

Next thing I know, stupid Sid is at the door to take me to the bus station.

Aaaaah….I see.

She couldn't call the police this time because the neighbours knew I was a nice daughter and 'mum' would look like the mad bitch she is….. SO she called Stupid Sid! So it looked like I was getting a normal lift.

So the neighbours would be none the wiser to her insane treachery.

"Why don't you get the S.A.S. too?" I said and sadly left with beefy Stupid Sid.

How could I know that she'd not be violent with my little siblings? Or let O'Leery hurt them? She was brutal to me and she was known to hit another sister from her first batch of children, on the head with a stiletto heel.

It cut me up inside to think of the little ones having no-one to turn to. I didn't have a phone they could call. I wrote to them that they must ask the neighbours for help if ANYONE hurt them, even if it's someone they see every day! Agonising to write as I didn't want to scare them about their only mother and father.

Elvis sang "Clean up your own backyard". My family was my backyard. How could I do anything if the family was fractured? I desperately wanted to fix it before I could do anything else. **The laws for siblings need changing.**

It destroyed me to know that they were being brought up with the idea that it's NORMAL to have a sibling removed by police. An innocent sibling! Insane! ALL OF IT NEEDLESS.

When **Fathers For Justice** came out in Superman costumes on high bridges with banners because they'd been denied access to their own flesh and blood, I sympathised entirely. Laws are often terrible.

This continuous rejection and ejection went on way past the end of this book until I couldn't walk or think anymore. Mum hated me so much she even let her guard down and crossed the room to hit me in the face as I was telling a sister about a sales job I briefly had.

Mum's lodger yelled, "Oi! That's out of order!"

For once a witness! I knew he'd been fed lies from how he looked at me suspiciously and I knew it was pointless to tell him my story against his 'posh' landlady's slander. Well for once the truth was out. Mum was a violent nut against me and he could see I hadn't done anything to deserve it.

No stone was left unturned to get my siblings and my mother back. Even to the point of putting scars on my face and getting to her door with scabby blood on my face and saying, "I'm ugly now, is that good enough? Can I come in now?"

People said she was jealous. It didn't work when Vincent Van Gogh cut his ear off, and messing up my face didn't work for me. I tried everything. Even wrecking my own average face. 'Mum' just saw it as a massive power trip.

(I'm finishing this book at around age 25-26. Except for the further appearance of Bob Crumpton in my 40s. Missing out my insane international stripping years which are a book in themselves).

But I'd not be able to see my siblings until they left school and until they were thoroughly brainwashed that I must be bad surely? At least a bit bad? Subhuman-ish, the kind of person you have to ban? They were bound to entertain that notion, otherwise they couldn't reconcile themselves to my mother's ban on me. Unless they accepted that she was an evil piece of work. It's very hard to see your 'Mary Poppins' guardian as capable of such treachery against her own child. I was the child she chose to be treacherous to and even I couldn't believe my own eyes for ages.

'Mum' gave me the biggest burden of my life.....for nothing. Just her own jealous obsessive spite. I'd been a stoical, generous daughter, "never any action", and been attacked in my sleep and banned from all I loved.

No choice but to learn to live in severe pain about my 'mother' for the rest of my life. Nothing was ever really right with my little siblings from the ban onwards. I never wanted to admit defeat, and for years forgave mum everything if she would just relent.

Mum would occasionally say, "OK you can come to see them". I knew I couldn't trust her but I'd no choice but to risk it as it was my only chance to see the little siblings. Mum would then call the police as soon as I arrived.

A cruel donkey and carrot game, knowing I couldn't afford it financially or emotionally to travel only to be chucked out. I pleaded with mum to be honest. She said, "You're a mug then aren't you?" For trying to see them.

I have to say that the psycho 'won'. Her prize was a deeply wounded daughter and a decimated family.

Seeing the little siblings playing in the summer street and seeing them notice me walking towards the family house, then running up to me clutching my leg, almost crying, "Ida they'll kill you!" I replied brightly,

"It's a lovely summer day, I'm your big sister! What could be wrong about a big sister seeing her own family, her own little sister and brother on a lovely day?" They agreed, smiling ruefully that nothing was wrong with that.

But sadly, they were right to worry. My visit lasted all of 10 minutes under extreme duress and ended in a police car.

As I type, tears spout out at the memory that the little children's minds had been so twisted by an evil bitch that they were SCARED for their own big sister's safety, should I try to enjoy seeing my family like anyone else on a summer's day. How fucking cruel.

As I was taken away one day by a policewoman and a policeman, my 'mum' yelled, **"Why don't I get raped? You deserve rape!"**

The policewoman said out loud, "That's a terrible thing to say". In the police car as we drove, the policeman asked me if my mum was mad. "Is she mad?"

I was too upset to speak. What could I say? She's allowed out! She walks freely among us.

Hey mum! Perhaps you'd like a fractured skull thrown in with a rape? You monster!

To know your own mother wants you dead and gone is a terrible burden to get used to. It's kind of tough to have any self esteem at all! Knowing that every breath you take is an affront to her. A driving factor of my getting back on TV after Bob's video was deleted by mum, was so that my siblings could actually see me in their home!

Mothers Day would have me laughing and crying in card shops, reading the saccharin rhymes.

Knowing that my mum would think I was taking the mickey if I sent one of the typical cards;

"Dear Mum you always care, dear mum you're always there. You wipe away every tear, I'm so glad that you're near". HAA HAAAA!!!!! AS IF!

Where's the Mother's Day cards for kids of psycho bitches?

What about Rosemary West's children? There's an untapped market! 'Mother as you banged my head against the wall, and kicked it like an old football, I knew you didn't care at all.

Mother you are a fucking psycho, as you and I both know'.

I could get rich on those cards!

For years if anyone disrespected their kind mum near me and didn't say please or thank you, it sent me livid, as they didn't know how lucky they were.

Even Bob Crumpton said to me, "Your mum treats you like a dog!" and he saw next to *nothing* of your full repertoire 'mother'.

It comes to something when psycho shark Bob is better than your own mother. I have to forgive her but I certainly don't care to ever see 'mum' again.

When the little ones grew up, a sister from the first batch had a party in Sandiford and invited me plus 1, Jeremy Paige the lead singer of Rumblefish and then Low Art Thrill. Lucy was there aged about 16 and I was about 32.

It was surreal and amazing to be in the same house with 2 of my sisters, my family. I'd almost made it from the bottom of a pile of shit to the top of it. Having been long forced to accept that I had no mother, I'd somehow gained some tenuous self-esteem.

Then somebody said to me as I was sitting upstairs with Jeremy and some kids at the party, "Your mum's here!" A cold claw gripped my heart.

I numbly went downstairs and there she stood in the lamp lit kitchen, surrounded by moody youths all sitting on the kitchen surfaces.

All I could do was stare. Then, after wrecking my life and health for years, she said in a creepy measured voice, “Aren’t you going to hug me?”

All I could do was stand speechless. She continued, “Jenny you ran away. You didn’t answer my letters”.

??

This was my cue to yell, “The solicitors letter banning me? That’s all I got from you, you mad cow! What? Run away in a police car?”, then I should’ve walked out of that kitchen!

But I couldn’t speak or move. Then a moody youth said, “Go on give ya mum a hug”. He knew nothing.

All I could think was, I cannot wreck my sister’s party. My arms hung limp, I couldn’t raise them, but I did a lame attempt with my limp arms, in total stunned disbelief that after all this time she could dare to publicly come at me with LIES!

‘Mum’ then had the brass nerve to *indirectly, through* someone else at the party, invite me for Christmas with the family.

How convenient!

Now my young cousin Phillippa was at B’ham Uni and regularly saw me, and the kids could see me legally on their own and all realised I was as alright as far as could be expected after a brutalised life of rejection.

So mum knew her ‘bad banned Ida’ story would look like the lie it was! So she wanted to pretend to them all that I’d improved and could now be allowed in! (I was fried by then).

The FIRST TIME I get to see two sisters in a happy setting in YEARS.......the beast turns up LYING! Expecting me to jump for her!?

Mum was years too late and without *ever even once* apologising in my *entire life;* not even to assure me *somewhat* that it wasn't another sick trick, a fake invitation so she could attack/spit in my face/remove me on arrival. She couldn't even afford me that basic A, B, C of respect. She couldn't even caveat it with, "I know this is very hard to believe but, would you...".

She still wanted to treat me as her puppet to yank around. A subhuman to summon or dismiss at will....with bold faced LIES in public! I was meant to respond positively to that. Zero honesty!? I never was her "mug", I had no choice if I wanted to see my own siblings. Unconscionable. She can tell God all about it.

It set me back 5 months mentally to know that, having achieved adulthood despite her abuse and having been forced to assimilate that she hated me and to live without my family... she actually thought she could command me back!? To suit her twisted narrative!....With lies about the past.... in public!

Her opinion of me was truly subhuman. She was worse than I'd imagined! I feel like hurling as I type it, just recalling the gall of the creature. There were so many low incidents from her that I've omitted.

Never saw her again until my Dads (second) funeral in 2010. She never changed.

BACK TO LUCY'S UPCOMING 7th or 8th Birthday and I'm 23

In my room, dimly lit from a street lamp through the curtains, I lay in bed sobbing to die from. I really wanted to live but had nothing left up my sleeve. No more cards to play. My endless resources had run out. It was all black and I was wiped out from endless abuse. Lucy and my brother could be being abused for all I knew. *(I hadn't*

figured out that it was 99.9% mainly directed at me). **NO LAWYER COULD HELP ME!**

It was the sweet little girl's birthday, I couldn't stand the pain anymore. I got out of bed and fell to my knees saying,

"PLEASE HELP ME! PLEASE SHOW YOURSELF IF THERE'S A GOD! ***I really want to live but I don't know how anymore!*** **I CAN'T TAKE ANYMORE.**

Buddha! Hari Krishna! Allah! Aliens! Father Christmas! ANYBODY! PLEASE!"

Laid in my bed my heart was dead, nobody came, sobbing like a death rattle, I figured Darwin was right all along and I was just a little ex-monkey about to die now.

Then a bronzey warm glow appeared at the end of my bed. A bearded man with long hair to his chest, in an ivory linen robe was inside the glow with his palms up in an open gesture. INSTANTLY I knew it was Jesus! Even though he was middle Eastern coloured and not white like our Catholic neighbours had on their walls.

(*If I see a strange hippy in my room in the middle of the night, my heart is usually pounding, I'm trying to talk my way out of rape, I'm thinking 'where's my axe?' But no, I was peaceful and my house was locked and He'd come through the wall!*)

Jesus said nothing at all. He just stood at the end of my bed in this warm glow that radiated in the glum room. I was mesmerised, transfixed and sat up. Then Jesus started walking towards the head of my bed and as He walked the glow came with Him and got closer to me until I was in the glow. He stood by the head of my bed and put his hand on my forehead.

From that touch I saw another dimension of light and ribbons of light and I was weightless, no pain, just bliss and pure love. It was the best experience I'd ever had. Better by far than any drug I'd tried.

It would be five years before I tried a millionaire's good quality cocaine and frankly it was shit compared to what Jesus showed me.

The next day I was still in the same terrible dilemma family wise, but I was now full of wonder! Enough to stay alive.

I kept thinking WOW! Jesus is REAL! He's not just a story! He really lived, was really killed and really came back to life and now really visits a heathen like me who's never been to church or read a Bible! WOW! There's more to this world than I've been led to believe.

It was bitter cold with no fires working in the house and seriously snowing until it came under the big gap under my back door. I cursed the fact that I'd run out of matches and didn't have a gas cooker igniter clicker thing.

Then there was a knock on my back door next to the cooker. Most unusual to be knocking on the backdoor.

On opening it, I kid you not, there was a little old lady holding aloft a gas clicker lighter thing! She said, "I thought you might want this?".

"YES! I really do, that's amazing thank you!" Then she toddled next-door.

Honestly, I had NOT been talking out loud about needing a clicker! She just appeared with one.

It was as if God was really driving home that there was definitely more to life than I'd ever known.

Then I mistakenly rationalised that maybe ALL the famous deities are real too, and Jesus was the only one who wasn't busy that night when He visited me? I had images and statues of Kali the goddess of destruction with her belt of skulls around her waist, which I saw as all the men who'd ever raped me. There was a statue of the Indian god, Ganesh who was supposed to remove obstacles. Buddha was in my house and all kinds of images of deities abounded.

What a mistake!

For years and years I fell into Aleister Crowley's and Madame Blavatsky's New Age TRAP that there are 'many paths to God'.

That's what they wanted people to think! So that people are wide open psychologically to their anti-christ. Defenceless!

Mme Blavatsky, Alice Bailey and Aleister Crowley set up the Theosophy Society and the Lucifer Trust publishing house in around 1900. They channelled spirits and called it 'externalising the hierarchy'. spirits <u>They didn't ask, check or care if the spirits were from God and believed Jesus died for us and beat death and Satan, as you always should ask them</u>.

Mme Blavatsky planned to flood the culture with as many cults, tarot cards, palmistry, ouija boards, 'angel cards' 'animal cards' and religions as possible, to flood people with everything we see today until witchcraft, sorcery and mediums are as normal as having a cup of tea; and all the Runes and IChing and astrology.

I was into it all for years at great cost and much haunting by spirits. Grown men would come out of my kitchen shaken and white. I'd be like, "Thanks a lot! Big men. I have to live here, a girl, by myself!"

A girl ran out of my house when a knife threw itself across the room. It was full on. I'd get home and say,

"Hi dead people, I'm home!"

Until my early 40s when I realised from Chris White on Youtube that it wasn't my old houses that were haunted, it was me!

So I threw everything in a rubbish skip, beautiful books on palmistry, velvet bags of Runes etc, ALL OF IT.

Then I went home and said "I rebuke you spirits in the mighty name of Jesus, GET OUT!" That night a man's voice said "Bye then". And I've never been haunted since

Those Satanists didn't want people to know that ONLY Jesus can visit you and defend you, because only Jesus beat death! Only Jesus rose again!

They don't care who you worship as long as it isn't Jesus! Because ONLY Jesus beat Satan, their prince of this world.

Muslims worship a warlord, Buddha sat under a bodhi tree and the rest were no better. **Only Jesus died for us and took on the worst of all humanity, then resurrected from the gruesome grave and beat Satan.**

ONLY Jesus visited me, because ONLY Jesus CAN! It took many lost years before I realised that.

Some Christians came up to me on the street, trying to get me to their church. I said,

"I'm IN church NOW! Do you like the pavement? Everywhere is a church! I've MET Jesus! He came to my house!"

They looked at me suspiciously and said they doubted it.

This surprised me. "I thought you were Christians and believed in Jesus! Are you saying that you don't think Jesus would want to know me?! Well HE DID visit me and He used to hang out with lepers and prostitutes, so there!"

In hindsight, maybe I could have got a Bible off those Christians if I'd gone with them and saved myself years of future grief by reading Proverbs and Psalms and much more. I've asked God a question and opened the Bible randomly and been AMAZED that the writing is so specifically telling me about my question! The Bible is ALIVE.

But Jesus had visited me SANS Bible study and that's what I clung to for many years. No Bible reading for me, ZIP, ZERO, NADA, ZILCH.

I reasoned that if EVERY book was burnt, Jesus would STILL BE REAL. If people are illiterate, JESUS IS STILL THERE.

But I *missed out* on some **VERY HELPFUL** CLUES and INSTRUCTIONS FOR EASY LIVING in the Bible.

Because I believed Satan's whispers that the Bible was written by blokes and was censored and edited and therefore it was no use at all. When *all of theBible*, even the Old Testament before Jesus was born, is all the inspired word of God, written through inspired men.

I struggled out of a hellish trap, fought onwards and upwards and became a twisted monster of sin, which cost me **greatly.** I could have avoided some of it by knowing the Bible.

HERE IN AUSTRALIA I was BANNED in 2021 by the only church I'd ever been a regular at.

Pastor Reg stood before the congregation saying he'd got a covid jab and for people to get one. He's always asking for money too.

I said "**Pastor Reg, WHO do you serve?**"

Privately I told him that we all love him and to come back to us. And as he'd been preaching about repentance, he should publicly repent of taking the jab and never take another. **BANNED.** How unChristian of them.

Did I tell you that here in Australia at age 50 I was diagnosed Bipolar? Didn't they call that condition 'artistic' a hundred years ago? Then it was manic depressive. Now it's bipolar. How handy to sell drugs to us. Especially as I survived drug free for 50 years. Then I made the mistake of telling a psychiatrist that I'd seen Jesus, which was the only reason I'd survived at all. Ohhh bad move. Never mix spirituality with big pharma. I was immediately diagnosed with 'Schizoeffective disorder'. But I know that's false. I've never seen anyone else walk through a wall in my whole life and only heard God speak once as you will see later.

BACK TO THE STORY

AFTER JESUS HAD VISITED ME IN SHEFFIELD

I wrote to **Richard The Hippy** who was back in Brighton with his family, asking him to rent a room in Beehive Road.

He arrived and was an angel in the house. He pressure cooked chickpeas and made hummus, he grew strawberries in the garden and built a wormery and a compost heap. He took the top attic room and grew cannabis in the roof space through a little doorway, by putting tinfoil around the roof triangle and putting lamps in there.

Richard is well over 6ft tall, blonde like a Viking and as the weather warmed up he loved to run about naked with his monster penis waving in the wind.

By this time my brain was overloaded with penises and I found it quite difficult, unlike before all the rapes. Oh I gave Richard hell about his dick. "Get in your DICK room, your shrine to your DICK!" Just because the poor young man had baby oil by his bed. But Richard was a fantastic person to live with.

I should NEVER have left Sheffield to go with Bob to Birmingham, but I reasoned it was closer to be chucked out of mum's house to go

45 minutes to Birmingham on the train, than it was to travel hours to Sheffield on the Mogadon bus.

No idea what machinations Bob had in mind when telling me to go to B'ham with him, and I'm sure he had some twisted reason, but I knew I needed to be nearer to the family in Sandiford, get a job and go to America and see Alan Schoenberger.

AUS UPDATE 24th May 2022.

Made friends again with Big Bill because he's my neighbour and has a sweet side. Bill said, "I really do love you very much". I love him too. Helped his relative to streamline his house and make it easier for him to perambulate around in it. The case against Shayne interfering with my privates whilst I was unconscious is closed. They won't prosecute because, as usual, it's word against word.

ALIENS AND JESUS & IDA SPUTUM.

Aged 23 in Sheffield, at Beehive Road the words, "I DISPUTE THEM" were looming in my head. Ida Sputum would be my stage name in a future life.

Also I went to a Sheffield hill overlooking the city in the late afternoon with a DJ. We saw two balls of shiny material whizzing from one side of the horizon to the other in milliseconds! We checked that we were both seeing this spectacle. "Uh huh"

A normal jet plane was creeping along in a straight low line, as if to show how fast the balls were.

Then a ball stopped dead in the air and started to trace a pattern, up down, left right. I said, "That's the sign of a cross!" Just like writing your name in the air with a sparkler on Guy Fawkes night.

Then blip! They accelerated and were gone!

I thought hard about it all; Jesus is real, aliens are real, well I guess there's room for them all.

Maybe the aliens made the sign of a cross to tell us that Jesus's teachings are a good way to live? But nobody worships Jesus anymore, I thought to myself, they worship false idols. So I had an idea to make crucifixes with Hendrix, Joplin, Monroe, Elvis on them. As all of them were killed by man's inhumanity to man. And we are all still prostitutes like Mary Magdalene, renting out our bodies for the currency of money. We are their fans, like Mary Magdalene was a fan of Jesus. My thought involved a lot of crosses, so I narrowed it down to one portable crucifix with the two biggest icons, Elvis and Marilyn mixed together in one body on the cross. All the things that killed them were collaged from magazines pasted all over the cross. Child abuse, junk food, exploitation, corrupt doctors, idolatry, exploitation, mafia, corrupt politicians etc.

In 1999 I carried it to the top of the Birmingham Bullring and planted it on top of the Horror Shop, run by my mate Stewart, the lead singer of punk band Contempt. It was my Millennium Artistic Statement.

Birmingham is the oldest centre of commerce in Britain and I was up on top of the Horror Shop as Mary Magdalene, naked except for banknotes on my tits and fanny, looking down at all the upturned faces below in the market. It was winter and the police took me away. Any newspaper items about it misreported what it was about. For some reason my good friend Patti Bell told a reporter I was 26 instead of 35, which is what I was.

Ms PATTI BELL

Patti Bell, the designer who featured in the Albert Hall exhibition of fashion through the ages, was a riot of colour and joy and we called ourselves 'Jolly Girls'.

Patti was born in exactly the same year as my mother and all through my early 30s we'd go out dancing to live bands every week,

with Patti remaining *exquisitely* beautiful, flamboyant, funny and youthful although 20 years older.

Patti made Christmas dinner for me in her flat one year whilst I was racked with sobs over another 'family' onslaught from a so-called sister from the first batch who should've known better.

Patti Bell was my REAL family and she went through a phase of creating clothes with pictures of Jesus on them. I was always in fine style thanks to Patti's talent and generosity

2 SISTERS from the 1st Batch; Esme born 1965. Rachel born 1969. (I wasn't going to put these two varmints into the book, *but in for a penny, in for a pound).*

Nature or nurture? Bah!

In hindsight both sets of grandparents were right when they all said quietly to me that I was the only kid who was any good from the first batch. As a child I couldn't conceive that my sisters were no good. I learned very hard.

My family was my false idol, I couldn't think bad of them no matter what! Always thought that being the eldest, they could do no wrong and I was their protector.

The only solidarity or defence I ever got from one of them was after mum crossed the crowded room to punch me in the face, Rachel, the sister who's 5 years younger said lamely, "Hey mum, I was enjoying that conversation with Ida!" That's all. A small mercy I was glad of. Even the lodger witness said, "OI that's out of order!" Then I was chucked out again. Inhuman. Rachel told me, "I look after number one".

Years later Rachel dumped me at the airport in Portugal on Christmas Eve, after inviting me there in my 30s for my *first 'family' Christmas in years*. Her husband, who knew NOTHING of my mum's relationship with me, harangued me for *hours* like a big bully, telling me that I must see my mum! I said patiently I understand that she's nice to you, but it's not the case with me. Calmly I repeated that I didn't want to get into it as it was Christmas. I ended up telling him that my Mum called me a 'MUG' for even trying to see my family and had me removed repeatedly by police!

I'd been awake for 48 hours, had loads of cheap red wine and couldn't take any more. Rachel lamely told him, "It's different for Ida".

That's all she said!

But he was deaf and nagged like a lunatic. So in the end I said, "You really are a total tosser". He went mad. "You're banned! Nobody calls me that in my house!" I apologised that I was wasted and drunk.

They went out the next day and I cleaned their house and created a Christmas tree out of a water bottle.

They returned and sat looking in amazement at the transformation. They said they loved it and the art I'd made for the wall out of Christmas cards. But the husband's mind could not be changed from his original idea to ban me. I pleaded with Rachel and her husband not to do this to me. But they did. Strangers at the airport said it was cruel.

In my very early twenties I never told Esme I was banned by mum, as I hoped it would end and I'd never have to worry Esme about it. Esme was working in the Channel Islands.

A family holiday at Esme's in the Channel Islands was being arranged. I'd love to have gone with the little children to see Esme. But mum said, "No way, Esme won't want you there!" "Of course she will, why wouldn't she?" I exclaimed.

I'd have loved the end of the ban and a lovely reunited family trip. But I was excluded as usual.

When Esme returned to Sandiford I saw her on another ill-fated mission to see the little ones. Esme announced that she *knew* I was banned as she'd spoken to mum on the phone and *encouraged it*!

"Why?!" I inquired, astounded!

Her answer could only have come from one born in the insanely jealous Snake year.

She said, "Because you were in Sheffield with Andrew Morton drugging it!"

WTF!? I hadn't seen Andrew Morton, the genius kid for years! Seven kinds of disbelief went through my mind.

Firstly, I'd never been in Sheffield at the same time as Andrew Morton. Secondly, what the heck difference would it make if I had?

Thirdly, it wasn't my fault that after I'd introduced Andrew to Vic, he had told her she was "pompous" and he didn't want to go out with her. Andrew wasn't the only person who called her "pompous". She was. It wasn't my fault! I knew nothing of Esme's personal business as I didn't live at home.

Seventhly, ALL THAT SHIT did not add up to any reason to encourage mum to *ban me from my little siblings!!*

Angela Gribbin, (the little sister of Alexandra) was at the house when all the family were talking about what a great time they'd had together at Esme's in the Channel Islands. Angela could see how sad I was and said, "It was a terrible holiday and it rained everyday".

Esme said, "You think you're Cinderella!" Which revealed where her nuts head was at, not mine!

She wasn't ugly except for her brain!

If I had a penny for every person who told me that I was nothing like my sister Esme, I'd have about 10 pence.

Mum told me when I was about 19 that Esme had come back from Liverpool Poly or Uni, crying that the lecturer had told her, "Nobody likes you".

(I put that in for context). I thought it harsh, and thought no less of her because she was my Esme and I was used to her.

The *one time* Mum had attempted to moan to me about Esme, I stopped her by saying, "Come on Mum, You know you don't mean that".

Being a total twat was rewarded by my Mum, but being rock solid was literally spat on.

Once, at school age, Mum was teaching Esme how to make a Victoria sponge cake. I wanted to know too but they barred the kitchen door, laughing.

For years people had said Esme was "horrible" about me behind my back. When I was at school, kids on the estate said,

"Esme slags you off, she says you're as thick as your make-up!".

I smiled as I knew I wasn't fully thick and neither was my make-up. I said, "Ha, you don't get her humour! Tired of Esme? Tired of life!"

They said, "Well *she doesn't stick up for you*!"

Living in hopeful delusion again. I couldn't cope with the idea that my sister was bad AS WELL as my 'guardians'!

But Esme put the boot in the moment my Mum banned me, based on NOTHING!!!

YEARS later Esme said she'd finally meet me in B'ham in my 30s. Despite everything I was wearily excited to be seeing her again. But she didn't show up. Every time I rang her at Mum's I got a busy signal. Rachel went to mums for me to look for Esme and found them both laughing with the phone off the hook. Even Rachel said it was, "Disgusting treatment"

Esme spitefully didn't show up and cut phone contact. Devastated. Didn't even invite me to her wedding. I was gutted from Ilford.

To her credit Esme at least sent a brief birthday card when I was in my 40s saying, "Sorry I was a shit sister". All I wanted was for her to see me again and be friendly but she wouldn't. I'd held her in hushed reverence for her ability to say the alphabet backwards. But it was misplaced affection.

At Dad's funeral when I asked Rachel why she hadn't been in touch, she answered, "I thought you wouldn't want to know me". I replied, "Of course I would".

Rachel then said I was "A great big sister".

I styled them and cut their hair and shouted at paedophiles. When I was 8 and Rachel was 3, I used to strap a cushion to my bike pannier and sit her on it and take her for bike adventures.

The whole remaining family drove off from my Dad's funeral without me, leaving me alone with my dead Dad. Dad's best friend Del said she'd, "Never seen such spite".

Those two so-called sisters gave me worlds of pain inside an existing world of pain caused by 'mum'.

<u>RANDOM **BOB GIG AT A COLLEGE; a microcosm.**</u>

In the dressing room, I was sitting on the counter with my back against the mirror, facing Bob on a chair.

A young student girl, my age came to collect her pot of loose face powder off the counter. She was very nervous and clumsily spilled powder all over the floor. She scrabbled on the floor and apologised.

I moved to tell her to forget it, but Bob looked at me with his mad leer, shaking his head, mouthing the word NO! He enjoyed seeing her squirm with nerves. I noted this as fucking weird.

Same gig, a young student came in offering Indian food from over the road or Pizza. I immediately said "Indian".

The guy said it was a really good Indian restaurant close by, as the pizza place was across town and it was raining.

Bob said "No, I want pizza".

After 45 minutes the poor dude came back soaking wet saying, "Here's your pizza, I'm glad I didn't have to get it". Obviously he had got it in the rain.

I like to put people at ease, whereas Bob actually **likes** people to suffer.

OK SO AGED 23 I GO TO BOB'S SHARED FLAT IN BIRMINGHAM...... SIGH.

It began alright. His flatmate was often out. Bob sent me to the bookies with betting slips and he made nice dinners for us. But when Bob went to play football, he'd leave me in the house and refuse to let me come and play. I'd no idea where he'd go as I didn't know B'ham at all.

(A man named Muppet told me that Bob was overly aggressive on the pitch. Years later some Brummie boys used to let me play on Sundays and I'd punish the ball, so happy to be playing. But no girls would come with me when I asked them.).

I went out and found a swimming pool on Alcester Rd. A tall handsome man called Ricki Stevens followed me out of the pool. (*Years later Ricki had hair like The Prodigy and used to make dinners for many, including me. I called him 'Fluffy' or 'Mummy'. He was very lovely and the best mother).*

Across the road from Bob lived a young man named who loved to play cards. He ran Bob's fan club and had a poster on his window saying, "A Haven For Women". He really was a very funny man who was good and friendly to women, without being a pervert. My brain was like Hiroshima by then, BOMBED, I was ashamed to tell anyone what Bob was like and I could barely string a sentence together. The fan club guy talked enough for everyone.

EARTH SHATTERING REVELATION of WHY BOB HAD ASKED ME TO BE IN HIS VIDEO, ONLY TO ATTACK ME!

The fan club guy happened to mention that the record company boss **had told Bob to get his girlfriend for the video, as I was already on the record.**

Bob admired him.

AHA!

So Bob had thought, '**DAMN! I can't say, well actually I'm a psycho and would rather bite my girlfriend's nose than have my girlfriend in public! So I better say, "Yes boss, no problem, I'm a normal boyfriend, honest!"'**

So Bob had come to Sheffield to ask me to be in his video, in front of all my friends, looking like a nice guy to all of us.

Then when the filming was happening in Liverpool, Bob did everything to make me cry and sabotage me.

At night in the pub scene I'd managed to do a composed close up despite everything he'd thrown at me all day.

So psycho Bob took me home and disfigured me as the only way to stop me!

WHAT A SNEAKY INSANE PSYCHO.

Nobody was any the wiser.

When Bob's flatmate came home, Bob began his reign of terror as usual. Making me cry before his mate arrived, also telling me my hair looked shit because I was doing it in a low bun like a Charlie Chaplin heroine, and it became apparent that I had to find a place to live pronto.

Bob put me with his pal, Sherry, an older girl. I'll call her Sherry because she said her name sounded like a fizzy drink. But she was more like Sherry, sickly saccharine and something insincere about her, with her long drawn out vacuous echo chamber syllables. Her flat mate was away for a little while so she had a temporary spare room in her pink house.

On the kitchen wall were photo portraits of the Kray Twins. I supposed she thought it was 'edgy'. How out of touch with reality do you have to be to have psychopaths on the wall?

Nobody who's known real psychos wants to be reminded of them.

Sherry seemed to be following me and corralling me. When I was brushing my teeth in the bathroom, I heard her voice saying, "That's rather vigorous brushing". When I got dressed to go down the road to go to the video pub, she said, "Oh no, you can't go there! Stay in!"

WTF? Why did it matter to her? I reluctantly thought I better comply as I had no place else to stay.

Sherry said, "You're nothing like I thought you'd be from how Bob talks about you. I thought you'd be more….." Her voice trailed off as she was being polite.

I knew she'd expected Dame Edna Everage and got Madge Alsop instead. Mentally I was wrecked.

I wished I could go to my family's house and told Sherry that I couldn't go home due to my mother's ban.

Sherry pouted, "My mother wouldn't come to visit me one time and I felt hurt".

Sigh. No point in saying anything. How about NEVER being visited by your mother, banned from your siblings with police deployment, beaten and told to kill yourself!?

Sherry lived in a fluffy world. That's fine. She'd done a degree and said all that she wanted was to have a baby.

NOTE; One afternoon, Sherry took me into her tiny bedroom and started giving me clothes that were nothing like my taste, but I accepted them graciously. She went out of the room and I was left standing by the door across from the bed where she was getting the clothes out. Next to the door I saw a large multi-coloured spiral bound book on top of the tall chest of drawers with the usual girl's stuff on it. So I picked up the book to look at it like I've picked up a hundred books in a hundred houses. It could've been sketches, who knew? Just as I was opening it, Sherry came in and said "*That's my diary!*" And took it off me. "Oh. I didn't know", I replied. It wasn't hidden or obviously a diary. I didn't see anything. No need to be so precious. I thought no more about it.

Sherry took me to a nightclub where I met some girls who needed to fill a room in the house they'd just rented. It turned out to be in Balsall Heath where Bob lived.

I moved in and one of the girls had a black guy friend who drove me to get my drumkit etc from Sheffield. He insisted on raping me in my Sheffield bedroom where I'd met Jesus. Grief! A GP gave me some pills to take and after taking them I couldn't get my head off the pillow. It made me very angry and I nearly broke the toilet in rage.

The girl's house was mad and one of them locked her errant boyfriend into the lounge and he broke down the door.

Bob phoned me up there, I said, "Hello, what do you want?" He seriously replied, "My friend Sherry said you read her diary!"

I said, "BOLLOCKS! No I didn't! Ringing me up with shit! You deserve each other!" And I slammed the phone down. Pathetic petty minded crap heads.

Sherry had a long swooping pointy nose like Rita Tushingham, or PINNOCHIO! What a snidey, shit stirring thing to do, to tell a psycho bullshit about me! Thanks a lot! Big help. As if I knew what that colourful book was!!! As if I gave a shit about her poxy diary. Bah!

The petty mean stupidity of lying about me to stupid petty Bob, always irked me about Sherry! Maligning me and making something out of nothing! So now it's in this book. Yes your name is like a fizzy drink and you're full of noxious gas!

MUNCHERS VIEW

The video pub was known locally as 'Munchers' and the house opposite it was run as a guest house by Dick, a man I knew from Bob's friends.

Dick asked me to paint a wooden sign for outside his house with 'Munchers View' written on it. I painted it with yellow 1930's rays of the sun coming out of bold lettering for either side of the sign. It looked great and I earned a bit of money. The council told him to take it down.

Our landlord at my shared house was a Muslim man who lived over the road and I'd often visit him and hear about his religion and how he'd wake up at exactly one minute later each day to pray, according to precise religious instruction. He was an Imam and his wife would always bring us delicacies to eat. Unfortunately he hadn't paid rates on my shared house and we all had to leave the property. He let me sleep for free in an empty building next-door to him, so I slept on the floor on my coat with my drum kit.

Dick had a room free in his house so I moved into it and all was fine, except there was no hot water and it was freezing December. Couldn't face the icy water. (It would be seven years before I started my 'FERRY DISASTER SURVIVAL REGIME' of freezing showers to avoid heart attack from the freezing sea if I ended up capsized in the English Channel like all the passengers in the newspapers that I used to read).

Bob saw me and smelled me and took me to his place for a bath then shouted at me.

An Australian couple, a girl and man lived there with Dick. Lovely surfies who said I was really smooth faced compared to their Aussie friends in the sun.

One day soon after I moved in, the Aussie dude said they'd been kicked out for no reason and had to move their stuff out. He said Dick was nuts.

Crikey, I hoped it wasn't a bad sign, but it obviously was.

When just myself and Dick lived there, he gave me a red dress. I said, "No thank you, as I don't want to be your girlfriend".

Dick stopped me from meeting Gary Hopkins at the pub over the road at 7pm. Gary was fun and sang like Elvis and he didn't want to be my boyfriend.

I was all ready and going out the door when Dick pushed me onto the kitchen floor and said, "You're not going out!"

Gary rang the doorbell to see where I was and Dick held a kitchen chair over my face and said "If you make a sound, this chair leg smashes into your face". I was convinced he'd do it and I didn't make a sound. Gary left! But I was determined to get out.

Dick blocked the door so I ran to climb out of the living room window but the sash window was nailed shut.

He grabbed me and chucked me on the sofa and hurled glass at the wall above my head so glass rained down on me.

Then he said, "I bought you a red dress! What more do you want?"

I said, "You only gave to receive and I don't want to be your girlfriend, so no thank you!"

I ran out of the front door and down the street hysterical. Rang the police from a phone box. Waited in the street with some Indian lads who pulled up in a car.

The police arrived and Dick did the old routine, "Hello gents, just the people I want to see, do come in, just a family argument. Just a 'domestic'".

The two policemen interviewed me in the wrecked living room with glass everywhere and asked if Nick was my boyfriend or husband.

"NO! He's my LANDLORD! I've only just moved in!"

The cop said,

"Well we've spoken to Dick in the other room and he says it's a 'domestic' and you're his girlfriend".

"NO I'M NOT! And it's terrible that the law says it's ok to do this to a girlfriend! Look what he's done!"

They went out of the room and spoke to Dick. Then they returned to the living room and said, "He says you're safe, he won't touch you again and you can leave tomorrow morning".

"You're not going to just leave me here!? I don't know what he'll do next!" The cops said I'd be alright until tomorrow.

They left and I was stunned and thought, *I don't care what they think, I'd rather be in the street than alone with this nutter* so I ran out of the lounge to thefront door and Dick was waiting outside the lounge door and grabbed me, saying,

"If you're leaving tomorrow I'll rape you tonight".

He dragged me upstairs to my bedroom, I grabbed the Cointreau bottle lamp and like in the movies, I smashed him over the head, but unlike in the movies he wasn't knocked out and the bottle didn't even break. He just had some blood on his head. He ejaculated in me and then blocked the door with his body by sitting against it.

After both of us were awake all night, he left at 8.00am to go to his job as a teacher. He put on a hat to hide his scratched bald head.

On ringing around I got into a women's hostel in Alum Rock. I somehow packed and got all my stuff over there. My head was a shed.

I begged my mother on the phone to let me in, she said, "No! He probably likes you!". I said, "I've got some clothes for the girls!" She replied, "They don't want your shit!" She slammed the phone down. Lovely 1950's dresses and great stylish stuff I had for my sisters.

ABOMINABLE ABORTIONS

The result of the pregnancy test was that Dick had got me pregnant. I'd been worried about the effects of the birth control pill after so many years so I'd stopped taking it as I wasn't with Bob. It was awful to think that my first child would be aborted, but I didn't see an alternative in those days. It was awful to think of that nutter Dick near a baby. I was in a homeless hostel without family or friends and just turned 24 in Birmingham. I rang Bob to tell him what happened and he whined, "*What can I do?*"

I put the phone down, pointless bothering.

The doctor booked an abortion for three months time. THREE MONTHS!! I walked to the clinic, vomiting in flower beds and when I came round from the operation my first words were, "I want to kill him". The nurse said, "Who? The doctor?" I replied in a very measured tone, "No, the man that did this to me". Loads of screams could be heard from women coming round to consciousness. But I was very cold and measured in my deepest semi-conscious state. I'd not realised that I felt so strongly against Dick until coming round after that abortion.

I now know that 3 months is A LONG TIME. Back then I thought the baby was just like a little water chestnut and my size was due to the fluid the baby was floating in. I didn't think it would be developed until it was at least 6 months.

Clueless about foetal development. It wasn't until a year later that I saw an Open University program showing how fast the baby grows that I was SHOCKED! A baby is fully formed in about 6 weeks!!

My soul was opened up to the reality of abortion and how horrible it must have been for that poor baby.

Next day I was on the loo and saw a vision of an angry charred baby running up the bathtub at me, holding a dagger in its little hand! I apologised to the baby and said, "SORRY BABY! Look where I am! It's no place for a baby!". It was a mouldy horrible flat. *(God would have provided for the baby).* Baby George Joseph.

But I still thought abortion was normal as I'd seen my mum have an abortion and it was deemed a part of life.

I'd go on to very reluctantly have 2 more operations and an abortion pill, aged 28 and 33 and 34 and a huge amount of morning after pills. The operations destroyed me mentally for years, and to this day.

But in all cases I didn't have faith in God to provide. In all 4 cases I didn't have faith. I didn't like the idea of leaving them with baby-sitters while I went out at night to support them by stripping and I had zero family. So many people said I was great fun with their children, but I had zero confidence in my ability to support them alone, I didn't want them to be on the dole and I felt the world was too bad for them.

The second man was singer/ designer/ nightclub host Mr Tony Baloney. I was due back in Athens to strip and didn't want to risk getting pregnant. Mr Baloney insisted he was gay and wouldn't even get it up. He did and I was pregnant again. At that time I didn't trust him with a hamster let alone a child. He WANTED the baby. He repeatedly said so, even telling me from the side of the stage of a rock gig I was stripping at. Mr Baloney is a beautiful and very talented man. A huge regret. We're very good friends and he would have called his daughter Verity.

The third time I was pregnant I honestly don't remember the man. I was early enough to go to the clinic and avoid an operation but was given a big killer pill. Then I had to sit a while before they gave me the next killer abortion pill. Baby Abigail. (What a dreadfully decadent life I led of killing, killing, killing and killing again).

The fourth man refused to even consider my having the baby, nagged me to have an abortion, also rang in the middle of the night telling me to kill the baby and drove me crying in a taxi to the clinic and waited until it was done. It devastated me. I had nightmares about the man. *Who he was is another story.*

Oh I may as well say here.

It was a black man from America, Franklyn Chancer, whom I thought was a true friend, as we'd done comedy gigs together for about a year. I was also still stripping. In retrospect I missed big clues, like him inviting me to his place to watch a video called 'Stag', in which some men hire a stripper then accidentally kill her.

Franklyn also bemoaned the fact that I'd been on TV but he hadn't. It all went over my head as I had no room for negativity in my head about Franklyn. I assured him that he'd be on TV no problem. Anybody could be. We talked a lot and I said that abortions were terrible and I'd never have a third.

(I'd given up the depot injection in my 20s as it made me ill and huge, the coil caused stabbing pain to my boyfriend Duddell and myself. I didn't see why I should have birth control just in case I got raped!)

Then one night I was invited to Franklyn's shared house for a party after I'd been out dancing.

But Franklyn was asleep and the only 'party' was his housemates. I said "Don't wake Franklyn, I'll just call a taxi".

But they insisted that Franklyn would kill them if they didn't wake him. Odd. Then Franklyn peeped round the lounge door and said,

"Ida, come with me, I want to talk to you". I went with him to his small box room that I'd never seen before. It was dark and he sat on the bed and I said "What's wrong Franklyn?" He then started kissing me and I thought, "Blimey! I didn't know you cared!"

We'd never so much as held hands for as long as I'd known him! From nought to sixty in one second! I was very drunk and allowed him to have sex with me. I was so drunk that in the morning I was half dressed, and it hit me!

"Franklyn, did what I think happened really happen last night? Do you want children?" He said "No". But that's how children are made!

My heart sank but I kicked into practicality and said "I must get to a morning after pill pronto".

Franklyn then blew my mind.

He started parading around the room proclaiming, "Oh my God I have been deceived!" (????) Like Martin Luther King without a soul. If anyone had the problem, it was me! If anyone had been tricked it was me! But I was being practical and casting no blame.

The Hungarian pill didn't work and a result came through a week later that I was pregnant. I sobbed in a world of pain as I couldn't bear another abortion. I asked Franklyn if he'd see the baby once a week? Send pictures? Let them know why they were a different colour to me? See them once a year? ANYTHING? He just blanked me. Like a staring stone wall. His family was in the USA and my family was nowhere. In fact my sisters Rachel and Lucy told me to "kill it". Terrible. The opposite of any type of positive support.

I had to do a TV show the day before the operation. I had to get up at 5am. Franklyn phoned me at 2am to tell me the baby had to die. Not to wish me good luck. He said, "You don't need it". He took his phone off the hook so I couldn't yell at him. I was so upset at this blatant mental sabotage that I drank wine to sleep at all and arrived in London hungover and utterly beleaguered. Somehow delivering some kind of show.

The main thing about that awful show is that I remembered my promise made to a little blonde girl at Moseley Festival a couple of months before.

She was 7 and I'd been dancing and she asked me if I was on TV. "A tiny bit", I replied. She said she was sad as it was the anniversary of Princess Diana's death. I told her Princess Diana was with Jesus, and I know because I saw Jesus at the end of my bed. The little girl's face became very serious. She stared into my eyes and said earnestly, "You've got to say that on TV!"

I replied, "Right! I will!"

As the awful exploitation TV show ended, I remembered to say "I SAW JESUS AT THE END OF MY BED!" It was televised.

Franklyn Chancer drove me to the clinic, we paid half each for an early abortion, which was bloody decent of me.

I was devastated, crying continuously, all the way. Afterwards, my 'friend' Franklyn was nowhere.

Didn't call once or visit.

Agonising months later I was ready to do a show over the road at the pub and got a call from Franklyn, (*wait for it*) telling me I **could not go on stage!** Somehow he'd found out I was doing a gig, He was now my self appointed jailer!

Not a word of support or any kind of contact since the operation, now this! I'd really hoped we could stay friends and it gutted me to find out what he was. We had problem mothers in common, but I didn't take it out on others.

Then it happened again! A few months later Franklyn called one afternoon to tell me **"YOU CAN'T GO ON TV!"**

Why on earth would he say that? None of his business! No TV was on offer anyway!

I went out and got very drunk to escape the fact that Franklyn, a so-called friend who knew I'd recently been through hell, was phoning me only to bully me!?

I got home the next day at 2pm after staying with Amy, my friend, and checked my answer phone. **Mrs Barbara Nice (Janice Connolly) had rung me and left a message to get to Manchester to appear in my favourite TV show 'Phoenix Nights' by Peter Kay.**

The time of the call was exactly the same time the day before as when Franklyn had rung to tell me I COULD NOT GO ON TV.

Maybe Mrs Nice had mentioned to him that she wanted me to appear in the show?

I rang Janice Connolly/Mrs Nice and she said I'd missed the bus! I was meant to be on it that morning! She'd wanted me spinning on my head in the splits in the Gong Show section of Phoenix Nights.

If I hadn't gone out grief stricken by Franklyn's horrible bullying call I'd have got Mrs Nice's call or message and made it in fine style.

I'd have LOVED IT! Janice Connolly was playing Bloody Mary in Phoenix Nights.

Mrs Barbara Nice was a popular regular performer at the Cheeky Monkey Comedy club, which I named for manager Martin Mullaney. Mrs Nice and compere/comedian Andy Robinson were my favourites. It was my great escape. I was part of the furniture there and would laugh hysterically every week. Except when comedians went on about Star Wars and Ikea as they were such commonly used subjects. I wrote about comedians like Mrs Nice for 69 Magazine.

Then Franklyn did something that stabbed my heart and churned my mind. I was sitting watching TV at a band's house and they were watching a stand-up comedy show. Franklyn appeared on the show and did his usual boring material.... THEN he ended his show in a new complete non sequitur,

"And if a woman wants a baby....I say HAVE the baby". He actually said that on national mainstream TV! How cruel.

I went home and cried, knowing Franklyn was trying to cover his ass, LYING on TV! He'd told me I had to kill the babies! But naturally I was distraught thinking maybe I could have had the babies and cried as I lay in the bath, my mind seared, crying.

Abortion is evil. Your body is all geared up for creating LIFE, then suddenly.....it's a grave yard. A desolate waste ground. Cut off! It takes a hell of a toll on your brain and body.

I knew from a pinging in my brain that Franklyn had given me twins. The word 'TWINS' suddenly pinged into my brain and a tarot reader told me they were twins inside me without my telling him about what had popped in my brain. Ezra and Delaney.

Aged 40 I dreamed I was a passenger in a car on a dark deserted highway with a faceless driver. Ahead on the side of the road the car headlights picked out a baby in a nappy crawling along by itself.

The car swerved to miss the baby. Phew! Then I realised the car was slowing to a stop and *reversing* to go back over the baby, I screamed, "DON'T KILL THE BABY!" I woke myself up with my own scream.

THEN an angry male voice thundered in my ears, **"Don't kill ANY babies!"** Emphasis on **"ANY"**.

I knew it was the voice of God. It was not my voice!

Then it hit me that....it wasn't just the dream baby that was killed. I'd had three abortions....and we also bomb babies in Iraq and kill them all over the world....we actually LIVE IN A DEATH CULT!

The only time God ever spoke to me was to tell me off. He's never spoken to me since.

GOD IS VERY ANGRY AT THE KILLING OF BABIES.

Aged 42ish I opened a Bible having asked God to tell me what I should know. It was horrendous! It said I'd been worse than a prostitute as I'd had loads of sex with loads of men for free! It said at length that I was a serious slag, worse than all my sisters.

I remembered a time in my early 30s when I'd lain spreadeagled on the bed yelling in my best Shakespearean villain tones, **"BRING ME FRESH SPERM!"**

"ONE DAY MY PRINCE WILL COME! BUT NOT BEFORE I DO!" I'd given up expecting love from men to avoid the pain, and was instead on a mission for the perfect orgasm.

I even photo-copied diagrams of vaginas with Latin terms and gave them out to an audience with instructions to tell their friends how to make women orgasm. I had a poster sized copy on stage.

"LABIA MAJORA, LABIA MINORA! Sounds like holiday destinations. DON'T BE FOOLED! YOU'RE THERE TO WORK!"

I repented fully of it all in tears and prayed for forgiveness, realising I'd been so far gone. The words in the bible said to cover my head when praying. So I did. I cried on my knees for forgiveness.

(After I'd struggled for years to get out of a hellhole of grief and abuse at Queenswood Road, I became a super fit rampant sex monster, I became an abuser of sex but that's another story).

ROCK 'N' ROLL DID NOT SAVE MY SOUL. ONLY JESUS CAN. In my early 40s I BECAME A BORN AGAIN VIRGIN. ONLY SEX IN MARRIAGE.

BACK AT PRISONER CELL BLOCK H HOSTEL

Aged 24 back in B'ham. To get a cheap Housing Association flat like Bob had, so that I would never have to meet another landlord, I wrote to every Hsg Assoc in town from the first hostel I was in. The horrible St Brigids.

I knew that hostels weren't long term and I dared to ask my mother if I could fill in the forms using her address, so that she could forward any replies to wherever I was, which I'd tell her.

Mum AGREED!!

An old woman's son came to take his mum to an Indian restaurant for Christmas Eve. He saw me sitting alone and took me too.

Time dragged on in this disgusting hostel St Brigids, with the manager withholding cheques that came in the post for a laugh, knowing I was desperate. Sheena, an old woman who seemed to live there, was best friends with the manager and used to stalk about, peering through windows in the dark like The Freak, a character in her favourite TV show, Prisoner Cell Block H.

Alum Rock was a hellish place. The life expectancy around the polluted Saltley viaduct was around 35. Seriously.

Salman Rushdie was being hounded for writing a book, and I'd chat to local Muslim shopkeepers who wanted to kill Salman Rushdie. "Have you read his book?" I'd ask. "No".

By request of the non-smokers I made a lovely sign for their area with curling smoke going through the letters. The manager stared at me as she ripped it off the wall and ripped it up. A sweet girl taped it back together and gave me a bottle of wine because I'd helped her in some way. I was thrown out of there for no reason and went to the Salvation Army where the manager went through my stuff and found the bottle of wine. She opened it, took it outside and poured it down the grid. Nice.

In my room were a mother and daughter who were homeless after a divorce. Everybody smoked. So when I was hassled by the boss for names of smokers, I refused. What was she going to do? Throw everybody out and have no rent?

Petty tyrants.

There was a box of clothes that had been donated and fortunately lots of stuff was left for me as everybody else was much larger than me. All the small stuff left were padded skiing jumpsuits in anorak material. Not much call for them in the B'ham Sally Army. So I took them to the market and sold them to a dealer. Otherwise I'd have had nada, zilch, zero money.

No news from my mum about housing, so I presumed there was no news. I was going nuts waiting for months in the hostels.

I wrote again to Moseley Housing Association to hurry them up, saying it was impossible in the hostel.

Moseley Hsg Assoc offered me a bedsit but it was so truly shitty that I turned it down. The Office wouldn't open again until Monday so I decided to keep the keys until then. It's a good job! I was thrown out of the Salvation "Christian" Army that night!

My boxes of books and everything were put in a black cab and purely by chance I had the keys to the shit bedsit still! Otherwise I'd have had no place to go.

The taxi driver said to the Salvation Army manager, "It's rush hour! Can't she leave a bit later?" No mercy.

All I had was about 12 pounds and the driver said he'd let me off a bit. It was 10 pounds to Moseley and the shitty bedsit on the first floor in Queenswood Road.

The ceiling paper in the bathroom was hanging off in ribbons of mould. The carpet in the bedsitting room was 50 plus years old and rank. It was a terrible place. I unstuck the edge of the carpet and found a newspaper from 1922.

(When I finally escaped the place 5 YEARS of helllater it was demolished and good riddance).

I arrived on a Thursday night with just a couple of quid left and slept in the empty room on the floor. Dared to ring 'mum' to see if I could use my 2 pounds to afford the bus to her place and stay for the weekend until the bank holiday was over on Tuesday, so offices would be open and I might get some money. "NO!"

On Woodbridge Road was an Indian looking man's grocer shop and I asked if I could do some cash work. He had me hauling sacks of spuds for three days and refused to pay. My stomach was still cut up from the abortion. Three times he sent me away, saying "Come back later". In the end I demanded money in front of all his customers and he said, "You've got a big mouth!" and he gave me a fiver! Bastard.

The Canon Hill Arts Centre let me clean it for a few more quid. Then I officially moved into the shit bedsit.

Resumed my mission to see the bambis at 'mums' and when I got inside her door I saw a MASSIVE pile of envelopes all addressed to me! Each one from different Hsg Assocs, all offering me 1 bedroom flats with gardens. The letters were dated to right back in January, just after when I'd first written to them. Followed by more letters saying, "We've taken you off the list because you didn't show up to collect the keys". (!!!!)

If 'mum' had forwarded the mail as she'd promised I could've had a decent flat MONTHS AGO and been saved from hostel bullshit.

It hit me that homelessness was too good for me in my mother's eyes. I had to keep my dismay under wraps as if I said anything about it to 'mum' it would've cut my visit down by about 10 mins. I never gave her any excuse to call the police at any time. But Police were duly called as usual.

Very depressed to realise I'd mistakenly trusted mum to pass on mail or ANYTHING for the LAST TIME.

VERY TOUGH TIMES UNTIL 30 WHEN I FINALLY GOT A SAFE ADDRESS. **RAPES BURY YOU and are tediously traumatic; you have to hold on and wait for time to dig you out. If you get no time before the next rape, it compounds the darkness and takes longer. TOTAL FLAT LINE EXHAUSTION. ZERO energy. Aged 23 my brain had started making sizzling noises. Then popping sounds. By 25 I was barely alive. Some squatter boys gave me speed and I collapsed asleep on the floor. "Oi! That's good stuff!" said one, pushing me with his foot. The speed had used up all the energy I had, which was all that had kept me upright. You can't kickstart an empty motorbike. I had zero reserves for the speed to use. Each rape would take me to minus 10 and I'd inch forward in desolation to maybe plus 2, barely staying conscious long enough to pay fuel bills to keep a roof over my head. Then unfortunately knocked back down to minus 5. I just didn't have a safe place to go to recover and desperately needed one.**

ELTON JOHN DIDN'T HAVE THIS PROBLEM. If I relayed it all, I'd need a regression hypnotist and it'd be another book, very turgid and I'd get more upset than I've already made myself. Will say, I made a big mistake once when Barry, a black neighbour of my artist friend Alex, was on top of me after trapping me; I gave a little wriggle to get it over with. Oh dear. Thought he was going to fracture my skull he looked so angry. They want you to be dead. They are the boss. The radio was playing 'I Wanna Sex You Up'. Whether you like it or not! When he left I cleaned his back yard of shit so his poor dog would be able to lie down. I'm a fucking hero.

Aged 25 I found myself on a garage roof, came to my senses before my foot went through the asbestos and climbed down. I went to see a doctor and said I was a tad concerned to find myself on a roof. Next day he came to my house and said I wasn't "Alright" as I told him. He wanted me to go to the hospital, Stratford ward, for a while. I protested that I wasn't well enough to go to hospital. Only if they promised to NOT give me drugs, and just give me food and a bed. After 3 days of bullshit distressing treatment in that hospital I left with Phill Duddell.

The COMFORT WOMEN of the Japanese Imperial Army of WW2, if they made it to old age, became opium addicts rolling on the floor in unimaginable grief. I saw pictures of them on the floor in an Observer magazine article when I was 21. Never foreseeing that I'd ever relate to them. I didn't even have any opium, I was fucked anyway.

Then my father rang me from the grave on the payphone in my communal hallway. Mother had lied about his death. She had told him we kids weren't interested in talking to him when he'd phoned her. So he didn't come forward to refute her claims of his death as he'd no idea she'd said that to me. I figured that he must be close to death for him to bother tracking me down.

I trekked to Arnhem in Holland where he still was and found him divorced and living alone in a government house filled with jumbled furniture and a little sofa in an alcove where he slept.

The HAPPY MONDAYS were blaring out of the MTV box, "He's gonna step on you again!"

My once strong dad was now frail and ill looking. He took one look at me and said "Your mum's done a demolition job on you". Dad had a plastic bag of rotten food on his back door step and said it was compost. The garden was just overgrown grass, nothing to compost! I disposed of the health hazard and scythed his grass, more dead than alive.

We went to a bar (surprise surprise) and a creepy man was standing at the bar staring at me as I sat at a table with my dad.

The creep was well over 6ft tall with stringy, thinning, shoulder length, greasy black hair slicked back. His black eyes had dark shadows round them and he looked like a giant version of The Penguin in 'Batman'.

My heart sank as he moved to our table, saying to dad "Hi Geoffrey! Who's this?" He feigned friendship with my dad, never taking his eyes off me. Dad greeted him like a long lost friend and appeared BLIND to the guys obviously creepy intentions towards me. Dad informed me that the man was going to come home with us to help dad move the jumble of furniture.

My worn down self was honed to survival mode and I was gutted to hear that El Creepo was coming with us. The creep helped move the furniture, set out the dinner table and cooked some food. Dad fell unconscious onto the sofa. The man wouldn't listen to my pleas as he pushed me back, pinned me with his weight and raped me. I was thinking of the old scared concierge at the Eros Hotel in Leicester Square, too scared by the sight of my fractured skull to help me.

Dad was no match for this giant and was far gone. The predatory creep left and I was devastated. Next day I put a knife under my pillow on the couch opposite my dad's couch. My dad said "You're nuts!" I told him that his so-called friend had raped me last night. "Dad you're one of the more harmless men I've ever met and it's a shame that you'll get it if you make one move on me, as I've reached a point where I can't take anymore!" (Dad was estranged from me for another 10 years, until he turned up in Hastings England). While in Arnhem I went with a gang of people to an old old quarry pit that had been turned into a lake. It was a nudist bathing site. I left my bikini on as I felt utterly wasted and vulnerable. The men said it looked sexier to be partially dressed. I COULD NOT WIN. I lay sunbathing, stoned and there was an image of myself in my mind as a barely alive maggot lying on the ground, hardly able to even move itself. The men's eyes had porno movies playing in them. Sure enough on returning to their house, the video they got out of their bag was a porno movie. My brain was so finely tuned that I knew.

BOB CRUMPTON TURNS UP AGAIN A FEW TIMES. OUT OF NOWHERE when I'm 25 in Queenswood Rd.

Aged 25 I somehow got a job drumming with some boys in a band called 'Julia Screamed'. We used to practise in a house in the dreaded 'video pub' street, Mary Street. We did a gig in somewhere like Leicester and when I got home I changed out of my baggy bodice, (that I'd go on to wear on Jerry Sadowitz Vs The People TV show with my invention of chest outplants and selfmade giant penis. The outplants were invented by me in reaction to all the botched boob jobs I'd seen in strip clubs. I created healthy outplants made of genuine plastic with life sustaining substances inside; beer, milk, korma in a D cup, beans, wine. You can hang them around your neck and easily remove them/consume them at will. Jerry didn't allow me enough time to show him my outplants.

The large penis I crafted was in reaction to the lack of penises on the top shelves of British newsagents, yet there were a plethora of vaginas on show. I didn't want to see penises really, it was the principle. All or nothing).

I got a knock on my flat door and it was BOB! He wanted to know why I was wearing Johnny Fingers pyjamas and not the outfit I'd worn on stage! *Still policing me!*

Bob wanted to know why I was seeing Phillip Duddell, a man who'd followed me down the road with a guitar, playing at me until I gave in to him after 24 hours solid busking all around town, never stopping still.

Bob said, "Has he got a big dick? Is that it?"

Bob turned up another day and lay on the old mattress and told me he'd just come off a tour of America, and how the women there were only interested if you had a car. Fat people were everywhere as food was cheap. But rent was expensive so there were a lot of fat homeless people.

Bob said, "YOU'LL like this story", and went on to tell me that he got a job on a building site in the heat with Mexicans. The boss came around with water and gave it to all the whites but not the Mexicans, who were saying "Agua agua!" Water water. Bob said he took a swig out of his bottle then spat it out, saying "PISS WATER!"

If Bob had wanted to impress me with his newfound social conscience he could have just passed his bottle to the Mexicans to share his drink. Instead of tipping it on the floor. Sigh.

(In my 30's in my illustrious safe address in the listed Brighton Place flats, I saw the lead singer of a band that toured with Bob. She said that Bob really was the most miserable bastard on that tour and I should sell my story).

Then Bob said, **"I still think about you and me in bed".** "Yes well", I replied archly.

Bob continued, ***"You've got to have my baby! If youdon't have my baby it will be a MONG!"***

What a terrible thing to wish on a girl, I thought. If anything, I'd be frightened of Bob's baby in case it bit me! *His words about my future baby echoed in my mind for years.*

Another time he knocked on my door and I told him **not to** come in as the 'Brew Crew' squatters from the flat beneath me had put crabs in my bedsit.

He insisted that he didn't care! He wanted to come in anyway. **I emphasised that it was NOT on my head if he caught crabs, he'd been strongly warned.**

He came in anyway and caught crabs. He went away after a while and I cleaned everything in the flat at the launderette at great expense and put lotion everywhere.

It was finally a crab free zone when Bob returned. He came in and started rolling around on my dilapidated furniture and mattress. Strange. He then said he'd got crabs.

I went mad! He said nonsensically and pettily in his favourite whining voice, *"Now you know how I feel!"*

I chased him down the street shouting *"WHY DON'T YOU KILL JESUS!? KILL THE KIDS!"* Then kicked in the door of the house he was staying in on Brighton Road and broke it! GOOD!

My drum kit was broken 3 times by different males. Even the new skins I bought from Musical Exchange, were thrown in the road under a truck before I could get them home! I found myself ripping my top off in the rainy grey Birmingham street and screaming, **"Why not take the flesh off my bones!"**

Then I realised where I was and quickly got dressed in case I got locked up. I was gutted at endlessly trying to be positive when wasted and in the face of such sabotage. A guitar I got at 25, (finally) was deliberately broken on me by a man. Couldn't any of them be happy for me? Or marvel at my resolve to keep trying to be positive!?

A third guitar I got in my 30s was also smashed by a man. I've got one now but I'm almost scared the guitar police will break in and smash it if I touch it!

Agz the lead singer of Sensa Yuma amazingly moved in a few doors away! He said "Ida it's a miracle that you can even stand to have men around you!" It was. But I refused to become twisted or victimised. To the point of stupidity. I trusted too much in reaction to everything, to prove I hadn't been changed. It took ages for me to learn that ***trust is earned***, not just given!

JACKIE.

I let Jackie move in as a mutually beneficial arrangement; he'd have a roof and I'd have a deterrent.

Jackie was always looking in the mirror saying how gorgeous he was. He was mentally abusive, giving me four orders in rapid-fire succession to mess with my head. Even if he was a boss and paying me, I'd leave that job. Not mutually beneficial at all and I made that clear.

So one day I was downstairs with the squatters and Jackie walked in saying, "Come on Ida! Tea! Toast!"

I just said simply "No". Jackie persisted, "Come on Ida!" A squatter called Joe Simmo said, "She said no, I think you better go mate". So Jackie left and I thought no more about it.

A few weeks later there was a knock on my flat door so I opened it thinking it was the squatters, and Jackie burst in with two vile pals.

They held me down on the floor while Jackie urinated on me. They let me up and I went into the kitchen which was by the bathroom.

My brain was racing. If I get a carving knife I'd have to be very strong with it to get three of them or they'd get back up, and that may mean one or more dies and maybe the other one would kill me or insist to police that I'd attacked them out of the blue and I'd be jailed for murder.

The effort to control my anger was about to TRULY send me insane and I went into the bathroom and cut off all my Pre Raphaelite locks to just tatty skinhead level and got an eyeliner and blackened my whole face with scribble.

I went back to the living room and they stared at me in surprise. "She's radio" said Jackie. (radio rental, mental). They left.

And I looked in the mirror and said, **"What a way to survive!"**

Don't get me wrong, remembering things for this book has got me crying on occasion, but I got over it enough again to write it down.

A lot of my time was spent with guitarist Phillip Duddell in his shithole flat listening and singing to his guitar and his excellent vinyl record collection, or cursing him for trying to make me as deaf as him. Cursing him for picking me up by my pants in a wedgie, "When I get my strength back you'll see my dust!" Otherwise he was a lovely man.

Or writing the perfect letter to my mum, as surely if I could just find the right words it would all be over. Just this last letter will do it!

I loved listening to **THE STONE ROSES** band, "Down down, you bring me down, I hear you knocking at my door and I can't sleep at night...." Ian Brown is great.

Put it this way, I had to sleep in my cowboy boots with a stick in my hand and one eye open when wasted.

Men would knock on my first floor window after they'd climbed on top of the bay window below.

In the day I'd emote desperately to **Alex Harvey's 'NEXT'** to anyone around, but I don't think they understood. If they read this, they might.

The man who lived downstairs next to the squatters had been released into the community after 30+ years in an insane asylum. Margaret Thatcher called it 'Care In The Community'. But the community didn't give a shit.

I tried to teach Geoff to read but that ended when I realised he was wanking and lying about not being able to read. He'd wank out of his window because there was nobody to tell him to take his pills.

I'd say, "You'll lose your flat Geoff and be sent back to the institution".

One day I'd lost my key and he broke my door down with the flat of his hands. I'd never seen such insane strength. His fag ends would be outside my door every morning. He'd lurk there in the night.

After a week at Duddell's I came home to see my building cordoned off by police. A girl in Queenswood Rd had been murdered by a care in the community patient. Everybody thought the girl in the poster plastered around the streets was me.

I must have asked the Hsg Assoc a thousand times to move me. Even the neighbour on my floor, a tall sax player, saw me leaving my flat door to go out one night and he grabbed my head and smeared my perfectly fresh eye make-up off with his massive hand, saying, "You can't go out!" I ran down to the taxi and went to the gig's toilets and cried that I couldn't even leave my own building without abuse. Then I fixed my face and danced.

One night I went out or rather escaped out in the car of a Scottish criminal called Tiger, because the boy over the road had smashed my window, which had to be boarded up, and he'd threatened to break my fingers. I was determined to go to this special event called 'Oscillate' which was run by Toby and Zilla whom I'd met aged 17 with Bob. I'd always avoided talking to any of Bob's associates due to fear of not being believed.

Tiger dropped me off and I danced like a dancing thing on national dance day in my survival skinhead haircut, 5 pound second-hand Rag Market cowboy boots, turquoise space bobble leggings and lemon yellow bolero quilted jacket.(?)

Then I saw **Lara** watching me and I went over to her. She said, "Ida you've got a hell of a lot going for you girl". I thanked her.

Lara said "Why didn't you come round?" Tears spouted and I said, "Because Bob was abusive and I didn't think I'd be believed and I knew I couldn't hold it inside!" Lara replied, "Oh you should've come round, we always doubted him". (WOW! Bob had said nobody would believe me).

The fact is nobody could help the state I was in unless they could control my mother. Or give me a home to rest in. If I'd gone to Lara's house, the dream lady, I'd have been in strong danger of being just a stain on the carpet, unable to speak or leave. So I didn't bother visiting Lara or Nicky.

"Nobody could help me!" I insisted to Lara. (Unless they could convince my mum to let me see my family)

A little while later Lara's band released a song about a girl needing some shelter who doesn't think anyone can help her.

I was so moved, knowing Lara. Wrongly or rightly I believed the song was about me.

Bob remained a monstrosity in my mind for many years. I made sure to never mention him at the comedy club or ever reveal my connection to him. His records that I was on, album, 12 inch and single were hidden out of sight as it gave me nightmares to look upon them.

Over the years the odd report would be told to me by musicians. One told me that I'd known some crazy guys and said Bob had a "poorly baby". I was sorry to hear that about any baby and shocked remembering what he had wished for me.

Another saw me in a pub and said hi and then dropped the info that it was a shame as, Bob's baby is always going to be ill. (Double shock!). Then someone told me Bob's baby was dead. Awful.

I didn't see Bob again until my early 40s when I was strongly led to buy my first 'TIME OUT' magazine in years. At home I opened it and saw Bob's face! He was to be playing at a pub the very next night.

As I read the article I was stunned and felt a cold claw in my heart when I read that he was now The Reverend Bob Crumpton and wore the white dog collar of a vicar!

NO WAY!?

It was like the creepy pastor at the door in the movie Poltergeist! Are all vicars satanic? The article went on to say that Bob overturned his lorry load on the highway in America. Bob driving?

Unbelievable.

Then I read that a concert benefit was being held for him called by lots of comedians! I was determined to get to the North London pub to see this 'Reverend' Crumpton.

On arrival I walked into the empty bar and straightway I saw Bob sitting with some mates. Bob bought me a pint and immediately confused me by saying, "Hello, I haven't got any money, I live in the projects".

WTF?! Weird thing to say! Money was not even in my head!

I said I saw you in Time Out, is it true you're a vicar and crashed your lorry? He said, "Ahhh don't believe all you read, you know that".

Bob asked about my littlest sister Lucy and my little brother James and I said he was at University doing animation. Bob said "Oh I thought he'd be wild!" I replied, "He is!"

(*When little Lucy was at University she put on an exhibition of clothes based on a nature theme. She said she got the idea from a 'nature picture' I did with her on a brief visit when she was tiny; I rubbed some grass and flowers and mud onto paper so their coloured stains remained and the idea stayed with her*).

Somebody at the table mentioned an appearance Bob made on a daytime TV show when I was a teen. I said, "I never got to see that show".

The guy said, "Oh it's on YouTube!" I asked him to spell YouTube so I could look it up as I'd never heard of it as I only emailed on the computer.

(At home I looked up Youtube and found Bob on the daily TV show. Then I wondered if my video would be there too. I looked under Bob Crumpton's name. But it's as if it never existed. Like my mum, Bob had eradicated all traces of me).

Bob asked me sneeringly, "How's your career?"

I didn't bother going into how I'd been kidnapped by Press agents for a week and my 2000 pound prize winning competition at The Cheeky Monkey was kiboshed along with my solid reputation.

My reputation was definitely a bit 'mad' but my integrity was rock solid. My show was the best I'd ever done and timed to fit the slot perfectly. I'd performed it in front of my friend Lucy Middleton and Emma and they laughed.

My I.T. teacher was getting a babysitter especially to see my show. It was my big glorious comeback back after the abortion hell. I WAS ON FIRE mentally and physically!

Then Aaron Barschak broke into Windsor Castle in a peach dress unbeknownst to me as I wasn't seeing TV. I was in Cannon Hill park practising my show when agent/comedian Geoff Whiting phoned me to say what Aaron had done.

I told Geoff I was rehearsing my crucial show for Tuesday, in two days time and that I hadn't seen Aaron for a year.

Geoff said, "It's serious Ida, Aaron is in a lot of trouble, I've got a reporter with me and I told him how you sent Aaron to me. Will you talk to him on the phone now?" A 'snake in the grass' feeling hit me on that sunny day. (I'd only just got a mobile phone and didn't even know how to text, now this).

Befuddled somewhat, but not wanting Aaron to go to jail and mainly out of my liking Geoff, (although I felt like saying, "That's not my problem Geoff"), I spoke to the reporter from The Daily Mail.

"He's a camp smelly man but not Camp X-ray material. Do not put a spoon in his mouth if he has an epileptic fit".

How do I know him?

"I met him by the cheese counter at a supermarket, we did an Irish play on Broadway, (Cricklewood Broadway!), aptly titled 'Lovers And Losers'. He stole my lines so I let him finish the run by himself. His family are excellent".

Have you got a picture from the play? - Yes.

Can you give it to an agent who will come to your house in twenty minutes? - Yes.

Awful tragedy struck me after I let agent Mark Islander into my house to take photos of my photos for The Daily Mail. It was like dealing with satan.

I signed a contract for the photos to be used by The Daily Mail. I'd no idea that he had his own agenda, separate from The Daily Mail phone interview. He lied and lied.

On that sunny Sunday he pressured me repeatedly to do a deal with him, citing examples of people who'd made money.

I admirably refused saying it'd be the *kiss of death*for me as I had my own show in 2 days with a massive prize and TV options, everything I'd ever wanted. NO WAY did I want to be on the coat tails of ANYONE otherwise I could've spent my life in newspapers!

I was so excited about my show that I showed him my props and did some of it for him. **Thinking I was untouchable.**

He went away and I concentrated on my show. Next day, Monday, I was going to Sally Issit's house at 12pm to rehearse with her. I *couldn't wait* to spring my eclectic and original show on the Cheeky Monkey club.

Comedian friend **Ian Cognito** told me "Enjoy what you do!" And I did! I often winged my shows but THIS ONE was scripted and timed to perfection as it was a crucial competition.

Next morning all was well, it was Monday and I was going to rehearse with Sally. Then at 7am Islander phoned and said The Daily Mail had a problem. They needed studio quality shots. I said, "Look, you can put me on the North Pole with today's technology with the shots you have! I'm really busy rehearsing with Sally today".

Usually by 9am I'd be over the road at the shop buying tobacco and I would have **SEEN** that he was **lying**! The Daily Mail had ALREADY done their article with the theatre shot of Aaron and I. It was out on the shelves in the shop!

But Islander intercepted me, he cut me off at the pass and I wouldn't know about The Daily Mail already being out until I was released from captivity a week later!

He persisted saying, "We need pictures of you in your comedy costume with your props. Good shots like that cost a fortune and *you can have them for free!* Get your stuff ready and I'll pick you up inhalf an hour and take you to the B'ham studio, then drop you off at Sally's house on time!"

Something didn't sit right, but I didn't know what it was. It was fair enough if he'd get me to Sally's on time.

I fatally thought, 'What can a little middle aged guy possibly do to me anyway?'

So I packed my costume and went downtown with him, down industrial back streets to the studio. As we got out of the car a youth in black took a picture of me and ran off. Seemed odd as the place was otherwise deserted.

Inside the studio was huge and full of youths in black with walkie-talkies. I posed in my costume and long black wig and was ready to LEAVE!!!

"Just a formality Ida, but we need a few shots of you in your street clothes. It's something we're expected to do with all sessions".

I complained that I wasn't ready for normal shots, my hair was all wiggy from wearing the wig and my clothes were combat trousers and T-shirt. This wasn't in the plan, I had to go!

"Just a formality, won't take a minute!" said Islander.

Reluctantly and looking very pissed off, I sat for the shots. Then it was definitely time to go. But no. They kept me waiting in a room.

Islander came in and said, "Slight change of plan, ring Sally and tell her you've got the awful inconvenience of needing to stay in a 5 star hotel for your own safety tonight and you'll be home tomorrow. It's carnage outside, there's stacks of press, we have to leave by the backdoor!"

Something wasn't right. The streets were empty not long ago except for some fake photographer. What was going on?

Islander said, "It's all par for the course, we're used to it and often have to relocate people for safety in cases like this. Nothing to worry about. Ring Sally".

Sally said it sounded mad. I agreed.

As I left with my props bag and crutches out of the back door, they took my stuff off me! I pulled it back off them! It was a tug-o-war! Why are you taking my stuff!?

They, several of them, insisted that it'd get damaged in the scrum and they'd bring my props to me later. (WTF!?) They promised to get it all to me a.s.a.p.

There was NOBODY out the back, no scrum. I said, *"I could easily have taken my props with me!"*

Driving through Birmingham the snake Islander had a smooth as silk patter. "We do this all the time, you like 5 star hotels right?" Actually I wasn't that fussed having been in them with my dad since I was little!

He insisted that I'd be taken home in the morning and would definitely be doing my show. That's ALL I CARED ABOUT! MY SHOW!

He said, "You've got your script, you can rehearse at the hotel and we'll get your props to you". **I told him how very important this show was, it was a one-off event! It was also for a breast cancer charity.**

(Tears are rolling down as I write. I'm sobbing. There was SO MUCH at stake! All my ducks were finally in a row. My show was my best! It was a competition in MY home club! I'd lost in other peoples home towns, but THIS ONE WAS MINE! It was the pinnacle of a triumph over every comedian that had ever bitten me, squashed me, bullied me! I had it in the bag! There was even a prize, and TV contract and it was for charity!!! I'd had to beg to be included in the competition! It could never be so perfect again! AND THOSE LOW SCUMMY BASTARDS STOLE IT FROM ME! I HOPE THEY DIE TORMENTED).

I totally believed I'd be delivered home for my show with my props and I'd win on the crest of this unique and unrepeatable wave, surfing to triumph over my WHOLE LIFE!

Islander drove through the suburbs, through the fields! Where the fuck was he taking me? For an hour he drove!

To a quaint olde worlde hotel with an effigy of a black crow outside it. It was more like a 3 star hotel. Inside was a casually dressed young man and a man in a suit who took me to the bar and suggested Pimms. I'd never had Pimms before so I knocked some back.

All I could talk about was my show and how much was riding on it and how great it was going to be.

(There's a pic from the comedy costume shots they took **when I thought everything was fine**, and my eyes looked on fire with excitement and my face fresh).

They wanted to talk about Aaron and I had nothing to say except that I'd told Aaron about Ian Cognito, The Rottweiler of Comedy, and

Aaron had said, "I'll be the terrorist of comedy". Then we both said, "The Comedy Terrorist!"

(R.I.P. Ian Cognito. I loved going on your refurbished barge down the countryside canal, through the weeping willows to the pub)

In the hotel room one reporter was doing Michael Caine impressions over and over. I found I was drunk and chatting away.

Then these reporter guys started bullying me. No other word for it. Insisting that I'd ruin the show for the other competitors if I arrived, as so much attention would be on me.

UTTER BOLLOCKS. I insisted that IF that was true and attention would be on me from the Press it would ENHANCE the show!

They said I was selfish. Wheedling voices saying I was unfair. I kept responding with "Those are the breaks!" I'd lost before in another person's town and that was how it rolled. NOTHING would stop me.

Tuesday arrived and the guys were at my door first thing and brought breakfast to me. I was ready to go. All day they kept saying my props were on the way. I was excited about the night's show.

I had no idea where I was and the hotel just had a black crow outside it and it was staffed by Eastern Europeans. I started getting angsty about my props but was SURE they'd get me to the show although it was 4pm! There was still time. 6 o'clock. No props. I ran into the carpark and three men followed me. Surrounded me.

Another suited bespectacled agent had appeared looking like an unctuous undertaker, telling me to calm down in syrupy tones. NO PROPS! NO LIFT! I was frantic.

7PM, 8PM, Martin Mullaney rang to ask where I was. "I DON'T KNOW! I'll be there!" Martin said he'd put me on last at the Cheeky Monkey Club. I was crying.

The horror of that day still haunts me. I'm crying again as I write. The creepy lying men. Being trapped! My whole life's work sliding out of view! NOT HAVING A CLUE WHY!

The day ended and I wanted to throw myself out of the window. I wanted to die. I screamed at the men in my room. "HOW CAN YOU LIVE WITH YOURSELVES!? YOU'VE DESTROYED MY LIFE!"

They said they did this work all the time but had never seen anyone so unhappy before. IT WAS EVERYTHING I DREAMED OF YOU EVIL CUNTS! I sobbed for days.

Jon Ronson, a Guardian journalist texted me. My basic Nokia phone was running down. I was unable to use punctuation in my reply and could only say 'GUTTED to miss my show'.

THESE PRESS AGENT BASTARDS KEPT ME PRISONER FOR A WEEK and I had no effing clue why they were doing it!

They bought me a hardback Harry Potter book and a Jackie Collins novel. I said, "YOU WRECK MY LIFE AND BRING ME SHIT!? I don't want these!" Then they brought me a Spike Milligan book. Better, but I could not read. I wanted to kill myself.

(AUS UPDATE. 6.6.2022. HOW EFFING APPROPRIATE that I'm writing about this killer twisted event on a day that = 666)

They took me to a cinema. When we sat down, I got up and left. They followed me and I pretended I was going into a toilet up ahead. I went into the toilet. Looked outside the door and they'd gone. SO I RAN OUTSIDE and started telling bypassers that I was a hostage. The men ran out and said, "Sorry, she's not well, we'll take care of it". They took me back to the hotel, forgetting the film.

They put Aaron on the phone. "Aaron, they've wrecked my show!" Aaron replied, "LOVE, LOVE, TAKE THE MONEY! There's always shows!" "Aaron you don't understand! They've wrecked my life!".

The hostage takers said, "There'll be other shows!" Not prestigious important ones like that PERFECTLY set-up show! I was suicidally depressed.

Time dragged on in a blur of drink until they finally dumped me outside my house on Sunday morning.

I RANG THE POLICE and said I've been kidnapped for a week by press agents! The police put me onto media lawyers Peter Carter Ruck.

Peter Carter Ruck took all my information and said I'd been treated appallingly and they'd take my case Pro Bono.

The Sunday papers were full of BS about me and Aaron, totally made up rubbish with a picture of me looking pissed off in my street clothes. In reality I'd been pissed off at the studio agents who'd forced me to be pictured like that before they could let me go! Then they kidnapped me instead of letting me go!

I had a really annoying man in my house Pete, who was a self-employed engineer and spoke like Jeremy Paxman. I must have let him in although he'd bothered me in the past but I wasn't thinking straight.

Pete knew I'd been bullied for a week and wasn't my happy self at all. He got in my way and wouldn't GO away! He was and probably still is the limpet from hell.

Jon Ronson phoned my landline and I told him I'd been taken prisoner and was dealing with it through Peter Carter Ruck lawyers.

Mr Ronson said, "Well I've never seen anyone win against them, they do it all the time. Will you send me what you're writing to the lawyer as I'm doing an article about Aaron".

I agreed as at least I could put the record straight and expose these gutter press agents!!!

BUT PETE SAID, "NO! DON'T TALK TO PRESS AGAIN! ASK THE LAWYER FIRST!"

I reasoned to Pete that Jon Ronson was a respected legitimate writer for grown-up press, The Guardian, and he represented my only chance to clear my name! What if the lawyers couldn't help?

Pete browbeat me that I'd "get into more trouble!" By this time I was so wobbly from my hellish week that I didn't trust myself anymore and reluctantly I did as Pete said and asked the lawyers.

Peter Carter Ruck said "NO" Don't send anything to Jon Ronson. I had another terrible feeling: it was a big mistake to trust the lawyers.

Jon Ronson phoned and said, "Have you sent it yet?" I told him that I'd been told not to by the lawyers. Jon asked if he could use my note, I think he meant my text, so I said, yes, no, I don't know! And hung up. I felt awful.

THANKS TO LIMPET BULLY PETE *who knew nothing*, I BLEW MY ONLY CHANCE to clear my name of being a kiss'n'tell! The only kiss'n'tell in history to get**zero** money to go with the ruined reputation!

All I'd agreed to was speaking to the Daily Mail reporter that Geoff Whiting put on the phone on Sunday in the park. It appeared the next day.

ALL the subsequent INVEIGLING and incomprehensible SUBTERFUGE I was subjected to was because Islander LIED and had done an EXCLUSIVE deal with whichever newspapers, and had to keep me under wraps AWAY from *all other press* until HIS DEALS were published the following Sunday!

SO HE TRASHED MY SHOW for that pile of defamatory*crap*. My personal integrity now with a huge question mark over it.

Exactly the reason why I'd told Islander NO from the start! (I'm still shaking my head in disbelief to this day)

ALL I'd EVER HAD TO DELIBERATELY AND FIERCELY CLING TO WAS MY OWN ROCK SOLID INTEGRITY.

RUINED!

(*A nasty rasping voiced American woman who had never taken up any of my invitations to the comedy club, suddenly decided to turn up to the club and mouthed the words "Low Life" at me. I tipped a quarter pint of beer on her lap and she tried to get me banned from my own club. She failed. She'd banned me from other clubs she ran previously for zero reason and actively sabotaged me. She'd even slandered me, so intoxicated was she by her own jealousy. She relished the idea of turning up at the club to put the boot in when I was down. Another woman trapped in the base level of the Snake year).*

Then I got a cheque from The Daily Mail, the only one I'd agreed to speak to.

But it was money I had not won. Money I had no pride in. I didn't know what to do with it. I bought a feather duvet. I eventually lost it. At least the Daily Mail were honest.

According to Peter Carter Ruck, Islander made **over 30,000 pounds off my misery and gave me not a penny in damages.**

Due to 'privacy clauses' on blacked out receipts, Peter Carter Ruck tried but couldn't bring Islander to justice.

Jon Ronson was right. I finally sent Jon what I'd sent to the lawyers with an overly egged section about Aaron's great family.

Jon Ronson said, "It's all a bit yesterday now". TOO LATE.

I cursed myself for being so broken down that I'd followed Pete instead of MYSELF! Jon Ronson could have cleared my name and cast light on the dark dealings of gutter press agents.

Back to BOB'S GIG at the pub.

No, I didn't bother telling Bob the above when he asked, "How's your career?" I simply replied, "I didn't do it, I had another abortion".

Bob quipped, "That could be a punchline!" Nobody was laughing.

I confided to the assembled mates that Bob was my mum who made me dinners and correctly informed me that my own mum treated me like a dog.

I told Bob I'd qualified as an aerobic and Pilates instructor. "How's that?" asked Bob. I lied and told him it was very hard.

Bob went into his act and riffed about fitness gyms especially for me, it wasn't very good.

The audience shouted out a request for the song I'd made with Bob. The one record I'd been on. They still remembered it.

I was right there!

But Bob said, "NO I DON'T DO THAT ONE NO MORE!"

After the show I gave a hearty handshake to Bob's wife, the woman brave enough to live with Bob. She met me with a tiny, limp fish hand.

Oh well.

Alone after the show I told Bob, "You've paid for your sins haven't you". He replied, "I haven't done any!" Whatever.

I asked Bob directly, **"Are you still possessed by Satan?"**

Bob looked into my eyes and grinned, making a gurgling chortling sound. The kind of sound a gargoyle would make. Clearly still demon possessed.

He said it wasn't his fault but he couldn't invite me to the big benefit show that night. I demanded that he give me a proper hug.

The last thing I did was blow him a kiss, tears in my eyes.

It is finished.

CONCLUSION. I HAD IT COMING. BAD KARMA

All that treachery, skullduggery and trickery I faced after the abortion I'd allowed Franklyn to bully me into, was well deserved.

I'd broken my promise to God that I'd never have another abortion; God had blessed me with the twins I'd always wanted and I killed them as I couldn't bear the thought of them having a father who ignored them and wanted them dead. Completely forgetting their Heavenly Father who gave them life and would never forsake them.

The treachery towards me began directly after the abortion. No matter how positive I tried to remain, I was dogged by demonic people. I was incapable of doing my regular week-long stint stripping at the Sunset Strip Porn Cinema. 5 shows a day, 6 days a week, 30 energetic shows a week. (Ooooh maths!) Often doing gigs after a day's work.

Often I'd cycle there on my ubiquitous bike.

The music I provided was eclectic including tapes specially made for me by musicians. The manageress tolerated them, but preferred Prince or Madonna. Radiohead surely owe me for the amount of average Joes who asked me who the singer of 'Creep' was.

The manageress had a mother who'd often be in the office with her catchphrase, "If strippers had brains they'd be dangerous!" I loved her spoonerisms and malapropisms. "All that cascara on your eyes!" It turned out that the Mrs Slocombe style mother had once stripped herself.

In the dressing room I wrote the doggerel poem;

'In Sunset Strip it's always night, with just the glows of cigarette lights and lurid pictures on the screen, projections of the money man's sex dream scheme.

House lights on!

Tape loop stops!

The male eyes stare at the space where it was.

The stripper enters left, takes centre stage, scanning faces every colour, wage and age. I see the rows of genitals shamelessly exposed like a vast meaty pronged sea anemone, waving frantically back at me.

As I get down to my thermal vest, it occurs to me, what if there were rows of oysters in this ocean I could see? What if women could share the same seabed? Imagine!

Alsorts of women given their head!

From sweet 16 to ancient old dears, playing with their privates, the music in their ears!

Free to come on a rainy afternoon as their old macs dry out and pension books loom. No fear, no shame, no reason to hide as they feast their eyes on young men's back and front sides.

Grey hair in curlers and as much fashion sense as some of the old men free to come in such dens.

I wish it were true but women are barred. The Chippendales are placebos and bingo balls are hard….and shiny...with numbers on the side... and it's not the same actually'.

Oh I was deeply obsessed with the disparity between the sexes and what was available to them. I couldn't stand to see even a flash of the films the porn cinema showed as I walked through the auditorium to the dressing room before a show. The Luciferian sex industry had enveloped me since childhood, but I remained observant like a secret agent.

(Table dancing was termed 'BATTERY STRIPPING' by me. It was labour intensive and physically far more dangerous due to the proximity of customers who may never have seen a naked woman up close before and couldn't be trusted to keep their hands to themselves. The clubs kept a big cut of the hard won wages. I preferred to be a FREE RANGE STRIPPER doing gigs, roaming the length and breadth of the stage. Far less work, more artistic scope and for more money).

Raw emotionally and physically after the deadly operation, I found myself accidentally in a small pocket of Moseley people that I'd never known. After the pub I'd gone with a little group to the Nasty American's pokey local house with dead dried plants.

To begin with I didn't know she was nasty and that she deeply hated me. She seemed nice enough, and kept topping up the glass of vodka that she supplied to me and everyone in a steady stream.

I was happy to be out and still alive.

She commented that I'd been on TV and she sounded like Franklyn. As I'd replied to him, I said the same to her, "Nearly everyone I know is on TV, it's no big deal".

In my bleary mind I thought everyone in Moseley was connected and she must know what I mean. But of course, she wasn't and she didn't.

She was quite new to Moseley as it transpired and nearly all the expansive inspiring stars of Moseley were long gone.

Except for the comedy club, Moseley had gone downhill. Patti Bell lived across town and worked in London every weekend. I'd been on the Homeswapper list for years and would often go down to London to see offers but they weren't good enough to move to.

The nasty American was born in the Snake year but I didn't hold it against her as lovely snakes existed like Jason. Anyway, astrology was surely rubbish, right?

She kept loudly imploring me to do a gig so she could film me as I could trust her better than a man to film me, and she rasped that she was just like me, "A boy-girl". Errr no, I was definitely a girl. But whatever, it was a kind offer and I explained I was in no state after an abortion a fortnight ago!

Every week she'd loudly nag me to do a gig regardless of my condition. In time I said I would. (In hindsight she was making herself look supportive to the assembly).

Every weekend for a few weeks I'd find myself in her small rectangular living room with the same people lining the walls. Initially it was quite a pleasant way to recover from hell in my fragile state.

But every weekend was the same, staying up until daybreak and prosaic conversation. Stagnant. Stultifying.

The room was bereft of original thought and there were no razor wits like in the comedy club. I didn't need speed to stay up, I'd given it up in my teens.

For all the speed consumed, the fastest thing in the room was the black stubble that sprouted from her chin at 5am. Totally at odds with her carefully dyed red bob haircut.

On perusing the room the words, "DEATH'S WAITING ROOM" came to mind.

Rather like my barren empty womb.

Eventually I booked a 5 minute gig for her to film so that I could send it off in time to meet the deadline for a competition. I gave the American a week's notice and had no cause to doubt her.

She picked me up on the night in question and said she had some band to film. She'd double-booked herself. I said it was OK as it would only take 5 minutes to record me.

I performed the gig and she sniggered that she hadn't turned on the camera. The kindly club manager let me repeat the same show to the patient audience. The Nasty Yank sniggered in her rasping voice that this time she hadn't turned the sound on, it was only visuals.

Most crestfallen after all she'd promised. I took the visual recording and recorded an audio at home on a cassette tape to send them together. What a fiasco. It was the last day to post them. What a waste of time. What a drawn out dirty trick.

Then after a lovely time talking with John Cooper-Clarke I took him to the pub then took him to a taxi outside.

On returning to the pub I was talking to a misogynist weak musician I knew, at the same table as the Nasty American and her friend. The thick friend suddenly lunged across the table at me pulling my long hair. The nasty American said "GO ON! GET HER!"

I didn't retaliate at all except to untangle myself and put out my arm. I touched nobody and didn't spill my pint. I just let them reveal their true selves.

To top it all, I later heard that the Nasty American was spreading lies that I'd attacked her!

Gosh, I mused, karma wise I wouldn't want to be her shoes, lying like that after I WAS attacked and did nothing!

A week later the American was in a wheelchair with a broken leg.

I knew enough about karma not to gloat.

(Years and years later, my hair was grey and I felt great. I travelled all the way to Birmingham after being invited to my punk friend's gig. It transpired that the Nasty American was on the door. I didn't care as it was a new dawn and a new day and I felt good, I've never been a grudge holder. But she barred me from the gig, asserting that I'd attacked her. Unbelievable obduracy. It was YEARS later and I was the only person to be attacked, while she cheered! And if I could move on, why was she still obsessed with me?!

I'd not met such a petty minded hardened obdurate since my mother. Don't look for any chinks of light, there are none. She's probably still living in her dark hole to this day. 'orrible! Shame).

Then Franklyn started dogging me with bullying phone calls. Sabotaging my chance of being on Phoenix Nights thanks to Mrs Barbara Nice. Then I met the crazy Aaron Barschak who was fun for a while.

I finally got fit again for my comeback competition show ONLY to be kiboshed by press agents.

Young Lucy, my little sister, was doing postgraduate studies in London and working as a stylist for The Sunday Times newspaper and other media, and I had to be with her.

A great flat swap came up in Little Venice right on time, huge with high ceilings and black wrought iron balconies. I was gone no question.

I met so many inspirational people in London including a magnificent and brilliant Snake! Too much to tell now. But after my Polish neighbour raved about Australia I just had to see it for myself. ALL GLORY TO GOD.

BUT WAIT! What about the VERY talented, VERY GOOD guy Dave Kusworth, the beautiful person, outside and in!?

As promised, here's a story of Dave leaving my house with his camera tripod, which I warned against as he'd lose it. I'm in my early 40s. It's London. I've got so many funny memories of Dave, but here's one. He was booked to play in Berlin. To avoid catastrophe I booked him to arrive a day early on the plane.

Dave had played all over the world and I was sure he could manage the airport by himself, as I put him in a black cab for the airport in the afternoon.

As I was going to sleep at 11pm my door buzzer buzzed. I went to the intercom and said "Who is it!" A soft familiar Brummie voice said, "It's Dave". Oh dear. I let him in and showed him to the couch and said "Don't speak. Sleep".

In the morning he told me the flashing lights on the departure boards had confused him and he was lost for hours in the airport with his Innocent Smoothie bottle full of alcohol. He'd lost his tripod.

I made another booking for him to DEFINITELY arrive that day in time for his show and took him myself to the airport on the train. Dave said it was "Superhuman" the way I whizzed him through all the desks. We were all ready for take-off.

When Dave went to the loo, I grabbed somebody at a desk and said, "I have to get Dave Kusworth to Berlin to play a gig, he's super talented on stage but cannot do normal life. We've already wasted one air ticket cos he missed the plane yesterday. PLEASE get him onto the plane, I cannot afford to go air side with him. He must get to his Berlin show".

They said "Leave it with us. When it's time to go, bring him through without queuing up and we'll sort him out".

Dave came back from the loo and we had a drink. Then the queue started forming to go air side. Dave was ready to queue but I led him straight past the queue and through to the other side. His tall frame grew visibly taller with the special rock star treatment.

The helpful staff told us to go to the room with staff in yellow jerseys. When we got there they whipped out a wheelchair and told Dave to get in it. His face and ego sank a bit but he took it in good heart and got in the chair with a poor innocent little boy's face. He looked like a huge squished spider with his gangly limbs sticking out of this chair and his guitar on top.

I looked at Dave and thought of the TV comedy sketch show 'Little Britain' featuring a man who faked needing a wheelchair and could barely control my laugh and said, "Think of LITTLE BRITAIN! BUT whatever happens, DO NOT GET OUT of this chair!" Dave promised and the staff assured me they would stick with him and get him on the plane.

I left that airport laughing my head off! I later heard the Ramones record and realised it had been done before. That night Dave's soft voice came on the phone, "Yeah, great I'm in Berlin. Yeah they even rolled me off the plane!"

ROCK'N'ROLL.

To err is human. To forgive, divine.

NOV 7th 2022. AUS UPDATE.

17 days ago by the grace of God, I escaped from Hancock Street after threats of violence from Big Bill's associate. Now I have a sea view and have accepted a proposal of marriage. To be continued.....

Printed in Great Britain
by Amazon